NATIONAL UNIVERSITY
LIBRARY   SAN DIEGO

D1121540

Planned Giving
for Small
Nonprofits

Also by Ronald R. Jordan and Katelyn L. Quynn

Planned Giving, Second Edition: Management, Marketing, and Law
(ISBN 0-471-35102-4)

Invest in Charity: A Donor's Guide to Charitable Giving
(ISBN 0-471-41439-5)

Planned Giving Workbook
(ISBN 0-471-21221-3)

Planned Giving
for Small
Nonprofits

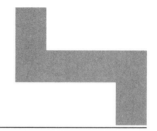

RONALD R. JORDAN
AND
KATELYN L. QUYNN

John Wiley & Sons, Inc.

This book is printed on acid-free paper. ∞

Copyright © 2002 by John Wiley & Sons, Inc., New York. All rights reserved.

Published simultaneously in Canada.

No part of this publication may be reproduced, stored in a retrieval system or trans-mitted in any form or by any means, electronic, mechanical, photocopying, recording, scanning or otherwise, except as permitted under Sections 107 or 108 of the 1976 United States Copyright Act, without either the prior written permission of the Publisher, or authorization through payment of the appropriate per-copy fee to the Copyright Clearance Center, 222 Rosewood Drive, Danvers, MA 01923, (978) 750-8400, fax (978) 750-4744. Requests to the Publisher for permission should be addressed to the Permissions Department, John Wiley & Sons, Inc., 605 Third Avenue, New York, NY 10158-0012, (212) 850-6011, fax (212) 850-6008, E-Mail: PERMREQ@WILEY.COM.

This publication is designed to provide accurate and authoritative information in regard to the subject matter covered. It is sold with the understanding that the pub-lisher is not engaged in rendering legal, accounting, or other professional services. If legal advance or other expert assistance is required, the services of a competent pro-fessional person should be sought.

Wiley also publishes its books in a variety of electronic formats. Some content that appears in print may not be available in electronic books. For more information about Wiley products, visit our Web site at www.wiley.com.

ISBN 0-471-21209-1

Printed in the United States of America.

10 9 8 7 6 5 4 3 2 1

Contents

Preface

Planned Giving for Small Nonprofits contains 20 chapters and a variety of exhibits, documents, and tables designed to assist small nonprofit organizations in developing successful planned giving programs. At small nonprofits, the director of development holds several positions. He or she may be the annual fund director, the major gifts officer, and the planned giving officer. Yet most directors of development are not trained in planned giving, nor do they have expertise in the field. This book is written with that in mind. *Planned Giving for Small Nonprofits* takes the reader through the steps necessary to prepare, implement, maintain, and expand a planned giving program. The authors have taken their more than 40 years of combined experience and applied it to meet the unique needs of small nonprofit organizations.

Planned giving requires careful analyses, commitment, and the support of several of the charity's staff members, officers, and departments. Unlike outright gifts, planned gifts must be administered for years. Nevertheless, planned giving is one of the most effective ways for the nonprofit to raise needed financial resources. *Planned Giving for Small Nonprofits* is designed to help small charities promote planned giving, step by step. This book answers these important questions:

- How do small charities start a planned giving program?
- What does the charity need to do before it begins?
- How do small nonprofit organizations staff the program?

- Which planned gifts should the nonprofit offer?
- How do nonprofits market to attract donors?
- Which planned gifts should be avoided?

The book is divided into seven parts, which are as follows:

1. Background Issues
2. Getting Started
3. Planned Gifts
4. Gifts of Assets Other Than Cash
5. Working with Donors
6. Marketing
7. Planned Giving and Taxes

We welcome your comments and hope you find this book to be a valuable addition to your planned giving program.

Ronald R. Jordan
Katelyn L. Quynn
June 2002

About the Authors

Ronald R. Jordan is the former Assistant Vice President of University Advancement and former Director of New Mexico State University's planned giving program. He has been a member of the bar since 1975 and is a graduate of the New England School of Law. As an assistant professor at the university, he teaches courses on financial planning and consumer economics. Previously, he taught courses in federal income taxation and estate planning. Jordan is the former Director of Planned Giving at Boston University. He also consults with nonprofit organizations.

Katelyn L. Quynn is Director of Development for Massachusetts General Hospital's planned and major gift program, and Director of Planned Giving for Partners Healthcare System. She was named Planned Giving Professional of the Year in 1996, is a past President of The Planned Giving Group of New England, and former board member of the National Committee on Planned Giving. She graduated from Tufts University and Boston University School of Law.

Acknowledgments

Writing a book takes teamwork, cooperation, and the participation of a number of individuals, each of whom makes valuable contributions to the manuscript and text. The authors wish to thank the following individuals for their help in the production of this manuscript.

- *Don Beasley, CPA, Beasley, Mitchell and Company, Las Cruces, New Mexico.* Don reviewed the technical chapters in this book and made significant contributions in improving the integrity of this book and in making difficult subject matter more understandable. Don is a skilled practitioner who appreciates the impact that planned giving has on a donor and a charity.

- *Dianne C. Jordan.* The authors wish to thank Ron's wife, Dianne, for her work as a production assistant in the development of the manuscript. The authors are indebted to her for her generous contribution of time and energy.

- *Diana Maria Garcia, Las Cruces, New Mexico.* Diana has worked with Ron Jordan for almost 11 years. As a volunteer, Diana has been involved in many aspects of this book, and the authors thank her for her able assistance and dedication.

- *PG Calc,* 129 Mount Auburn Street, Cambridge, Massachusetts, 617/497-4970, *www.pgcalc.com.* The authors wish to thank PG Calc and their fine staff for their generosity in allowing us to reprint PG Calc calculations and for creating such a wonderful product.

- *Our families.*   The authors thank their families—Dianne C. Jordan and Derek Jordan and Barry, Henry, and Andrew Smith for giving us the time to develop and write this book.

- *John Wiley & Sons, Inc.*   As usual, it is always a pleasure to work with the staff of John Wiley & Sons.

- Last, we thank our employers and our donors, who provide opportunities for us to grow in our profession.

Planned Giving for Small Nonprofits

PART ONE

Background Issues

CHAPTER 1

Planned Giving in a Small Charity: The First Year

INTRODUCTION

Starting or expanding a planned giving program in a small charity is an exciting and rewarding opportunity both for the charity and the donor. The addition of planned giving as a component of a development program demonstrates to donors that the nonprofit organization is maturing and that the charity is making a commitment to its future. Adding a new program is a challenging experience for small nonprofit organizations that are already short-staffed.

At a small charity, the development director performs a variety of development functions. The director may be the primary fundraiser for the entire organization, meaning that the director meets with the trustees, runs the annual fund, raises major gifts, and writes grant proposals to foundations and corporations. The director also crafts the solicitations, organizes the volunteers, makes the personal visits, and manages the staff. Increasingly, the director or a designated staff member is asked to take on new duties as the planned giving staff member. Alternatively, a development officer or other staff member may assume the duties of a planned giving officer. Without a planned giving program, the development program is incomplete. To stay competitive with peer organizations, planned gifts must be offered. In addition, planned gifts must be offered to meet the nonprofit's ever-increasing demand for financial support. The employee charged with the responsibility of the planned giving program must balance an array of other duties and begin to familiarize him- or herself with planned giving concepts.

The development director needs to feel confident that a planned giving program can be managed without being a financial expert, lawyer, or accountant. Some parts of planned giving have technical components, and the development director or staff member assigned to planned giving will learn the specifics as he or she goes along. A good planned giving program is built on solid, basic development principles, some of which may already be in place at the charity. This solid basis can include a managed pool of prospects, an annual giving and major gifts program, active volunteer leadership, and a willingness to engage in programs that benefit the nonprofit. A support network needs to be built so that other staff members can assist the development director as situations and questions arise. To learn what other small organizations are doing for marketing bequests, the development director may want to contact professionals who are working in similar situations and discuss the specifics of their brochures, advertisements, and bequest societies. Join a regional planned giving group to learn more about what other charities are doing.

Start by setting very specific personal and program goals. Be realistic about what can be accomplished, taking into consideration other work demands. It is important to begin a planned giving program, however small, because the rewards of such a program are worth the investment of time and resources. This chapter introduces fundraising principles and concepts covered more fully in other chapters.

Throughout this book, educational institutions, healthcare organizations, and arts and cultural organizations will be referred to as examples of small charities. These examples are used because more people in the business of development and planned giving are familiar with these models and because these models translate well to other charities. By no means is this book limiting its scope of planned giving to those organizations. Rather, through example, employees who work for other types of small charities can emulate strategies and techniques employed by these charities. Those in development graduated from a college or university (alumni), visited museums (patrons), or had loved ones benefit from care at a hospital (grateful patients). Examples of alumni, patrons, and grateful patients as prospects and donors exist at every charity. While sometimes they are not as obvious, and often they are not as easily managed as they are at educational institutions or healthcare organizations, there are ways to organize, identify, cultivate, and solicit every small charity's many planned giving constituents.

MANAGEMENT PLAN

The first step in developing a management plan for the planned giving program is to determine the goals that should be accomplished in the first year to year and a half of the program. Then, divide the plan into different areas including offering gift vehicles; marketing, including mailings, events, and brochures; identification and solicitation of planned giving prospects; and support areas, such as management of gift vehicles, computer software, and gift crediting.

For the first year, marketing bequests may be sufficient, although the charity may be ready to establish a pooled income fund or offer charitable gift annuities. To market these vehicles, begin by selecting one publication and run an ad or column in each issue. If a development newsletter is already being sent to donors, include marketing materials in it. Also target several donors who are good planned giving prospects and solicit them for a planned gift. Be realistic about what can be accomplished in the first year in a one-person shop. Do not promise more than can be delivered.

EDUCATION

Planned giving staff members need to present themselves as trained, experienced professionals with knowledge in several areas including law, banking, and finance. They must be able to anticipate questions and solve gift-planning situations. Planned giving officers should present themselves as experts in this field to instill confidence in donors and coworkers. Consider taking courses in estate planning, financial planning, and federal income taxation, and become skilled as a writer and effective speaker. Courses in communications and speech can improve presentations, while courses in entrepreneurship, business, and marketing provide important perspectives to invigorate and successfully continue a planned giving program. Perhaps the best skill successful planned giving officers can have is the ability to work well with all different types of people. Planned giving officers need to be good listeners and conversationalists. Cultivating personal interests such as travel, sports, and literature will help when having conversations with donors who share similar interests and allow points of commonality to arise. Conversational ease helps in negotiating the terms of a planned gift.

One of the first goals for the staff member assigned to the planned giving program is to obtain an education in planned giving. Many fine organizations, such as the Council for the Advancement of Support of Education, the Association of Fundraising Professionals, and the National Committee on Planned Giving, offer formal planned giving training programs. Attend one of the courses designed as an introduction to planned giving. A good planned giving course can provide an overall picture of the planned giving basics, including the life income vehicles, marketing, and working with planned giving donors. By attending a course, the director of development will meet colleagues with similar problems and concerns. The unfamiliar legal and financial language will soon become familiar. Planned giving also can be learned from reading books and monthly newsletters and by attending one-day programs and seminars. Day-to-day, hands-on experience, however, offers the best education.

Join a professional organization that holds monthly or quarterly meetings where speakers discuss planned giving topics. Every state is part of a district that offers a planned giving council. For example, the Planned Giving Group of New England was established to serve the states of Maine, Vermont, New Hampshire, Massachusetts, Connecticut, and Rhode Island. Some states, such as Rhode Island, offer their own planned giving group, while other states, such as New York and California, have more than one planned giving group located in different parts of the state.

Joining a professional planned giving organization is important for at least two reasons. First, planned giving requires continued learning because of changes in the tax laws, new estate planning techniques, and new gift opportunities and ideas. Second, regular interaction with planned giving colleagues is extremely important because colleagues can provide referrals to lawyers and financial managers, share marketing ideas, and provide preliminary advice before one calls a lawyer or a financial advisor. Building a network is an important and necessary way to share information about planned giving.

MOBILIZING THE SMALL CHARITY'S ADMINISTRATION

Planned giving programs can be instituted by the nonprofit's president or vice president of development, or they may evolve as part of a development office initiative, promoted by staff members. Regardless of the way the program originates, the nonprofit's officials and the development office staff will have to work cooperatively to develop the program. Chances are that there is very little room in the budget for additional staff, so determine who will provide assistance both inside and outside of the organization in helping develop a viable planned giving program. First and foremost, the president and board of trustees must support the creation of a planned giving program that works. The president and the board, by their actions and speech, communicate the importance of planned giving. They support the program financially by allocating funds for planned giving. The president and board also have a great deal of influence over the vice president for development in making the planned giving program a priority. If the president and board of trustees are not knowledgeable about planned giving, the development director may need to initiate the action and educate them about the benefits of such a program. Work with board members individually on specific planned giving assignments, and try to speak at a board meeting about the importance of planned giving or bring in an outside speaker or consultant to discuss planned giving.

Also consider selecting volunteers to help develop the various components of the program. Do not establish any formal board or committee until the role of the members and the scope and direction of the committee has been determined. Consider creating a Planned Giving Exploratory Committee by selecting individuals who are truly interested in planned giving and are committed to raising money either through planned gifts or by donating their professional skills. For example, a trusts and estates attorney could contribute to the program by answering donors' questions about estate planning as they arise. Or an individual who wishes to help raise money and has made a planned gift to another organization could speak to staff members or to a group of potential donors about the benefits of planned gifts. As the program grows, consider establishing a planned giving advisory board. The advisory board can help shape the program and educate the nonprofit's constituents. Identify support staff who can learn the basics of planned giving and help with the administration of the program.

BOARD OF TRUSTEES AND PLANNED GIVING

To begin a planned giving program at a small nonprofit organization, staff members need the support of the organization's board of trustees. If the organization does not have a pooled income fund or does not offer charitable gift annuities, board approval may be required to spend the necessary money to draft legal documents and pay for management of a planned giving program. Board members will need to see estimated costs outlined and fully described before they approve and are likely to have questions about planned giving program revenue versus the money spent each year to keep the gifts invested and managed, and to service donors.

It is very important to educate trustees on the importance of planned giving and what is required from outside legal counsel and an administrative manager for the planned giving vehicles. Most likely the board of trustees is made up of many distinguished, successful, and accomplished business leaders, all of whom have different professional strengths and connections in the business world, although they may not be familiar with planned giving. Be clear with board members about what is needed to run a successful planned giving program, a program that can handsomely support the organization for which they serve as trustees. Tell them about the cost to start a program, administrative fees, and legal costs. Individual board members will likely have opinions about the program and what firms should be used for legal counsel and investment services. Be clear about what the program needs, and do not select service providers based on an individual trustee's preferences. While one law firm or bank may do a superior job in some areas, not too many institutions specialize in charitable giving or planned gift management. In the end, the nonprofit may end up paying for hours of work that could have been done more quickly by an experienced charitable gift planning lawyer or planned giving manager. Planned giving staff members need access to experienced counsel who can recommend creative solutions to complex problems.

CREATING OR RESTRUCTURING FINANCIAL SUPPORT AREAS

In the first year of a new program, closely examine the current or potential planned giving financial support areas for the program. For the planned giving program to run smoothly and progress, the program and its staff must be supported by a number of individuals who are either employees of the nonprofit or outside managers or consultants. At most charities, support is needed in the following areas:

- Financial administration of the gift vehicles
- Investment of the principal of the planned gifts
- Life income payments
- Planned giving prospect management
- The creation of policies and procedures

If people or systems are not in place to support the program, take time to establish the necessary support areas. If the organization decides to establish a pooled income fund and offer gift annuities to prospects, determine who will manage the gifts. Charitable gift annuities can be managed in-house, but if gift annuities are new to the program, the development director needs to educate the treasurer thoroughly about them. An outside manager, such as a bank or trust company, also can be selected to manage the program and provide planned giving information and advice. If the organization selects an outside manager, determine what is needed from the planned giving manager and communicate those needs to the individual assigned to the account at the chosen outside institution. Be sure that all expectations are addressed up front. A professional outside planned giving manager also can provide information on real estate, financial, legal, and tax matters. The size and willingness of the organization's treasurer will help determine whether it is best to manage the program in-house or outside. If the nonprofit decides to seek assistance outside of the organization, work to help the treasurer understand why assistance is needed from outside providers. In the beginning stages of a program, small nonprofits may be better off using outside managers to administer, manage, and invest planned gifts. Later, as the program grows and becomes more savvy, the nonprofit can revaluate whether support should be provided in-house or by outside managers.

LEGAL ISSUES

Next, determine who will handle legal issues. These issues include drafting and approving endowed fund agreements, drafting planned gift agreements, tax considerations, and determining the appropriateness of accepting assets other than cash in addition to reviewing or drafting estate planning provisions in donors' wills and trusts. Even if the organization has experienced in-house counsel on staff, it is unlikely that he or she has expertise in charitable giving or the time to devote to learning it. When donors call, questions need to be answered quickly, and the development director does not have time to wait for the in-house attorney to research the topic. It is essential to have access to talented legal counsel when various legal issues arise, as they will when the program grows. Negotiate the need and cost of legal counsel with the in-house attorney and, if necessary, the charity's president.

Occasionally in-house attorneys are threatened by the presence of outside counsel and want to discourage the appointment of or control the selection of the outside counsel. It is also likely that the in-house counsel is responsible for legal bills and will want to negotiate fees. Work with in-house counsel and educate him or her about the specialized body of knowledge involved in planned giving, knowledge that may be beyond the scope of a traditional law practice. If possible, try to include money for legal fees in the planned giving budget so that outside counsel can be called as necessary, without advance approval from the in-house counsel.

USE OF A PLANNED GIVING CONSULTANT

Many organizations retain the services of an outside consultant when creating a planned giving program. A consultant can help to focus on the most important areas of the program and educate the staff members about planned giving. Planned giving consultants are readily available. Large, planned giving consulting companies employ many consultants, while others work alone, on an independent basis. Ask colleagues to recommend planned giving consultants, and interview several before making a selection.

Before hiring a consultant, work with him or her to define the consultant's role. The consultant may offer training to board members and staff, help to identify and solicit donors, market the program, select an outside manager for administering life income vehicles, and meet with individual donors when necessary. As the program progresses, do not rely too heavily on the consultant to do the work development staff members should do, but work with him or her to learn the basics of planned giving. Over time, as the planned giving program grows, the consultant's role should decrease.

ESTABLISHMENT OF GIFT VEHICLES

Begin the planned giving program by simply learning how to handle bequests, charitable remainder trusts, and gifts of securities and cash. Small charities can accept these types of gifts with very little effort, and the organizations probably have received these types of gifts over the years. As the program matures, determine whether the donor base merits the time and expense of creating a gift annuity program or pooled income fund. If a choice needs to be made between gift annuities and a pooled income fund, start with the gift annuities; they are easier to administer and less expensive to operate. They are also more popular with donors.

Planned giving is a method of funding a gift rather than an end in itself. Planned giving offers life income streams and favorable tax consequences, which provide financial incentives to donors to help make gifts materialize. The majority of planned gifts are major gifts. When donors make a planned gift, they have chosen to fund a major gift using a planned giving vehicle or using assets customarily associated with planned giving, such as real estate, securities, and tangible personal property.

A planned giving program offers several gift options, including life income gifts, endowed funds, assets other than cash, and gifts from the donor's estate.

Life Income Gifts

This major gift classification includes charitable gift annuities, deferred gift annuities, pooled income fund gifts, and charitable remainder trusts. Each of these options, covered in detail in Chapter 9, provides a stream of income to a donor, to his/her spouse, if applicable, or to another beneficiary, and a charitable income tax deduction. The charity receives the remainder of the gift upon the donor's death. A life income gift is truly a living gift, one that supports a donor during life and benefits the charity in the future.

Outright major gifts are more valuable to charities than planned gifts, but for many donors, an outright gift is not feasible. For example, an outright gift of $100,000 in cash can be used immediately by the charity to support operations, programs, or capital projects. A planned gift of the same amount cannot be utilized until the death of the beneficiary, which may not occur for 10, 20, or 30 or more years. A way to compare the relative value of gifts is to compare the amount of the charitable income tax deductions. An outright gift of $100,000 in cash produces a charitable income tax deduction of $100,000. Because it is an outright gift, the charity can use the gift immediately. In the case of a planned gift, such as a charitable gift annuity with two beneficiaries, ages 61 and 59, a donor receives an income stream and a charitable income tax deduction of $20,715, or almost 21 percent of the value of the outright cash gift. In this case, this planned gift could be considered on its face to be approximately one fifth as financially valuable to the charity as compared to the outright gift. When considering gifts, donors should be advised to consider making a planned gift that is four or more times greater than an outright major gift. Chapter 9 covers life income gifts in detail.

Endowed Funds

Planned gifts also can be used to support endowed funds in the name of the donor or to memorialize or honor a loved one. Planned giving staff regularly works with donors to draft endowed funds. Chapter 8 discusses the use of endowed funds and suggests ways to draft agreements governing the use of these gifts. The principal of the endowed fund is managed in perpetuity, and a portion of the earnings from the principal is distributed to support the donor's wishes. Endowed funds are part of the charity's endowment that provides financial stability and strength.

Assets Other than Cash

Many planned gifts are made with assets other than cash, such as real estate, stocks, bonds, mutual funds, and tangible personal property like art, collectibles, and collections. Planned giving officers specialize in gifts of these assets. A donor may own assets that are far more valuable than cash and prefer to make a gift of that property rather than cash. The choice of asset depends on the donor's needs and resources and the ability of the charity to accept these gifts. For example, not all charities accept gifts of real estate, and those that do should have restrictions.

Gifts from the Donor's Estate

Included within gifts from an estate are gifts through bequests by will or distributions from a trust. Bequests, a planned giving staple, are used by donors who wish to make a major gift upon their death. These gifts provide either a specific dollar amount, such as "$100,000 to XYZ organization," or all or a stated percentage of the donor's estate, such as "50 percent of the residue of my estate to XYZ organization." For donors who are unable to make an outright major gift, a bequest is most appropriate. In addition, many donors who have made planned gifts during their lifetimes make an additional gift to the charity through a bequest. Bequests often fund a project dear to the donor. For donors who make major gifts through their estate, there is no greater way to show commitment than to share one's estate with the charity. Because of the donor's gift and the support of many other donors, the charity can deliver services to its many constituents.

MARKETING

In the early stages of a planned giving program, it is important to develop ways to market to different audiences. The audiences can include donors, prospects, key administrators, faculty, staff, family, friends, and professional advisors. The marketing may be in the form of printed materials, programs, or electronic communications.

The nature of planned giving requires a high level of visibility. Planned giving officers can understand all the nuances of specific, technical planned gifts, but if they fail to reach and attract prospects and donors, very few gifts will be closed.

Examine existing marketing efforts. Is the program marketed correctly to achieve a heightened level of awareness to increase its visibility? Which methods are used to increase this visibility? Are staff members segmenting proposals to achieve a personalized message? If the organization buys newsletters from an outside source, are they too generic for the charity's constituents? Are new publications being produced at the organization that can include planned giving? Is the staff focused on working with others who can help market the program to acquire new donors? Do not forget outreach efforts to professional advisors who can be a vital source of new donors. Remember to work with them to identify their clients and service their business needs.

EVENTS

In the first year to year and a half of a planned giving program, the non-profit may not wish to invest the time and money necessary to run an event for planned giving donors or prospects. Instead consider "piggy-backing" with another event that the nonprofit is already running and include planned giving donors and prospects as invitees. For example, at a dinner to honor annual fund donors who give at a certain level, such as $1,000 and up, invite planned giving donors or prospects to attend through a formal invitation or mailing. The host of the event, a trustee, or the president can welcome these new attendees and talk briefly about the benefits of planned giving and how planned gifts help the organization. As the program matures and the number of planned giving donors increases, consider sponsoring a luncheon program that is geared strictly toward planned giving donors and prospects. A planned giving event creates opportunities to recognize donors as a group.

SOFTWARE

As discussed earlier, planned giving software is required to offer a complete range of planned giving options. Such software programs are specific to planned giving and are not linked to other development or financial planning software. If the organization offers charitable gift annuities or a pooled income fund, planned giving software can determine the specific financial and tax benefits donors receive by making different types of planned gifts. Outside gift managers under contract with the charity may run planned giving calculations at no cost. Select a software program that is easy to use, and attend a training program to learn how to use it.

Planned giving software allows a development officer the ability to compare the type of charitable gifts a donor may make and illustrate the various benefits the donor receives by making these gifts. For example, if a donor wishes to make a gift through a charitable gift annuity, with planned giving software calculations the development director can learn the rate of the donor's return from the gift, how much actual income the donor will receive each year, the donor's charitable income tax deduction, and the amount of ordinary, capital gain, and tax-free income the donor receives. See Chapter 9 for an exhibit that illustrates the benefits for a donor, age 75, who makes a gift of $10,000 of appreciated securities with a cost basis of $3,000 to fund a charitable gift annuity. Using planned giving software, this information is prepared in an easy-to-read form and can be explained and presented to a donor or financial advisor. Several planned giving software programs are on the market; the development director should explore all options to determine which package is best for the organization's needs.

GIFT CREDITING

In the beginning of the program, determine how the organization will credit, recognize, and acknowledge the various planned gifts. How gifts are credited internally may be different from the credit given to the donor. For example, the nonprofit may credit a donor who made a $25,000 bequest to the organization by thanking the donor for the gift through a personal letter. The donor's name may be published in a gift roster listing those donors who have made contributions to the organization through a bequest over the amount of $25,000. In addition, if the organization is currently in a campaign, the donor receives campaign credit. However, the organization may choose not to credit the gift at all, knowing that donors can change their minds regarding bequests. Determine how to credit planned gifts and keep the crediting and recognition consistent from year to year.

CONCLUSION

It is challenging and rewarding to establish and run a planned giving program while being responsible for several different programs in a development office. However, for a charity to grow and attract gifts at higher levels, a planned giving program must be offered. Focus by putting the basics in place and build toward creating a larger planned giving program as the program matures. Carefully examine the ways that the program can be started using both in-house staff and outside managers. Define the scope of the program and determine which gift options to offer. Select consultants and planned giving software. Be prepared to honor and acknowledge all planned gifts. Once the basics are established, the charity can begin to be fully involved in the planned giving program, which is the subject of the next chapter.

Checklist of Action Items

- ❏   *Establish a timetable with goals.*
- ❏   *Take a course on planned giving.*
- ❏   *Mobilize the small charity's resources.*
- ❏   *Secure legal counsel.*
- ❏   *Retain a planned giving consultant.*
- ❏   *Determine which planned gift options to offer.*
- ❏   *Market to attract business.*
- ❏   *Develop financial support areas.*
- ❏   *Evaluate and select planned giving software.*
- ❏   *Establish gift-crediting guidelines.*

CHAPTER 2

Planned Giving and the Charity

INTRODUCTION

One of the major jobs of the development director or staff member assigned to oversee the planned giving program is being an advocate for the program. As an advocate, it is important to present the many possible benefits that planned giving offers to nonprofit organizations while anticipating the concerns of staff members and central administration. The director also must be prepared to deal with objections or myths about planned giving. Further, adding a new program like planned giving can create potential conflict and some uncertainty among existing staff members. This chapter discusses issues that impact planned giving in relation to the charity. It examines the way planned giving should be viewed within an organization, some problems that arise related to planned giving, and some specific actions that can be taken to make a planned giving program more successful.

PLANNED GIVING FROM THE ORGANIZATION'S PERSPECTIVE

As discussed earlier, a nonprofit organization attracts more donors and gifts by offering a complete range of giving options, including different planned gift vehicles. Most life income arrangements, including charitable gift annuities, pooled income funds, and charitable remainder trusts, pay an income to a donor for life. This means that the organization must invest the gift to produce a yearly income stream to the donor and does not have use of the principal of the gift until the donor dies. This unique relationship between a charity and a donor allows an organization to build its endowment and its future through its relationships with its donors. Based on actuarial tables, the charity pays an income stream while continuing to preserve the value of the gift and, at the same time, investing the principal to generate growth. In the case of charitable gift annuities, when older donors make planned gifts, the organization pays a higher rate of return, assuming that the donor will live for fewer years. The charity benefits by committing to an arrangement that brings a donor into the organization and strengthens a relationship that often produces additional planned and outright gifts.

A charity that embarks on a planned giving program needs to adopt the concept of organizational patience. Organizational patience is the recognition that it takes time for a planned giving program to work and to secure planned gifts. Too often charities are unrealistic about their expectations of the planned giving program. Often a charity's central administration values the demand for current cash more than the promise of future support through planned gifts. This attitude can create conflicts for the planned giving staff member at a small charity. Sometimes because it takes time to work, charities become impatient and disenchanted with the planned giving program and its staff. Instead, charities need to understand that a planned gift is often a larger, more complex gift that involves a number of financial, tax, and estate-planning decisions. Often donors are assisted by a variety of advisors, such as attorneys, financial advisors, accountants, and family members. Because there are many considerations involved in a planned gift, the gift takes time, but once the planned gift closes, a satisfied planned giving donor is almost always a repeat donor further benefiting the charity.

PLANNED GIVING PROVIDES FIVE DECADES OF SUPPORT

While most of the development staff members at a nonprofit focus on the need for current income and outright gifts, planned giving staff members focus on its future. A development program must balance its efforts to bring dollars in today while building a foundation for the future.

There may be no greater way to provide for an organization's future than through planned gifts. Many experienced professionals know that the difference between fundraising and development is planned giving. A successful planned giving program stabilizes and balances a development program. During economic downturns, annual giving programs and major gifts may suffer, but planned giving programs generally prosper since planned gifts provide such substantial financial benefits to a donor. Planned giving focuses on gifts that will materialize over a 50-year period, although most gifts materialize over a shorter, 3- to 5-year period. The need for current cash can shortchange the ability to produce larger, more substantial planned gifts that must be nurtured and cultivated over time, causing charities to lose financial support. Rushing the process produces disillusioned and often alienated donors.

PLANNED GIVING PROGRAMS ARE COST EFFECTIVE

Some organizations decide not to begin a planned giving program because the program appears labor intensive and expensive to operate. While it is true that there are significant challenges for a staff member to learn and manage, and even greater organizational start-up costs for software, marketing, and staff education, there is usually an excellent return on the organization's investment for a planned giving program. If an organization does not offer a planned giving program, it cannot compete for support among its peer organizations that offer such programs and its ability to raise support in future years is hampered.

It is important to remember that those charged with raising planned gifts also raise many major gifts. Many donors are motivated to make a major gift to a charity after reading its planned giving marketing pieces. Planned giving staff members also develop close relationships with professional advisors, specifically those practicing in estate planning, taxes, and investments. Charities need to look broadly at the many benefits a planned giving program can bring to a development program in addition to the actual dollar value of those planned gifts.

ELIMINATE COMPETITION AMONG PLANNED GIVING, ANNUAL GIVING, AND MAJOR GIFTS

Some nonprofit officials may mistakenly believe that planned gifts diminish support for the charity's annual giving or major gift programs. They falsely argue that planned giving does not attract new sources of support, but existing sources are reallocated among the development programs. Planned giving does attract new sources of support and new donors. While annual giving donors often become planned giving donors, planned giving donors also often become new annual fund donors. In fact, most annual fund donors who become planned giving donors continue to support an organization's annual giving program. The organization greatly benefits when the $50-per-year annual fund donor becomes a $20,000 planned giving donor. In addition, major gift donors make planned gifts and vice versa. Annual fund, major gift, and planned giving programs should complement rather than compete with each other. After all, all large nonprofit organizations include planned giving as a central part of their development programs. Failing to offer planned giving will result in a loss of gift revenue now and in the future.

CHAMPION THE PLANNED GIVING PROGRAM

Many professionals who wear a planned giving hat also wear several other development hats, which cause a dilution of the planned giving effort and eventually may lead nonprofit organizations, especially small ones, to become dissatisfied with planned giving efforts. To build a successful program, the charity should appoint one person to champion the planned giving effort. This individual still can have other duties, but he or she must be encouraged to spend as much time as possible to make planned giving a priority. Planned giving programs sometimes fail because no one is ultimately responsible for them, given the charge to provide leadership, or given the time to make it work. Once the person is appointed, he or she will need to build collaborative networks with other development staff, volunteers, and leadership.

Planned giving has evolved from a misunderstood and often underutilized development function into a mainstream development function. At many small charities, planned giving has not been fully incorporated into the development program. While the planned giving field is technical, a successful planned giving program is built on solid development principles. Planned giving specifics can be learned, and the planned giving officer does not need to be a lawyer, banker, or accountant to be successful. Planned giving should be an integral part of the overall development effort, working closely with other development functions to further office and organizational goals.

CLARIFY ADMINISTRATIVE RESPONSIBILITIES

Over a period of time, administrative responsibilities can virtually paralyze a planned giving program. Nonprofits usually operate with fewer staff than necessary so employees must perform a wide variety of work assignments and an even greater number of administrative duties. While it may be difficult to avoid these types of assignments, planned giving staff members need to stay focused on the job at hand. Any interruption in the program accentuates the lag time for a gift, and the lag time grows exponentially in proportion to the interruption. Today's efforts produce tomorrow's gifts and the gestation period for planned gifts is a minimum of 6 months and can be as long as 5 to 7 years or more.

Remember that the president of the organization and the vice president for development are concerned about the bottom line: money raised. Try to maintain a balanced level of independence with respect to assignments that take time away from raising money. Educate all key internal players about the nonprofit's expectations for the planned giving program.

TRAIN AND CHALLENGE THE NONPROFIT STAFF

Has a planned giving training program or workshop been presented to the development staff or the nonprofit organization's key players? If not, try to offer at least two planned giving workshops a year. In-house training programs keep development staff current with planned giving concepts and remind them of the importance of offering planned giving vehicles to donors. Consider using case studies as an effective way to involve other staff members in the process and to publicly commend colleagues on their planned giving work. The planned giving staff member conducting the seminar may learn as much from the session as the attendees.

There are a finite number of hours that can be worked each week, and productivity must be evaluated. Once the staff is trained, encourage them to become proactive with donors and prospects. Define which activities are donor related and which are not. This exercise helps to focus staff, increase productivity, and encourage success. Make a chart that lists the names of donors and where they stand on the program's priority list. Focus activities on those donors who are closest to making a gift or need some attention.

BUDGET AND STAFFING

A planned giving program can flourish when it has an adequate budget and sufficient resources. Resources need to be allocated and accessible for marketing, training, and other planned giving necessities. Programs also fail when staff turnover is so great that the constant flow of employees in and out of a program disrupts it and its donors. Management needs to focus energy on keeping its staff. At many charities, salary constraints and an absence of opportunities to advance provide disincentives for staff members to stay. Planned giving is a revenue-producing area, and staff members should be given financial incentives to remain. Competition for experienced staff is great, and employees often change jobs because of higher salaries offered by other organizations. With the tenure in a development job approximately 2 years, a charity is just beginning to get a return on its investment at about the time the employee is looking to move on. Charities should reward good employees with financial incentives and encourage them to stay.

THE BOTTOM LINE

The bottom line is how much money is raised. After 1 year, a planned giving staff member should be able to raise a minimum of two or three times his or her annual salary; successful staffers who have been on the job for 3 years or more at the same organization should raise approximately 10 times their annual salary. In addition, staff members should have quantifiable goals, such as producing a minimum of 15 significant planned gifts per year, which converts to a little more than one gift per month. These measures are helpful in refocusing priorities to raise money.

Gifts do not happen accidentally. Gifts occur primarily because staff members pursue prospects and there is a formal program or follow-up. Encourage staff members to pursue prospects that have become stale and remind them that the organization seeks their support.

CONCLUSION

Part of a planned giving job is to educate the charity about the differences between planned giving and general development. The rewards of a planned giving program can be considerable; however, the program requires patience and time to be successful. Long-term planned giving programs provide a solid foundation to a nonprofit organization, and planned gifts offer attractive options to many donors. Cooperation and a mutual understanding of the roles of development and planned giving can well serve a nonprofit organization.

PART TWO

Getting Started

CHAPTER 3

Mobilizing the Nonprofit Organization's Leadership, Boards, and Volunteers

INTRODUCTION

To fully develop a planned giving program at a small organization, planned giving staff members must build successful working relationships with a variety of the nonprofit's internal constituents. They must work with many of the charity's senior administrative staff members, boards, and volunteers on planned gift options and on expectations the planned giving office has for them. Focus primarily on the organization's president; vice president for development; board of trustees; volunteers, including board members; and other key personnel within the charity such as deans, physicians, department heads, and administrators. In addition, develop business relationships with the treasurer's office, general counsel, and business office. This chapter focuses on mobilizing the people and departments within the nonprofit who can help the planned giving program to succeed.

PRESIDENT AND CHIEF EXECUTIVE OFFICER OF ORGANIZATION

Support for a planned giving program begins at the top. The way that the president of a small nonprofit organization feels about the planned giving program can add significantly to the program's success. An enthusiastic president can have a great impact on the way the vice president for development values planned giving efforts and how trustees and key volunteers view planned giving. The president is most likely to feel positively about planned giving once a valuable planned gift has been made to the organization. A president who has personally made a planned gift is uniquely qualified to speak about the value of planned gifts to other donors and employees of the organization.

If possible, work with the president of the organization to round out his or her knowledge of the benefits of planned giving. Take the opportunity to talk about specific gift situations and illustrate how planned giving helped to close the gift. Talking about specific financial benefits, such as the stream of income, charitable income tax deduction, and the elimination of capital gains taxes available to donors, educates the president and trustees about planned giving benefits and establishes the planned giving officer or solicitor as the resident expert. The aim is to have the president of the organization promote the planned giving program at appropriate opportunities. A president who does so puts others on notice to take the program seriously and to support planned giving efforts. A president's backing can result in more help from trustees, increased gifts to the program, and an increased budget to fund the program.

VICE PRESIDENT FOR DEVELOPMENT

Most vice presidents have a basic understanding of planned giving vehicles. They know that to compete successfully with other nonprofits and to provide donors with a full range of gift options, the charity needs a planned giving program. The vice president for development should encourage the development staff to solicit donors for both outright major gifts and planned gifts. If the vice president truly values the planned giving program, staff members will be encouraged to take the time to set up a proper planned giving program. The attitude of the vice president for development directly affects others' perception of the planned giving program, including development staff and employees in related offices. The vice president for development can provide support to the planned giving program and the staff person charged with implementing it by:

- Providing direct access to the president and trustees when necessary and appropriate. Support at this level demonstrates that planned giving is important.

- Providing a sufficient budget to run a planned giving program.

- Being patient enough to allow marketing efforts to translate into gifts over time.

- Creating opportunities for continued professional training and education for the planned giving staff officer.

- Promoting participation by the planned giving staff at meetings that include the president and trustees, and an opportunity to speak about planned giving.

- Offering full credit for planned gifts within the nonprofit. This is important for donors and development staff, because it emphasizes the worthiness of planned gifts.

ROLE OF THE BOARD OF TRUSTEES

One of the most critical duties of any member of a board of trustees is fundraising. It takes money to drive nonprofit organizations, and organizations should be direct about their expectations. After all, raising money is one of the major reasons for having boards of trustees. When they join the board, members should be told about their financial obligation to make gifts. At many organizations gift giving or getting is a condition of board membership. Board members should feel good about their financial support and know that their contribution can be very influential in encouraging others to give.

Importance of Trustee Giving

Nothing quite validates a planned giving program as having a trustee make a planned gift to the organization. This action serves to generate additional planned and major gifts from other trustees and donors. A trustee's planned gift is a wonderful marketing opportunity because the trustee can be profiled in planned giving newsletters and brochures. A trustee's personal planned gift demonstrates commitment to the organization, the program, and its objectives. Making a gift is a trustee's best opportunity to step beyond a policy and oversight role to become an active philanthropic player. Trustees who make planned gifts can discuss planned giving with donors and prospects and solicit gifts more comfortably because they have already given. For any planned giving program to succeed, prospective donors want to know that board members are fully behind the effort. If not, prospects ask, "If the board members have not given, why should I be asked to make a gift?" Educate trustees about the value of planned giving. Ask for their support when making decisions that affect the scope of the program. Invite trustees to identify and solicit donors and to become donors themselves.

Trustees as Planned Giving Fundraisers

Statistics show that most successful campaigns had significant trustee involvement. The ultimate responsibility for an organization rests with its board of trustees. Because the board is responsible for the spending of funds, it follows that board members need to play an active role in raising funds. Trustees know the most about the organization's hopes for the future and how the organization plans to achieve its goals. They are in the best position to tell the organization's story to others and to raise the level of awareness of donors, prospects, and community leaders. Trustees have developed other relationships, outside of their connection to the organization, that can provide financial resources for the planned giving program. To increase planned giving totals, trustees must be willing to help identify and solicit prospects who can make planned gifts to the organization. Because fundraising at the trustee level often is performed by peers, trustees should be willing to solicit some of their friends, acquaintances, and business associates who might be interested in the nonprofit organization and be willing to make a gift.

VOLUNTEERS

Some standard fundraising models believe that volunteers drive the leadership, direction, and implementation of a development effort. The theory is that staff-driven programs are unable to access, cultivate, and solicit an organization's constituents. It is true that many major gifts come directly from volunteers themselves, and this is to be encouraged. But to support and sustain a volunteer-driven development program requires staff. In the end, it takes both staff and volunteers to build successful nonprofit organizations and fundraising programs. Volunteer-driven programs work well at small nonprofit organizations, such as small private schools, community healthcare organizations, and arts programs. Volunteers usually best serve planned giving programs by screening prospect lists for new donors, agreeing to solicit some key individuals for gifts, or making necessary introductions for staff members to solicit planned giving prospects. Volunteers who can work on their own and bring new donors into a program who do not have a connection to the organization are the most sought after.

Sometimes volunteers misunderstand the nature of development. They see an organization's volunteer activities as a way to accomplish their own social and political goals. The volunteer may attend volunteer meetings to meet with old friends and have lunch, rather than focus on fundraising. Staff members may need to redirect volunteers' efforts to preserve the budget for appropriate development events and programs, such as educating volunteers about the importance of development and planned giving and suggesting ways to promote development efforts.

WORKING WITH DEANS

Deans are usually grateful for any assistance received from the development office. Yet a development officer who is based at one school within the organization often is in conflict with the various roles the development officer is asked to play, one of which is to secure planned gifts. Staff members must design fundraising strategies, identify prospects, interview faculty, and provide development leadership to the dean and the school. The dean, however, may feel differently. Some deans have little knowledge about what a development officer can do and often see the development officer as an adjunct to their office, a staff person. Staffers should educate deans about what is expected from a development standpoint. Encourage deans to discuss the strengths of their college and discuss their vision for the future. Visions are often expensive; that is where the planned giving officer comes in.

Like some presidents, deans also may consider fundraising to be a low priority; a few view it as beneath them. A savvy staff member can educate deans as to the dean's respective role and can provide leadership to run a successful campaign. The goal is to maximize the dean's development activities. Keep the dean focused on the relationship between financial support and project enhancement and the need for additional scholarships and recruitment. Schedule a weekly appointment with the dean or an associate dean, who reports to the dean, as a way to keep communication open and to develop a relationship with the dean and learn about the school's priorities. Develop an agenda for each meeting and work through it. Regularly scheduled meetings enable staff members to report successes and to stay in touch with specific priorities and ongoing prospects.

WORKING WITH PHYSICIANS

Doctors can be invaluable to development success in a healthcare setting. Most often patients want to make their gifts to the doctor who helped them. If their doctor is willing to assist in raising money, this is ideal. Staff members need to convince the physician that he or she can help raise money for the physician's own programs. All programs need money, and doctors will be more helpful if they know that they and their programs benefit from the money raised. Try to maintain regular contact with a physician by telephone and written correspondence. Success with patients often follows from having a physician sign a letter, telephone a prospect, or agree to personally solicit a patient. Encourage as much participation as possible because it can make a great difference to the bottom line, raising money.

SUPPORTING OFFICES WITHIN THE ORGANIZATION

Several key offices within an organization can have a very significant impact on a planned giving program. Three such areas include the treasurer's office, office of the general counsel, and business office.

Treasurer

To build a successful planned giving program, the treasurer and planned giving staff must work together. Together they will deal primarily with investment and administrative issues for the planned giving program. If there is a planned giving program in place, the treasurer may be intimately involved with the administration and investment of the charitable gift annuities and charitable remainder trusts, as well as making decisions about the use of an outside pooled income fund manager or its activities. If the treasurer is managing the charitable gift annuities and trusts in-house, first determine if this is in the best interest of the planned giving program.

Consider the following:

- Are the donors and development staff best served and serviced by keeping the management of these gifts in-house?
- Are the donors receiving the best possible rates of return while the remainder is protected for the organization?
- Is the treasurer's office interested in continuing the arrangement of managing the planned gifts in-house?
- If management of planned gifts is moved outside of the organization, who will pay the cost?

It is important to determine if the arrangement is working for all players. If the planned giving program is new, discuss how the treasurer's office feels about administering the program. Educate the treasurer and the treasurer's staff about the needs of the planned giving program and its impact on the organization's bottom line. Let them know what they can do to help the program flourish. For example, the treasurer's office is often a starting point for inquiries from donors. Suggest that donor-related calls regarding planned gifts be directed to the development office and thank the treasurer's office regularly for the work they do on behalf of the development program.

Office of the General Counsel

Many smaller nonprofit organizations use an outside law firm for their legal work. However, some may employ a single attorney to handle large issues, including those that arise in development. Work closely with the general counsel's office to help the planned giving program to run effectively. The general counsel's office may want to control much of the planned giving legal work, but unfortunately many attorneys at nonprofit organizations are overworked and kept extremely busy with more pressing issues. Charitable giving sometimes can be a distraction to the general counsel. Although it is unlikely that the general counsel has much experience in charitable giving, he or she may feel strongly about trying to do the work in-house to keep control over planned giving activities and keep outside legal costs down. The planned giving officer needs to educate the general counsel about the legal complexities of planned giving work, stressing the technicalities of the different financial vehicles, gifts of real estate, and the various tax implications for donors. It is hoped that the general counsel will see that he or she cannot manage all or most of this work in-house.

Suggest a law firm or attorney to use, and discuss the firm's experience with planned giving. Stress that when a donor needs an answer quickly, the planned giving officer needs to have the independence to call an outside attorney without having to clear the request with the general counsel. Additionally, the outside attorney will not second-guess everything the planned giving officer does, which affords some independence. Keep the general counsel informed of the planned giving work, but remember that it is the planned giving officer who is ultimately responsible for the planned giving program.

Business Office

The business and the planned giving offices work together on gifts of real estate. A strong relationship is helpful when an organization goes through the complex process of accepting a real estate gift. Bring the business office into the process early by educating business office staff members about what the planned giving office does and the benefits to the organization of receiving real estate gifts. Walk through the gift process from the beginning to the end. Do not let the business office immediately reject a piece of real estate because of complexity or the time involved in closing the gift. Consider working with the business office to design a questionnaire for the development staff about accepting gifts of real estate. In this way the planned giving office is in a better position to navigate the potentially treacherous waters of real estate gifts. See Chapter 12 for information on gifts of real estate.

PLANNED GIVING TRAINING PROGRAMS

A successful and productive planned giving training program should be used to educate internal constituents, including development staff members, about planned giving. It should define what planned giving is, alert audience members to the profile of a planned giving prospect, show how gifts can be funded, discuss various planned giving vehicles, show ways that the internal constituents can support the planned giving program, and provide attendees with handouts that can be read after the training program is over. A sample planned giving training program follows.

Sample Planned Giving Training Program

I. What is planned giving?
   A. A planned gift is an irrevocable gift. A donor transfers cash or property to a nonprofit and the gift cannot be retrieved.
   B. A creative way to give, using many different types of assets.
   C. A way for donors to make gifts to an organization and receive financial benefits.
   D. A way for donors to make larger gifts than they thought possible, and for some donors the only way to make a major gift.
   E. A way to help donors achieve philanthropic and financial objectives:
      1. Make a major gift.
      2. Obtain a charitable income tax deduction.
      3. Avoid or reduce paying capital gains taxes, currently at a maximum rate of 20% for most investment assets.
      4. Avoid probate costs, often 2% to 8% of gross estate.
      5. Reduce estate taxes, currently at 37% to 50%.
      6. Reduce federal income taxes.
      7. Increase current yield from stocks and bonds.
      8. Plan for retirement and family.
      9. Provide permanent support to <ORGANIZATION>.

II. Who is a planned giving prospect?
   A. A planned giving prospect usually shares one or more of the following characteristics:
      1. The donor is philanthropic.
      2. The donor is motivated to make a gift to the nonprofit.
      3. The donor desires tax benefits.
      4. The donor is looking for income.
      5. The donor is looking for an increase in current investments.
      6. The donor is interested in establishing an endowed fund.

       7. The donor has no children.

       8. The donor is a surviving spouse.

III. How can a planned gift be funded?

    A. Ways to fund a planned gift:

       1. Cash

       2. Pledge: If in a campaign, over the years remaining in the campaign

       3. Securities: Stocks, bonds, mutual funds, closely held stock

       4. Life insurance

       5. Tangible personal property: Antiques, jewelry, books, art, planes, automobiles, computers

       6. Real estate: Personal residence, farm, summer home, commercial property, and vacant land

       7. Retirement assets: Individual retirement accounts, pension plans

IV. What are the most commonly used planned giving vehicles?

    A. Charitable gift annuities

    B. Deferred gift annuities

    C. Pooled income funds

    D. Charitable remainder trusts

       1. Annuity trusts

       2. Unitrusts

    E. Charitable lead trusts

    F. Bequests

    G. Life insurance

V. Definitions and benefits of planned gift vehicles

    A. Charitable gift annuity: A gift option primarily for donors 72 years old and older.

      Definition: A charitable gift annuity is a contract between a donor and the nonprofit organization. The donor makes the gift, and the organization agrees to pay the donor a fixed income for life.

       1. Minimum amount for a charitable gift annuity at many organizations is $5,000.

       2. The donor receives a charitable income tax deduction in the year the gift is made.

NOTE

Inform the attendees that when they think about the various planned giving options, they should focus on different age groups and the benefits that donors in each age group receive in making a particular type of planned gift. After the next section, define each type of planned gift and describe each vehicle's financial benefits.

3. A charitable gift annuity provides the donor a fixed, secure rate of return for life. The rate is based on the age of the donor.

4. The best rate of return is for donors 72 years old and older; the older the donor, the better the rate of return.

5. A portion of the income the beneficiary receives is tax-free.

6. The donor can fund a charitable gift annuity with appreciated securities, but capital gains taxes cannot be completely avoided.

7. At the donor's death, the organization has use of the principal.

B. Deferred gift annuity: Best suited for donors 55 years old and younger as well as for donors who want to make a gift and defer receiving income for a number of years.

Definition: A giving vehicle most like an IRA. A donor receives an income later in life, often at age 65 or older, when income is needed more or when the donor is in a lower tax bracket. Sometimes an older donor may want to make a gift, but not receive any income for a certain number of years.

1. Minimum amount for a deferred gift annuity at many organizations is $5,000.

2. The donor receives a charitable income tax deduction in the year the gift is made. The charitable income tax deduction is based on the donor's age and the age at which the donor begins to receive the income.

3. The donor receives a fixed, secure rate of return in the future.

4. Excellent giving vehicle for younger donors. High rate of return and opportunity to become a big donor at a younger age.
5. The income received by the donor is partially tax-free.
6. The donor can make the gift with appreciated securities, but capital gains taxes cannot be completely avoided.
7. At the donor's death, the nonprofit has use of the principal.
8. The deferred gift annuity can also serve as a retirement benefit or as a way to pay children's tuition.

C. Pooled income fund: Best for donors 50 to 70 years old and for those who want to make a gift of appreciated property and completely avoid paying capital gains taxes.

Definition: A type of trust that is similar to a mutual fund. A donor makes a gift, the gift is pooled with other donors' gifts, and the donor receives a variable rate of return for life.

1. Minimum amount for a first-time pooled income fund gift at many organizations is $5,000.
2. Additional gifts to the fund can be made at a lower rate.
3. The donor receives a variable rate of return for life. Each year, based on investment performance, the income stream to the donor varies.
4. The donor receives a charitable income tax deduction in the year the gift is made.
5. When there are two beneficiaries, the rate of return stays the same; this is not true for charitable gift annuities.
6. The donor can make a gift of appreciated securities to a pooled income fund and completely avoid capital gains taxes, a significant advantage in making a pooled income fund gift.
7. Upon the donor's death, the nonprofit has use of the principal.

Some organizations offer several different pooled income funds to meet donors' various financial objectives. These different pooled income funds usually include:

a. High-income fund: Pays the highest rate of annual income to a donor; provides the lowest charitable income tax deduction.

    b. Balanced fund: Offers a balanced rate of return and charitable income tax deduction.

    c. Growth fund: Provides the highest charitable income tax deduction; lowest rate of income.

D. Charitable remainder trusts

Definition: A donor can make a substantial gift through a personal, individualized plan. The donor receives a stream of income for life or for a term of years.

1. Minimum amount for a charitable remainder trust is usually $100,000 or more.

2. The donor receives an income for life or for a number of years not exceeding 20. The donor selects the rate of return, between 5% and 7%, in conjunction with the organization's investment policies.

3. The donor avoids paying capital gains taxes when funding a charitable remainder trust with appreciated property.

4. The donor receives a charitable income tax deduction based on the amount of gift and payout rate selected.

5. At the donor's death, the nonprofit receives use of the principal.

6. The gift of the charitable remainder trust is excluded from a donor's state and federal taxes, and is also removed from probate.

There are two types of charitable remainder trusts: the charitable remainder annuity trust and the charitable remainder unitrust.

1. Charitable remainder annuity trust

    a. Pays a fixed dollar amount based on a percentage of the initial contribution, not less than 5%, chosen on the date the gift is made.

    b. More secure for the donor; less secure for the organization.

    c. A donor cannot make additional payments to a charitable remainder annuity trust after the initial gift is made. The donor can, however, create more than one charitable remainder annuity trust.

2. Charitable remainder unitrust
   a. Pays a variable rate of return based on the principal of the trust as valued annually.
   b. The donor selects the payout rate, not less than 5%, chosen on the date the gift is made.
   c. Less secure for both the donor and the organization, but the charitable remainder unitrust offers a greater chance for a higher return over time.
   d. A donor can make additional contributions to a charitable remainder unitrust after the initial gift is made.
   e. Gifts of real estate
      Donors can make gifts of real estate in several different ways. The four most common ways include:
      1. Outright gift
         A donor makes an outright gift of real estate and receives a charitable income tax deduction.
      2. Retained life estate
         A donor makes a gift of real estate, but remains in the property until her death. The donor continues to pay all expenses and taxes, but obtains a charitable income tax deduction and has the property removed from probate and her estate.
      3. Charitable remainder trust
         Through a charitable remainder trust a donor can make a gift of real estate, receive a stream of income, and, once the property is sold, obtain a charitable income tax deduction. A donor can avoid paying capital gains taxes on a gift of appreciated property made to a charitable remainder trust.
      4. Bargain sale
         A bargain sale arrangement allows a donor to sell a piece of property to a nonprofit for an amount less than the property is worth. The donor receives a charitable income tax deduction for the gift part of the bargain sale.

E. Bequests: One of the largest sources of income to nonprofits. Definition: A donor makes a gift to a nonprofit in his other will. The donor must draft a new will or add a codicil to an existing will to make a bequest.
   1. Through a bequest a donor can make a substantial gift to a nonprofit without depleting current assets.
   2. A donor can change his mind and revoke the bequest if desired.
   3. The gift avoids state and federal estate taxes.
IV. Integrating planned giving into the development program
   A. Identify individuals who fit the planned giving profile, and notify the planned giving office about such prospects.
   B. Use a planned giving check-off form to obtain more information on all solicitations, and include it in various publications.
   C. Work to upgrade annual fund donors to planned giving donors.
   D. Aggressively market planned giving vehicles in all available newspapers, magazines, bulletins, and other publications. Include planned giving ads, donor profiles, and financial, estate planning, and tax articles whenever possible.
   E. Introduce the concept of planned giving at all appropriate meetings, events, and gatherings.
   F. Share travel information so that planned giving prospects and donors can be visited by representatives of the organization.

When organizing a planned giving training session, consider using overhead projections or handouts to demonstrate the financial benefits that donors receive from making a planned gift. Supply audience members with handouts so that they can read materials after the presentation is completed. The handouts can be a summary of the session and should include planned giving calculations and perhaps a newspaper article of interest in this area.

Be sensitive to the length of the presentation; one hour is probably sufficient. Select a time of day when most people can attend, and give lots of advance notice. Keep the presentation interesting and fun, and avoid becoming too technical. Show attendees how interesting planned giving is and how planned gifts can help donors make gifts they did not think possible and help the organization to raise more money.

CONCLUSION

Educating the organization's internal constituents about planned giving is critical to the success of a planned giving program. Keeping these constituents educated and involved is a very important aspect of a planned giving program. Communicate regularly with all of these individuals to help the program prosper. The nonprofit's leadership, board, and volunteers become the planned giving program's ambassadors, conveying information about planned gifts to those who need to know. Staff, particularly other development staff members and key administrators such as deans and physicians, also can become allies as they learn more about planned giving.

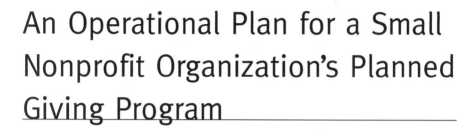

An Operational Plan for a Small Nonprofit Organization's Planned Giving Program

INTRODUCTION

At a small nonprofit organization, beginning a planned giving program or building an existing one requires a solid plan. An operational plan needs to be developed to identify the types of activities to be undertaken in the first 12 to 18 months of a new program. Before beginning the operational plan, the planned giving officer must fully understand the organization's style, pace, and politics. An operational plan needs to be realistic and well organized, and to reflect a wide range of planned giving ideas depending on the maturity of the program. The plan must be revised periodically to add new initiatives and ideas, and eliminate those that do not produce a reasonable return. This chapter presents issues to consider in creating a plan.

PLANNED GIVING AS A START-UP BUSINESS

When examining the planned giving program, adopt a fresh perspective. The nature of planned giving differs from almost every other area in a development office and is best exemplified by an entrepreneurial spirit and attitude.

Consider the following:

- *Research.*   Where does planned giving business come from?
- *Product or Service Development.*   What types of planned giving products or services should the nonprofit organization offer?
- *Marketing.*   How can the planned giving options be promoted through marketing?
- *Outreach.*   How can continued visibility be achieved with the community or nonprofit organization's constituents?
- *Identification of New Business.*   Who are new planned giving prospects? Which existing donors or prospects need attention?
- *Staff Management.*   Is the staff challenged, and are assignments delegated appropriately?

PURPOSE OF THE PLANNED GIVING PROGRAM

Start the operational plan by stating the purpose of the planned giving program, such as: "The purpose of the planned giving program is to raise funds through planned gifts such as life income gifts, gifts through estates and trusts, and endowed funds, and to raise funds through assets other than cash." Include a statement indicating what is needed for the program to succeed, such as: "To succeed, a comprehensive educational, marketing, and outreach program must be established to inform donors, prospects, trustees, physicians/deans/administrators, staff, and friends about the benefits of making planned gifts."

GOALS OF THE PROGRAM

Outline the broadest goals of the planned giving program in four steps:

1. Identify new and solicit existing planned giving prospects and donors.
2. Establish a strong marketing effort to promote planned gifts.
3. Raise the visibility of the planned giving program internally and externally.
4. Restructure existing support areas to provide services to the planned giving program.

Next take each program goal and further define the goal through specific activities. For each goal, specify the following five areas:

1. Target goals for money raised
2. Number of planned gifts to be raised
3. Marketing initiatives
4. Events, programs, and activities
5. Staff training

DONOR CONTACT

Planned giving staff, as well as other development staff, needs to maintain regular contact with prospects and donors. Is the planned giving program connecting with its constituents? Is the program building a foundation to maintain a continued presence over a five-year period? How will contact be maintained? Staff members usually stay in touch with prospects and donors in three ways:

1. By letter
2. By telephone
3. By personal visit

While meeting in person is the most effective way to build a relationship, planned giving staff members can supplement formal visits with letters and telephone calls to promote contact with donors on a regular basis. Development, especially the business of planned giving, is a people-to-people business. Planned giving by definition requires regular contact over an extended period of time. Many planned gifts materialize only after a series of integrated efforts conducted over several years.

IDENTIFY NEW PROSPECTS AND SOLICIT EXISTING PLANNED GIVING PROSPECTS

Because planned gifts often take years to materialize, it is necessary to build a large pool of prospects. To build this pool, consider the following steps:

- Assist other development staff members with individual planned giving cases.

- Identify and meet with existing donors to introduce them to planned giving concepts.
- Upgrade bequest donors by asking them to consider a life income gift.
- At an educational organization, identify members of a class who have made planned gifts and/or approach members of classes celebrating significant reunions, such as 25th, 50th, 55th, and 60th. At other nonprofits, target other groups of donors (e.g., patients, patrons, attendees) and organize them around an event or activity.
- Identify and work with one or two key volunteers who are willing to solicit others for a planned gift.
- Establish bequest societies or planned giving committees.

ESTABLISH A STRONG MARKETING EFFORT TO PROMOTE PLANNED GIFTS

Through publications, mailings, and events, establish a strong marketing effort to promote planned gifts. Even though the budget at a small nonprofit may be small, marketing is the best way to reach new prospects and donors, especially when only a few staff members work on planned giving. Remember to space marketing appeals so that an appropriate follow-up can be accomplished. The following is a comprehensive list of marketing appeals. Select those actions that work best for the program.

Publications

- Draft planned giving advertisements and articles for existing development newsletters or publications.
- Create a planned giving letter to send to planned giving prospects and donors.
- Run planned giving, financial planning, and estate planning columns in a development or planned giving newsletter.
- Revise annual fund reply devices to include a planned giving appeal.
- Create a general planned giving brochure to offer to donors and prospects.
- Identify and publicize organization-wide funding opportunities and needs through various existing publications.

- Draft an "Inventory of Assets" booklet to help donors with estate planning matters and to identify assets that may be used to make a gift.
- Create an endowment book that lists existing endowed funds at the organization.

Mailings

- Segment the database to develop a targeted population of donors who have made annual gifts of $25 or more for three or more years to send planned giving mailings.
- Segment the database to select donors or prospects who are 75 years old or older to send specific planned giving information, such as information on charitable gift annuities. If the donors' ages are not known, present a table showing payouts for donors at ages 65, 70, 75, and 80.
- Send donors 50 to 70 years old and donors who have made gifts of securities to the organization information about the organization's pooled income fund.
- Target donors 25 to 50 years old for a deferred gift annuity.
- Select all donors who have given $5,000 or more cumulatively to the organization to receive planned giving information.
- Target geographical areas for mailings by selecting donors living in zip code areas that indicate wealth.
- Prior to year-end, send existing planned giving donors and prospects a year-end tax letter that highlights the benefits of charitable giving and current tax tips.
- Mail a publication four times per year to all planned giving donors and prospects.
- Mail a "Ways to Give" brochure to retired faculty, staff, and administrators along with a letter showing the benefits of making a planned gift during retirement.

Events

- Host a series of seminars for donors, prospects, and friends of the organization to focus on preretirement planning, retirement planning, and financial planning to attract people who may be capable of making a planned gift.

- If appropriate, conduct seminars in regions of the country where many older donors live or vacation, including Florida, California, Arizona, and elsewhere.
- Host a luncheon for all donors who have made a planned gift to the organization.
- Speak at a local retirement home about the benefits of planned giving, estate planning, and financial planning.
- Conduct planned giving seminars for area professional advisors.

RAISE THE VISIBILITY OF THE PLANNED GIVING PROGRAM INTERNALLY AND EXTERNALLY

Educate internal and external constituents about the ways to create planned gifts:

Internally

- Educate development officers about trends in planned giving to make them feel comfortable about options they can present to donors and prospects.
- Interact with key internal staff, including the general counsel's office and representatives from the financial affairs and business offices, treasurer's office, and comptroller's office, to discuss the goals of the planned giving program and to educate them about planned giving needs.
- Train and educate researchers, telefund callers, and annual fund staff to identify planned giving leads.
- Meet with department heads, administrators, physicians, deans, and program leaders to talk about planned giving and ways to identify planned giving prospects.
- Conduct screening meetings with volunteers, staff, and trustees for local and international planned giving prospects.
- Work individually with development officers to include planned giving in their operational plans.
- Assign staff members to serve as planned giving liaisons to particular departments. For example, in a medical setting, assign a major

gifts officer to focus on grateful patients of the Neurology Department to close a certain number of planned gifts each year.

- Clarify priorities for private support in each department, outline planned giving strategies to help accomplish priorities, and target specific prospects as potential planned giving donors.

Externally

- Contact representatives from the banking, financial, and legal communities who can provide new business to the planned giving program. These representatives include trust officers, bankers, financial advisors, certified public accountants (CPAs), and attorneys.

- Create a professional advisory committee to assist in marketing planned gifts. Invite committee members to the planned giving office to attend workshops on charitable gift planning.

- Conduct charitable gift planning, estate planning, and financial planning seminars in select geographical areas for donors and prospects.

- Create and distribute a professional advisor's manual to lawyers, CPAs, trust officers, financial advisors, and others who may need information for clients or who can provide planned giving leads to the nonprofit. The booklet can provide information on estate planning, including wills, trusts and estates, and charitable gift planning. Include the organization's logo on the cover.

- Host an annual luncheon/event for outside professionals to educate them about the organization and provide them with a social event outside of the office.

RESTRUCTURE SUPPORT AREAS TO PROVIDE SERVICES FOR THE PLANNED GIVING PROGRAM

Evaluate and restructure those areas that provide services to the planned giving program:

- If the nonprofit has in-house planned giving services, determine if those services should be moved to a professional manager outside of the organization. If new programs need to be started, such as a pooled income fund or charitable gift annuities, determine what various outside providers offer and prices charged.

- Create or update existing documents, such as a charitable gift annuity contract, pooled income fund trust agreement, and instruments of transfer.

- Determine what area in the organization manages bequests and decide whether the planned giving office should take over management.

These ideas may be incorporated into an operational plan or used as background information to support current goals.

INVENTORY EXISTING PLANNED GIVING TOTALS

Inventory existing planned giving files, if there are any, to establish a baseline starting point for the program. Determine the total number of planned gifts including bequests, endowed funds, life income gifts, and gifts of assets other than cash, and their amounts. Use Exhibit 4.1, "Planned Giving Baseline Totals," to inventory planned gifts.

Look at the overall quantity and quality of existing donors, and determine their financial capacity and interest in the organization. Using the model provided in Exhibit 4.1, list the total number of each type of gift, the total amount of those gifts, and the average size of that type of gift. Identify the years in which each gift closed to develop a sense of how many and what types of gifts close each year, so that priorities can be established.

EXHIBIT 4.1   PLANNED GIVING BASELINE TOTALS

Total Number	Total $	Average Size $
Charitable Gift Annuities		
Deferred Gift Annuities		
Pooled Income Fund Gifts		
Charitable Remainder Annuity Trusts		
Real Estate Gifts		
Bequest Intentions		
Total Baseline of Existing Planned Gifts (from Inception of Program)		

PLANNED GIVING DATABASE

If a computer database retrieval system does not exist, consider purchasing a planned giving software package that retrieves information about each planned giving donor and prospect, including the donor's and prospect's address, telephone number, type of planned gift made or considered, age, and connection to the organization. Place all files on a mini-database and convert files to a system that enables the planned giving office to retrieve and sort data. The mini-database enables the planned giving office to communicate more efficiently with donors and to identify and target donors for seminars, cultivation, visits, mailings, and solicitations. To save money, create a database using one of the many software programs that are available on the market.

PLANNED GIVING BUDGET

An operating plan should include a one-year planned giving budget. Exhibit 4.2 presents a sample budget.

Consider the following expenses to include as budget items in the operating plan.

Travel

If the nonprofit has a national donor base, include local and national visits with donors and prospects as a travel expense. Remember to budget for airfare, hotel, meals, rental cars, taxicabs, telephone calls, and parking costs. Travel should be considered a high priority, because one-on-one meetings with prospects, followed by a solicitation, are more likely to produce gifts.

Programs and Events

Budget for recognition events, outreach programs, and donor-related functions. Count on producing at least one donor event each year. When budgeting for an event, include the costs of food, rental space, parking, alcohol, if applicable, invitations, postage, flowers, token gifts, an honorarium for the speaker, and marketing the event.

EXHIBIT 4.2 PLANNED GIVING BUDGET

1000	Office Supplies/Materials		$
1001	Letterhead	$	
1002	Postage	$	
1003	Business Equipment	$	
1004	Files/Folders	$	
1005	Furniture	$_____	
	Subtotal	$	
1010	Training/Education		$
1011	Conference	$	
1012	Subscriptions	$	
1013	Professional Memberships	$	
1014	Seminars	$_____	
	Subtotal	$	
1020	Travel		$
1021	Air	$	
1022	Hotels	$	
1023	Restaurants	$	
1024	Rental Cars	$_____	
	Subtotal	$	
1030	Computer Hardware/Software		$
1031	Planned Giving Software	$	
1032	Computer Laptops	$	
1033	Service Contracts	$	
1034	Telephone Fax	$_____	
	Subtotal	$	
1040	Professional Services		$
1041	Consultant	$	
1042	Legal Services	$	
1043	Financial Service Fees	$	
1044	Outside Administrators	$_____	
	Subtotal	$	
1050	Marketing		$
1051	Design Change	$	
1052	Printing Typsetting	$_____	
	Subtotal	$	
1060	Programs and Events		$
1061	Workshops	$	
1062	Recognition Programs	$	
1063	Events	$	
1064	Outreach	$	
1070	Salaries		$
1071	Director	$	
1072	Planned Giving Assistant	$	

Marketing

Include the cost of printing and designing newsletters, ads, year-end letters, holiday cards, stationery, targeted mailings, business reply envelopes, and other marketing pieces and expenses.

Postage

Include postage costs for targeted mailings, individual responses to donors, newsletters, and invitations.

Legal Fees

Include funds in the budget to cover the cost of outside legal fees. The ability to call an attorney to answer questions is very important to a successful planned giving program. This is especially true for a new program or when building a program. As the program matures, legal fees should increase. Estimate this amount based on the expected number of gifts to close in a year, with a close look at which ones may require outside legal assistance. Overbudget rather than underbudget this expense. This cost should be separate from any legal advice obtained from the general counsel of the nonprofit organization.

Outside Administration Fees

The budget should include the cost of planned giving services provided by an outside money manager. The administrative fees will likely include costs of maintaining the pooled income fund, gift annuity program, and charitable remainder trusts. Remember that as the program grows, so do the administrative costs. Budget additional amounts, if necessary, for outside consultants.

Professional Development

Budget attendance for at least one professional seminar a year, individual one-day conferences, and the cost to attend local planned giving group meetings. If the organization offers charitable gift annuities, become a member of the American Council on Gift Annuities, which charges a modest annual membership fee.

Conference attendance is especially important when resources are limited. The planned giving officer needs to have as many resources available as possible.

Computer Software

Planned giving software must be updated and costs for upgrades and annual maintenance fees should be budgeted. If necessary, budget for an introductory training session to learn how to run the software.

Books and Professional Newsletters, Subscriptions

Planned giving requires current reference materials, including books on planned giving, the Internal Revenue Code and Regulations, and various tax, financial planning, and legal references. Keep money in the budget to pay for planned giving reference materials as needed. Subscribe to at least one professional outside planned giving newsletter or service that is produced monthly or bimonthly. This will help provide information on current trends in planned giving and tax law changes. Also consider subscribing to the *Wall Street Journal*.

CONCLUSION

Everyone gets caught up in day-to-day office routines. With some frequency, however, it is important to step back and assess program progress. Although it is so easy to become distracted, constantly analyze productivity and focus on the bottom line, raising money. Develop an operational plan—one that is helpful and likely to be used and reused. Once developed, give it time to work and commit to it for at least one year. Read the plan quarterly and adjust accordingly, if appropriate. Make the plan the key working document and distribute it to staff and select nonprofit officials.

CHAPTER 5

Gift Acceptance Policies for a Planned Giving Program

INTRODUCTION

All nonprofit organizations with planned giving programs need to have a written gift acceptance policy to address issues involved with accepting planned gifts. Outright cash gifts are straightforward, offering very few challenges to a development program. But because many deferred gift arrangements have long-term implications and obligate a charity to make payments to a donor for life, prior to accepting a gift the nonprofit must consider the consequences, in order to protect both the donor and the charity. This is even more important at small nonprofit organizations where opportunities for gifts may be more limited.

Through a life income gift, the nonprofit is obligated to pay a stream of income for life to a donor or another beneficiary. For example, if a 65-year-old donor creates a charity gift annuity, charitable remainder trust, or pooled income fund gift, the gift has the potential of running for 25 years or more for the benefit of the first beneficiary, often the donor, and longer than 25 years if payments are made to a younger, second beneficiary. Other types of planned gifts also can obligate a charity for years. Gifts of real estate can obligate a charity to act as a landlord and broker, sometimes for out-of-state property. Gifts of securities also have specific rules for acceptance and valuation. Tangible personal property gifts may need insurance, storage, and special display cases. The gift acceptance policy should specifically address gifts of tangible personal property to protect the interests of both the donor and the nonprofit.

A gift acceptance policy is a written compilation of guidelines and suggestions for everyone involved in the gift process to understand and honor. Development staff members need to understand the difference between a planned gift that is truly a gift to the charity, given by a donor who really wants to benefit the nonprofit, and a "gift" that is motivated by personal financial gain, which could obligate the charity to a lifelong arrangement that is not in its best interest. A written gift acceptance policy helps everyone involved to understand the difference.

Turning Down a Gift

Sometimes inexperienced planned giving officers may be overly enthusiastic about a prospective gift of real estate. Unfortunately, the development officer may spend valuable time pursuing the gift, only to discover that the property would provide little benefit to the charity or, worse, be a burden on it, requiring substantial financial outlay and management.

Planned giving staff members also may need to counsel financial advisors who suggest that the charity create a charitable remainder trust for a donor who wishes to receive a very high payout rate from a trust, such as 15 percent. The staff member may feel that some gift is better than no gift at all and not realize that the trust is likely to be depleted by paying a high annual rate to the donor, a rate that diminishes the remainder, or gift, to the charity. Such gifts often require significant management, time, and expense on the charity's part.

A gift acceptance policy provides a way for nonprofit organizations to turn down such arrangements graciously. Nonprofit organizations can cite a policy that prohibits certain types of gift arrangements or payout rates higher than a specified percentage. The policy also provides guidelines for staff members to follow for most planned gift arrangements.

Donors need to understand that a gift policy exists to protect the charity because some so-called gifts provide only an incidental benefit, if any at all, to the charity. If the transaction is a way for the prospect to unload burdensome property that cannot be disposed of in any other way, or if it is made as a way to recoup lost principal through a charitable income tax deduction because of falling real estate prices, a gift acceptance policy can help the donor see that the gift would not benefit the charity. This is especially helpful if the donor has a strong relationship with someone at the charity, such as a trustee or high-level administrator, dean, or physician.

A sample gift acceptance policy is included in the *Planned Giving Workbook,* by Ronald R. Jordan and Katelyn L. Quynn, published by John Wiley & Sons, Inc. This chapter outlines the elements of a gift acceptance policy for gifts of cash, securities, life income arrangements, bequests, tangible personal property, real estate, and life insurance. It concludes by exploring administrative issues that can arise in a planned gift program that should be included in a gift acceptance policy.

Who Should Draft the Policy

Several departments should be involved in drafting a gift acceptance policy. The need for the policy is likely to originate in the development office and should be reviewed first by the vice president for development, the director of development, and the planned giving director. Legal counsel, whether inside or outside the nonprofit, then should review the draft to offer legal opinions on certain gift arrangements, especially gifts of real estate, life insurance, and tangible personal property. Outside legal counsel also can offer insight on what other charitable organizations include in their gift acceptance policies.

The treasurer's office and financial administrator should be involved in the drafting process to protect the charity from entering into gift situations that are financially questionable for it, such as establishing charitable remainder trusts with extraordinarily high payout rates or gift annuities with rates that exceed those suggested by the American Council on Gift Annuities. The treasurer's office or business office also can assist in creating parameters for endowed funds by establishing how much income should be paid out on a fund and how much, if any, should be returned to principal, and by outlining procedures for accepting gifts of real estate.

Flexibility

A gift acceptance policy must be flexible because exceptions in the gift acceptance process always arise. Planned gift situations can be unique, very different from annual fund gifts. A donor's relationship with the nonprofit can create a reason for the charity to deviate from the policy. A trustee or administrator at the charity may propose a gift option that is not terribly attractive to the charity, but the donor's connection to the organization may sway the charity to accept the gift. So, too, a charity may want or need to make an exception for a donor who has a giving record that includes substantial gifts over a long period of time. Development officers also may wish to deviate from an existing policy because of potential future gifts to the charity. Deviating from the existing policy is a decision that should be made by the organization's restricted gift committee, if one exists, or informally after consultation with members of the development staff, treasurer's office, and legal counsel. No policy should be written that does not allow for exceptions.

CASH

Gifts of cash (including checks) of all sizes are regularly accepted by nonprofits. All checks should be made out in the legal name of the charity; although it seems self-evident, checks should never be made payable to an individual working on behalf of the nonprofit.

A charity should turn down gifts of cash if a donor tries to place restrictions on the gift that are unacceptable to the charity or potentially illegal, such as excluding or including members based on race, ethnicity, or gender, from benefiting from an endowed fund or establishing a fund to benefit an individual selected in advance by the donor. A charity also may want to turn down a cash gift when a donor asks it to use the gift in a way that is incompatible with the charity's mission or long-range plan. For example, a small nonprofit hospital might choose to turn down a gift from a donor who wishes to establish a fund to provide medical training for physicians to study abroad if such a program is beyond the scope of the nonprofit's mission. Such an arrangement could be costly to administer and dilute the nonprofit's resources.

SECURITIES

Publicly Traded Securities

All charities accept marketable securities, including those readily traded on national or regional stock exchanges. Before the gift is made, the development professional involved in a transfer of public securities should tell a donor who wishes to make the gift that in all likelihood the gifted securities will be sold. Donors often want charities to keep a gift of securities, especially if donors believe that the stocks are likely to increase in value or because they feel the stocks are a good long-term investment. For ease of management and strategic investing, most charities do not keep small blocks of stocks representing many different corporations gifted from donors; generally, the stocks do not match the nonprofit's investment objectives or may duplicate the charity's existing portfolio, which is likely to contain a diverse range of investments. A nonprofit may hold a stock that is compatible with its acquisition criteria, so long as it has the right to sell the stock at any time in the future.

It is the charity's right, as owner of the gifted securities, to decide whether to sell them, and the planned giving officer should remind the donor of this in the beginning of the gift process to prevent misunderstandings or ill will. Having a gift acceptance policy that mandates the sale of gifted securities as soon as they are received helps if a donor criticizes the charity's decision to sell securities that later increase in value; it also helps prevent donors from tracking the price of the securities, staying involved with the gift long after they should.

Closely Held Securities

Closely held securities, which are not publicly traded, can be accepted by most nonprofit organizations so long as there are no prohibitions on transfer. Many gifts of closely held securities represent gifts from donors that are private or family-owned businesses. Before accepting a gift of closely held securities, the charity should explore how the securities could be redeemed, such as whether they will be bought back by the company itself or by one of its shareholders. Many types of closely held stock have restrictions on transfer, as most closely held businesses do not want to see ownership pass from a small group of owners. Many companies will work with nonprofit organizations to arrive at a price to buy back or redeem the securities. However, charities have a limited number of options when deciding who will buy back the shares of stock and may have little bargaining power.

No written prearrangement with respect to the sale of stock should be in place before the gift is made. The charity must have full discretion to decide whether and when to sell and, to the extent possible, to whom. Nevertheless, it is important to locate a potential purchaser who may buy back the shares of stock. At that point the charity can move forward with accepting the gift and completing acceptance of the gifted securities. Once the charity is holding the closely held stock, it can negotiate with the company or individual the price per share to be paid. While redemption of stock to the company can be a quick process, at other times it may take years, depending on how long the charity is willing to hold out for a specific price. A commitment for sale or redemption of closely held securities should not be entered into before the gift to the charity is completed, as this amounts to a preexisting agreement and could cause the donor to be taxed. A gift acceptance policy that addresses gifts of closely held stock should include determining who will buy back the shares of stock and the necessity of working with the charity's treasurer, business, or legal counsel's office before accepting the gift. The charity also may want to include its restricted gift committee in its decision-making process. See Chapter 11 for a complete discussion of closely held securities.

Life Income Gifts

Because of the charity's lifetime obligation to a donor in the case of life income gifts, such arrangements should not be entered into lightly. Life income gifts can cause conflict between a donor and the charitable organization that is offering the gift arrangement. The charity must have an investment strategy that allows it to meet its financial obligation to pay lifetime income to the donor as well as absorb administrative costs that must be maintained for many years into the future. The charity must balance the desires of the donor to make a gift, the development staff's wish to receive it, and the nonprofit's goal to build endowment with its need for current income and its willingness to spend time and money on administering a gift for many years without use of the principal.

A typical challenge presented by a life income gift is illustrated when prospects want their young children or grandchildren named as beneficiaries of a pooled income fund gift. Although legal, such an arrangement can result in a small gift received by the charity well into the future, because of the life expectancies of the young beneficiaries. The charity also must be alert to life income arrangements that primarily benefit the donor, leaving little or no gift for the charity. Such instances often are seen when individuals wish to establish charitable remainder trusts with high rates of annual payout that could be difficult or impossible for the charity to meet and would, over time, result in erosion of the trust principal.

The following sections examine issues that affect charitable remainder trusts, pooled income funds, and charitable gift annuities. These issues include amount of initial and subsequent gifts, payout rates, and ages of beneficiaries.

Amount of Initial Gift and Subsequent Gifts

Most nonprofits require a minimum life income gift because, among other things, the cost of investing and administering such gifts is high. The following subsections suggest typical gift minimums, which vary depending on the size of the charity's development program and the wishes of its vice president for development, board of trustees, treasurer's office, and outside money manager. Most charities need to balance the management and administrative costs of the gift (fees charged by the asset manager for investing the assets and the administrator for sending income payments and tax information to beneficiaries) with the possibility of discouraging donors from making a gift because of high gift minimums.

Charitable Remainder Trusts   Many charities that have their programs managed by asset managers feel that charitable remainder trusts cannot be established for less than $100,000 because of the time required to manage separately invested funds. The asset manager may be willing to accept a charitable remainder trust for $75,000 if the trust's assets can be combined with the financial institution's common trust funds, reducing the expense involved in managing a small account.

Some nonprofits manage their own charitable remainder trusts in house and elect a lower gift minimum. At a small nonprofit organization, charitable remainder trusts can be managed in house if the gift is at least $100,000. Additional gifts cannot be made to a charitable remainder annuity trust, but additional gifts can be made to a charitable remainder unitrust. Many charities prefer not to establish gift minimums for additional gifts to charitable remainder unitrusts and allow donors to make additional gifts of any amount. Other charities, especially those that have older, more established development programs, set gift minimums for additional gifts to a charitable remainder unitrust as low as $10,000 or even $5,000. Many organizations find that the time and expense associated with processing the additional gift justifies a specific minimum dollar amount.

Pooled Income Funds   Many charities choose $5,000 or $10,000 as a minimum gift amount for donors to enter the pooled income fund. This figure is lower than most gift minimums for charitable remainder trusts because the large number of beneficiaries in a pooled income fund reduces the number of investment decisions and administrative responsibilities (compared to those of a separately invested charitable remainder trust where decisions are made for just a few beneficiaries). Selecting $10,000 as a gift minimum can set donors' giving sights higher, but it should not be done at the expense of losing gifts that might have been made if the minimum were $5,000. Many charities that offer pooled income funds set $1,000 as a minimum additional gift amount, whereas other charities set no minimum for additional gifts, taking into the fund whatever amount the donor chooses to give.

Charitable and Deferred Gift Annuities   Many charities follow a gift minimum of $5,000 to establish a charitable gift annuity or deferred gift annuity; others have increased that amount to $10,000. Again, the charity must balance the administrative cost of the gift with the potential loss of a gift when establishing a higher gift minimum. Because a donor cannot add to a charitable gift annuity (although additional gift annuities can be established), many organizations choose to keep the minimum of a second charitable gift annuity at the same level as the first gift annuity. To encourage subsequent gifts, however, some charities allow donors to establish a second charitable gift annuity at a lower amount. Charities that do so should determine how much benefit they receive from smaller subsequent gifts after considering the cost of administration.

Payout Rates

The charity must decide on a policy for dealing with the payout rate on life income gifts because donors and their financial advisors frequently ask about the maximum payout rate allowed. The nonprofit must be sure that it is comfortable with the guidelines it establishes because they are likely to be challenged often by donors seeking high payout rates. The desire to receive a high payout rate can encourage donors to shop around at different charities, creating competition among charities and undermining the spirit of philanthropy. Planned giving staff members, disappointed by a prospect who made a gift to another charity that offered a higher rate, should remember that this prospect was not motivated by donative intent.

Charitable Remainder Trusts Although Congress has established 5 percent as the minimum amount for a charitable remainder trust payout rate, the minimum payout rate is rarely ever the issue with donors; more often the discussion revolves around the maximum rate selected by the donor. Many charities are comfortable with a payout rate of 5 or 6 percent. A donor may choose a payout of 7 percent or higher if the youngest beneficiary of the trust is older, if the size of the trust is quite substantial, or if the donor has a special relationship with the charity. A donor also can select rates between whole percentage points, such as 5.5 percent.

Higher payout rates may be acceptable for trusts that are established for a term of years rather than a donor's lifetime. Trusts established for a small number of years, such as fewer than 10 years, may be higher, such as 7 or 8 percent, especially if the donor has a specific objective that can be accomplished in a small number of years, such as paying college tuition for four years. The size of the gift also can be a factor when choosing a higher payout rate because, although more income will be paid to the beneficiary, the remainder amount to the charity will still be significant because of the gift's size.

Pooled Income Funds Because the payout rate from a pooled income fund is based on the income earned by the fund and is always variable, determining a maximum payout rate is not applicable. A charity can, if it wishes, establish several different pooled income funds with different investment objectives that pay different rates with commensurate charitable income tax deductions. When the funds are first established, investment objectives must be considered so that approximate rates can be met.

Charitable Gift Annuities The need for a written gift acceptance policy that establishes maximum payout rates allowed by the charity for donors at certain ages is important because, as mentioned earlier, some donors shop for the highest gift annuity payout rates among charities. Chapter 9 discusses the American Council on Gift Annuities (ACGA) and the reasons that nonprofits may wish to follow its suggested gift annuity rates. The suggested rates are based on actuarial information that factors life expectancies, inflation, and investment returns.

The planned giving director, consulting with the organization's treasurer, should decide whether to follow the ACGA's suggested rates. Many charities choose to do so, but place a cap on their highest payout rate at a number lower than the ACGA's current highest rate. It is helpful when working with donors to refer to the ACGA's suggested rates and emphasize the importance of following them when prospects challenge the charity to provide them with a higher rate of return.

Deferred Gift Annuities   As with charitable gift annuities, the charity may want to include a policy statement that addresses the payout rates to pay an income to the donor beginning at a point in the future, often many years later. The charity should consider whether rates should be capped at a certain amount and whether it will establish deferred gift annuities for donors who are quite young, such as 25 or 30 years old. The charity may want to devise a formula that places a cap on the payout rate of both deferred and regular gift annuities.

Ages of Beneficiaries

Many nonprofits establish age minimums for donors who wish to make life income gifts. Charities do not want to commit to pay income to donors who are very young because there is a great chance of depleting the principal of the gift, leaving the charity with little or no gift. This situation happens most often when donors wish to include their children as successor beneficiaries, extending the obligation of the charity. Each charity needs to decide, based on the type of life income gift, the minimum age of the youngest beneficiary.

Charitable Remainder Trusts   The minimum age allowed for a beneficiary of a charitable remainder trust should be determined on a case-by-case basis, if at all. Many donors want to benefit their children in their estate planning, which may include naming the children as beneficiaries of a charitable remainder trust. The younger the beneficiary, the longer the trust will run, incurring greater administrative costs and, because of the length of time the trust must pay an income stream to beneficiaries, perhaps a smaller remainder gift left to the charity. Factors to consider include

- Whether the trust is being established for a term of years
- If the charity has a special relationship with the donor
- The total number of beneficiaries of the trust
- The trust's proposed size
- The expected total return of the trust

Many charitable remainder trusts are established without involvement from the charity, so the planned giving officer who is brought into the planning process by the donor must be diplomatic in making suggestions but remind the donor about the size of the gift that eventually will go to the charity. A donor who really wishes to benefit the charity will strike a balance in taking care of individual beneficiaries and making a gift to the nonprofit.

Pooled Income Funds   The nonprofit should consult with the manager of its pooled income fund(s) to determine the minimum age for donors to the fund. Allowing a young (40- to 50-year-old) donor to become a beneficiary of a pooled income fund reduces the remainder gift to the charity. A wise strategy is to create several different pooled income funds, each with a different investment objective. Donors will choose which fund they wish to enter, based on how much they wish the charity to receive at their death, their need for annual income and a charitable income tax deduction, and their desire to preserve the principal of the fund. Ideally, a pooled income fund should have a balance of different-aged beneficiaries; for example, if a fund contains only older beneficiaries and most of the beneficiaries die, the pooled income fund risks extinction.

Charitable Gift Annuities   Payout rates to donors who establish charitable gift annuities are highest for older donors because the rates are based on actuarial tables. The older the donor, the higher the rate of return. Financially, it is generally not worthwhile to younger donors who wish to receive a high annual payout rate to establish a charitable gift annuity because the rate they will receive is low. Donors aged 40 to 55 who wish to receive a high rate are likely to do better joining a charity's pooled income fund.

Deferred Gift Annuities   The charity may choose to establish a minimum age for donors who make deferred gift annuities. With deferred gift annuities, the younger the donor and the longer the payment is deferred, the higher the rate to the beneficiary. Because donors often select retirement age to receive their annual income payments, the charity may consider a 30-year-old donor too young to pay what appears to be a high rate of return for such a long time, even though the charity invests the donor's gift for many years. The charity also needs to consider the burden of the administrative responsibility of tracking the gift for that length of time.

Number of Beneficiaries

All life income gifts require that the beneficiaries be alive at the time the gift is created.

Charitable Remainder Trusts Too many beneficiaries of a charitable remainder trust may be unwieldy for administrative purposes and are likely to reduce the ultimate gift to the charity. The charity may wish to limit the number of beneficiaries of a charitable remainder trust when the charity is involved in its establishment.

Pooled Income Funds It is smart to have many beneficiaries owning an interest in a pooled income fund. Multiple beneficiaries in a pooled income fund result in more gifts going to the charity and allow the charity to invest larger sums at lower cost. It is unwise, however, to have one beneficiary own a disproportionate number of units in the fund because when that donor dies, the fund will shrink considerably. More donors in the pooled income fund reduce this risk.

Charitable Gift Annuities The Internal Revenue Service (IRS) allows a maximum of two beneficiaries for a charitable gift annuity. For example, a husband and wife who create a charitable gift annuity cannot also include their children as annuitants.

Deferred Gift Annuities Like a charitable gift annuity, no more than two annuitants are allowed by the IRS.

BEQUESTS

Gifts made through a bequest can benefit a charity without any involvement from an organization's development staff. If, however, a development professional is asked to respond to an inquiry from a donor who wishes to make a bequest other than a cash gift, guidelines should exist for the planned giving officer to follow. Guidance is needed most often when a donor wants to make a gift of real estate, tangible personal property, or other noncash assets to the charity.

Unwanted Property

It is helpful to both the charity and the donor if the charity is involved when a donor makes a noncash gift by bequest to the charity. For example, a charity should discourage a donor from making a gift of a home located in another part of the country that may be difficult for the charity to sell, although this problem may be minimized if the donor's executor is authorized to sell the home and give the proceeds to the charity. The planned giving officer should explain the burdens and costs that the charity will have to bear. Although the intent may be charitable, a donor who resides in Florida and leaves his entire estate, consisting of an old car and motor home, to a Massachusetts charity makes only a minimal gift to the organization. The charity will have to retain counsel in Florida to probate the estate and sell anything valuable. Similarly, a vacation home located in an undesirable part of town is property that a charity is unlikely to be able to sell quickly. Insurance and maintenance costs make such a gift more of a burden on the charity, and such a gift probably should be disclaimed.

Disclaimed Requests

When a donor dies and makes a bequest of some type of property that the charity does not want to accept, the bequest should be disclaimed according to procedures established under applicable state and federal laws. A bequest recipient can refuse a gift made by bequest, but laws vary with regard to filing requirements, timing, and procedures for disclaiming unwanted property.

GIFTS OF TANGIBLE PERSONAL PROPERTY

Gifts of tangible personal property can present special challenges for a charity. For a complete discussion of gifts of tangible personal property, see Chapter 13. A gift acceptance policy should include restrictions on accepting such gifts. The charity should examine a potential gift of personal property for its financial value, its potential use by the charity, and its ability to be sold quickly and converted into cash. A comprehensive gift acceptance policy also should establish a committee to review gifts of tangible personal property (including jewelry, art, collections, computers, and equipment) before they are accepted.

Gifts Used by the Charity

Before acceptance each nonprofit should consider whether the gift is appropriate. Some charities set minimum values for gifts of tangible personal property. Some charities may choose to accept only gifts of tangible personal property that relate to their mission, such as books to a university and medical equipment to a hospital. Gifts with a less directly related use, such as a stamp collection to a hospital, may cause more expense than value after considering moving and display costs, and insurance. The collection could attract few buyers if the hospital eventually decided to sell it.

Liquidity of the Gift: Gifts Not Used by the Charity

The charity also should determine if it will accept gifts of tangible personal property that it will sell. The charity must consider whether significant costs will be involved with holding and selling the asset; if it cannot sell the property immediately, can it afford the maintenance, insurance, taxes, and management costs for the property? How expensive will it be to hire a specialist, if necessary, to sell the property? Will the property require sale at a special auction held in London only once a year? These and other questions should be explored before accepting a piece of property that the charity hopes to sell.

Acceptance of the Gift

An individual or group of people should have the authority to accept gifts of tangible personal property on behalf of the charity. If the planned giving officer is undecided as to whether a piece of tangible personal property should be accepted, an individual or governing body should be available to help make the decision. Remind the donor that the charity follows rules issued by the IRS relating to accepting gifts of tangible personal property, including filing forms 8282 and 8283. See Chapter 13 for a full discussion of tangible personal property.

IRS FORM 8283

A gift acceptance policy that deals with gifts of tangible personal property should include a statement about whether the charity will send, as a matter of course, copies of IRS Form 8283 to a donor. Donors attach Form 8283 to their tax return in the year they make a gift of noncash property over $500 to a charity. The charity is not legally responsible for sending the form to donors, but for stewardship purposes the charity should routinely send it.

GIFTS OF REAL ESTATE

Because gifts of real estate can be challenging, even for the most experienced planned giving professional, guidelines must be established to handle them. These policies will help deal with the many complex and multifaceted issues associated with gifts of real estate, including whether to accept the gift, use of an outside appraiser, and environmental concerns.

DECIDING TO ACCEPT THE GIFT

A number of factors determine whether to accept a gift of real estate. A full discussion of real estate is found in Chapter 12. Threshold guidelines should be established to determine whether the charity should even explore taking the potential gift of real estate. Issues to consider include

- Estimated value of the real estate
- Likelihood of selling the property
- Whether the property is mortgaged
- Location of the property
- Likelihood of the nonprofit using the property
- Relationship of the donor to the nonprofit

Selecting an Appraiser

The nonprofit should establish guidelines for valuing a potential gift of property by an outside, independent appraiser. If the charity is unsure of the appraiser's figure, it should analyze the appraisal thoroughly and speak with the appraiser. If it is still unsatisfied, the charity may want to conduct its own appraisal to determine the real market value of the property. Appraisers also can help determine the property's potential for resale and discover environmental problems with the property.

Environmental Concerns

If the charity decides to accept a gift of real estate, it should include in its gift acceptance policy the necessity of hiring a specialist to do an environmental study on the property to rule out any hazards that, if discovered, would require the charity to reject the potential gift. When an environmental hazard is discovered on a piece of property, the current owner is generally responsible for curing the problem, including any charity that was given damaged property as a gift. If the state determines that a piece of property was once the site of a toxic waste dump or was located next to a gas station and underground gas tanks have contaminated the property, federal law could cause the charity to assume millions of dollars of liability for cleanup. This potential liability, which can turn a gift into a financial disaster, makes an environmental examination of property absolutely necessary before acceptance.

Procedures for Accepting Gifts of Real Estate

Because various departments at the charity have to be brought into the process, all charities must have a system in place to accept gifts of real estate. The planned giving officer should speak with someone in the charity's real estate or business office to determine whether the charity wishes to accept the property. A professional with real estate experience representing the charity should make a site visit to examine the property, indicate its estimated value, and note any potential problems associated with it. This initial visit should take place before the charity hires an appraiser and makes an environmental examination of the property.

LIFE INSURANCE

For the donor to make a completed gift of a life insurance policy, the charity should be named as both the owner and irrevocable beneficiary of the life insurance policy. Gifts of life insurance that require the charity to accept a donor's premium payments as gifts and send them to the life insurance company on a regular basis should generally be discouraged because the administrative burdens often outweigh the benefit to the charity. If the donor stops making premium payments, the charity is confronted with an awkward decision as to whether to continue the payments.

Under no circumstances should a member of the development staff give a life insurance agent a list of the nonprofit's donors for the salesperson's marketing efforts. Donors solicited by a life insurance company who discover that their names were given to the insurance agent by the charity could become angry and choose not to make additional gifts.

ADMINISTRATIVE ISSUES

Each charity should establish how it will pay various expenses, such as management fees for administration of its planned gifts, including charitable remainder trusts, pooled income funds, and charitable gift annuities. Charities need to determine whether the fees will come from a department budget set aside specifically for this purpose or from income generated from the gift.

If the nonprofit pays the administrative fees from a budget set aside for this purpose, the donor does not obtain a charitable income tax deduction for the cost of administering the gift. Under certain circumstances, donors can take charitable tax deductions on their tax return if the administrative fees are paid directly from the income generated by the gift. But if the charity pays the fees from income earned on the charitable remainder trust, pooled income fund, or charitable gift annuity fund, donors' annual payments ultimately are reduced.

Some organizations take administrative fees from the income earned on the trust or gift annuity fund; if the trust or fund is large, administrative fees are spread to more donors, causing less of a financial impact on each donor. Smaller charities or new programs without many participants may choose to pay the administrative fees out of a separate budget so that their few donors will receive as much income as possible. They may wait to pay the administrative fees out of the income earned when their planned giving program includes more donors. Although donors rarely ask how administrative fees will be paid, the charity's gift acceptance policy should address this.

Legal Fees

Charities also must decide if they will pay any legal fees on behalf of donors and should address this in the organization's gift acceptance policy. Some charities are willing to pay for drafting trust documents for donors who name the charity as primary remainderman of a charitable remainder trust. The charity should require that donors have their own legal counsel review the documents to avoid having donors say later that they were not satisfied with the way the charity's attorney drafted the document. Some charities feel that they should pay legal fees for drafting a donor's will if the charity is the sole beneficiary under the will. But doing this could cause the charity to be in a conflict-of-interest situation; a donor also might change his or her mind and revoke the interest to the charity.

Charities should insist that donors pay their own appraisal costs. Otherwise, charities run the risk of displeasing donors if properties are sold at a price donors are not happy with. Donors often can deduct appraisal costs as a miscellaneous deduction on their tax returns, to the extent that this expense and other miscellaneous deductions exceed 2 percent of their adjusted gross income.

Charity Acting as Trustee or Executor

In limited circumstances, a nonprofit organization may serve as a personal representative for a donor's estate or as a trustee for a donor's trust. Most small and large nonprofit organizations are not equipped to make the decisions that an individual or professional trustee can make, although the charity may have the right under the donor's will or trust to appoint an individual to serve as executor or trustee. For example, a nonprofit should not act as a sole trustee making discretionary payments from a trust to an income beneficiary. Also, a nonprofit generally should not accept the duties of executor, settling a donor's estate and collecting, securing, and distributing a donor's assets, unless it is the sole beneficiary of the donor's estate or the donor's family wants the nonprofit to assume that duty. A charity that acts as executor of a donor's estate also creates a conflict of interest between the rights of any individual beneficiaries and the charity. A well-drafted gift acceptance policy should include language that strongly advises a charity about assuming this fiduciary responsibility.

CONCLUSION

A properly drafted gift acceptance policy protects the nonprofit organization and the donor. The policy should govern all planned gifts and gifts of cash and noncash assets. Policies adopted before a specific need arises prevent a donor's hurt feelings and provide the charity with a way to politely refuse a prospective gift. The policy should consider broadly the needs of the nonprofit and its mission. Only gifts that are compatible with the nonprofit's mission should be accepted.

CHAPTER 6

Managing Time: Planned Giving in a Small Charity

INTRODUCTION

Are there ever enough hours in a day? Technology has made today's employee efficient, but also has created increased demands and expectations. We are bombarded daily in our planned giving and development jobs with electronic mail, faxes, telephone calls—on both traditional and cellular phones—and regular mail. Our personal time has become more complex as many families have two working spouses, children attending school, and both participating in a multitude of personal and professional activities and lessons.

The planned giving world is faster paced than ever. Planned giving staff members at small charities are performing many functions. Expectations are high, as many planned giving staff members are responsible for some or all of the following:

- Raising significant sums of money
- Identifying new planned giving prospects
- Meeting with donors and prospects
- Stewarding donors
- Working with outside advisors
- Drafting proposals and letters

- Attending donor events
- Managing staff
- Mentoring new hires
- Attending local planned giving council meetings
- Staying current on tax changes and planned giving updates
- Reading planned giving journals, loose-leaf services
- Drafting marketing materials
- Delivering planned giving presentations

Are professional goals being accomplished for the day, week, month, or year? This chapter focuses on how to work most efficiently to accomplish work priorities.

GET ORGANIZED

For the big picture of a planned giving program, create an operational plan (see Chapter 5). Regularly read the larger operational plan to stay on track, to ensure that each day, week, month, and year larger goals are closer to being completed. This chapter will help determine shorter goals and objectives in the next day, week, month, year, or five years.

ORGANIZE THE DAY AND WEEK

At the beginning of the week or at the end of the previous week, make a plan for what should be accomplished in the following week. Write the plan on paper, on the computer, or on a personal digital assistant (PDA)—whatever works best. Next determine and record the objectives to be accomplished each day of the week. People who are organized (and a bit lucky) can organize their week efficiently. Be proactive and take charge of each workday and the workweek.

BLOCK OFF HOURS

For organizing the week, make a list that includes "free" time, reserved as time to work on a specific project or to leave some time to write. Much can be accomplished during these blocks of time. For these hours of work to be successful, find a way to avoid interruptions and distractions.

Consider closing the office door, disconnecting or forwarding the telephone, and turning the computer off to avoid reading e-mails if they are distracting. Anticipate the usual interruptions. To cut down on colleagues stopping by to chat, consider establishing "office hours" and limiting access to staff during those hours. Also discuss with colleagues, family members, and friends about how they can help with better time management, and ask them for their understanding and support.

MANAGING THE CALENDAR

Establish certain rules that control day-to-day office life. When setting the calendar for the day or week, adhere to the following:

- Hold no more than a certain number of meetings per day, such as three.
- Hold all meetings at a certain time of day, such as mornings or afternoons, so that work can be done at the beginning or end of the day.
- Leave open the day or afternoon before a trip to help prepare for it.
- Leave open the return day from a trip to catch up on e-mail and correspondence.
- Have lunch brought in when meetings are scheduled at the lunch hour.
- Block out time to concentrate on work.

KNOW THYSELF

Everyone has certain weaknesses that cause a loss of work time. Determine how to work most efficiently by focusing on strengths and weaknesses. Is the best time of day to work morning or evening? Are there times when a walk outdoors is needed? Are e-mails a distraction? Should personal telephone calls be reduced? Are conversations with colleagues distracting? Are hours before and after the workday good times to get things done? Is a day or two out of the office needed to meet with donors? Identify personal weaknesses and strengths to help schedule the day.

DO THE MOST DIFFICULT TASKS FIRST

If there is a project or assignment due at the end of the week, or a task that is difficult to perform, perform that work in the earliest part of the day or week. If other tasks are done first, one will waste energy dreading doing that other task as its deadline draws nearer. Try to finish that activity while energy is still available (in the morning for morning people) and when there is still time to work on the task (say at the beginning of the week, before things become less predictable). For example, if a first draft of a planned giving presentation must be completed by the end of the week, begin the draft on Monday. By Friday the draft should be near completion. If there is a difficult donor who must be called this week, call early in the week rather than waiting until Friday.

CONTROL THE OFFICE ENVIRONMENT

While juggling a series of assignments, find ways to organize the environment to be most productive and efficient. Two practical suggestions to work smartly include:

1. Hire great staff
2. Delegate

Hire Great Staff

One of the most important keys to success when hiring staff members is to hire people who can work together as a team. The planned giving staff can run calculations, handle donor calls, visit with donors, work on projects, and almost everything else that comes along. Competent and capable staff members can grow in their jobs as more responsibilities are shared with them. Good staff members will begin to close gifts on their own as they handle donor situations. When hiring, look for individuals who are bright, flexible, conscientious, adaptable, and quick learners who can multitask. Potential hires do not necessarily need planned giving or development experience; look for solid characteristics that can transfer to the planned giving environment.

If the budget allows, a great associate director can help the planned giving program and director tremendously. Let this person grow in the position to be able to handle almost everything. Also play to this individual's strengths and put him or her in charge of various functions, such as the bequest program, endowed funds, or presentations. Associate directors should be given lots of autonomy and allowed to do the job in their own way. If the budget does not permit the hiring of an associate director, cross-train a member of the staff to handle part of the work as the program grows.

If the budget permits the hiring of a good assistant, productivity will soar. Once a team learns how to work best together, the assistant can handle many responsibilities, such as:

- Make travel arrangements
- Manage the calendar
- Start and perhaps finish letters
- Sign letters
- Talk with other departments at the charity
- Handle telephone calls
- Act as a gatekeeper to protect the director's time
- Summarize highlights of planned giving journals
- Run planned giving calculations
- Respond to select voice-mail messages

Be sure to provide good staff members with incentives to stay at the organization. Give them as much responsibility as they are comfortable with and be sure to thank them often, publicly and privately.

Delegate

The ability to delgate is vital to the success of the planned giving director. Before immediately moving to handle a task, see if it is a job someone else can perform. Ask:

- Who should be the representative at this meeting?
- Could an associate on the planned giving staff attend the meeting on investment policies?
- Where does this meeting rank on the priority list of meetings? If it is near or at the bottom of the list, can it be completely eliminated?
- Could someone else draft this letter or proposal to the donor?
- Could another staff member handle the donor interaction from start to finish? Perhaps there could be a policy that certain staff members handle prospective gifts at different levels.
- Does one staff member handle something better or most efficiently?

ORGANIZE THE PLANNED GIVING STAFF

Meet regularly with the planned giving staff as a team to get everyone moving along productively. On a semiregular or weekly basis, gather the team together to see who is working on what and which assignments can be delegated to other staff members both inside the planned giving team and in the development office. In this way employees can equitably redistribute workloads, and tasks can be accomplished more efficiently. These regular meetings also give everyone an idea of the nature and scope of the work being done by individual team members.

MEETINGS

One of the greatest challenges in managing time is office and organization-wide meetings. While all meetings cannot be eliminated, consider the following ways to reduce the number of meetings attended:

- List monthly meetings. Rank them in order of importance. Eliminate those meetings located at the bottom of the priority list.

- Determine who really needs to attend the meeting. Can someone else be the representative at this meeting? Can that person be asked to handle the entire project?

- Suggest that the meeting take place by e-mail or conference call, cutting down on travel time to and from the meeting and perhaps reducing the amount of discussion time.

- When meeting with others, go to their office so that you can leave at the end of the meeting rather than continuing the discussion because the other person does not leave.

- Consider reducing hourly meetings to 50, 40, or 30 minutes.

- Suggest, where appropriate, that weekly meetings change to biweekly or monthly meetings.

- Combine some individual meetings to one group meeting where appropriate.

- Stand at meetings. Meetings at which people stand are shorter than meetings at which people sit.

- Discuss with the vice president or other supervisor the need to reduce meetings, with the goal of spending more time with donors and being responsive to their needs.

- Draft an agenda for every meeting to keep people focused on priorities.

TRAVEL TIME

Make the most of travel time. Many planned giving professionals travel regularly to other parts of the country for donor visits and planned giving conferences. Designate those hours in the air as time to work: complete proposals, read planned giving journals, work on staff evaluations, and so on. Working hard for three hours in the air or at the airport can accomplish a lot.

WORKING FROM HOME

In today's telecommuting environment, more development professionals are having the opportunity to work from home at least part time. Working from home can provide some significant benefits:

- It eliminates commute time.

- No colleagues dropping by the office to chat means more time for work.

- One can control e-mail and telephone calls at a regular pace.

- One can enjoy a block of uninterrupted time to work.

- Home provides a conducive environment for reading, writing, and working on projects that require more thought.

How to Begin

To make working from home viable, consider the following:

- Discuss the concept with the vice president for development. Cite the number of people, nationally, working from home and/or those in the office who work from home. Explain the major advantage: being fully accessible to staff via telephone and e-mail while accomplishing more work from home.

- Start slowly. Try to work at home in small blocks of time. If it works out well, gradually increase the time working from home. One or two days a month from home can be increased to one day a week from home.

- Make sure that children are either at school or have someone in the home to care for them. It is impossible to get work done from home if children constantly interrupt.

What Is Needed

To work from home successfully, a number of items need to be assembled, including a computer and work supplies. Have a computer installed at home, complete with printer and fax machine, to draft planned giving letters, proposals, and other documents and to respond to e-mail. Before the computer is installed, work with the charitable organization's information systems department to determine the best type of hookup to access the charity most easily. Find a clean, private place to keep supplies handy and a desk area to work from. Be sure to have a filing cabinet. Decide what supplies are needed and have them conveniently located and organized. Determine the office's policy on bringing supplies home.

To make the most of a day at home and to help the workweek run most efficiently, consider saving projects that require the most focused attention for the work-from-home day, such as writing a planned giving proposal that has many technical components, digesting a new tax law, preparing a planned giving presentation, or drafting a colleague's performance evaluation. Also consider blocking off time to read and respond to lengthy e-mails from home.

Telephone Calls

Depending on how one divides one's time between working at home and in the office, and on the charity's financial position, one might consider installing a separate telephone line for business calls to avoid being interrupted by personal calls when working from home. Consider purchasing a portable telephone. Also consider using a caller identification system, available from the telephone company, to screen incoming calls.

Technology

Make the most of technology that has been designed to help work life run more efficiently. Take a closer look at the following technological advances:

- *Hands-free headset:*   Use this in the office while on the telephone so that hands are free to work on the computer, write, or clean off a desk. This is especially helpful when speaking with long-winded callers.

- *Hand-held or personal digital assistant:*   The technology in hand-held computers is growing and changing rapidly. Many offices use PDAs to coordinate calendars office-wide. Excellent features include space to record engagements as well as to-do lists that keep running lists in one place, grouped by topic, rather than spread out on different slips of paper. Consider including donors' names, addresses, and telephone numbers as well as personal information to remember about them.

- *Portable computer:*   The new lightweight computers allow one to work on documents while traveling out of the office as well as to correspond with the office via e-mail during business travel. It is so much easier to read e-mails at the end of each day rather than return from a business trip and be faced with hundreds of e-mails.

- *Business telephone credit cards:*   These cards allow calls to be charged directly to, and paid by, the charitable organization. They are very helpful because users no longer have to process receipts for reimbursement checks. If policies permit, charge expenses directly to the charitable organization.

- *Home computer:*   This is perhaps the most important piece of technology to help with the work effort. A good home computer allows flexibility, which is of paramount importance when trying to balance home and work life. Consider saving long e-mails from work to read and respond to from home.

- *Cellular phones:*   Cell phones save time in numerous ways, as when one is

  - Traveling to meet with a planned giving donor and running late

- Out of the office and needing to touch base quickly with a boss or assistant
- Boarding an airplane and wishing to check in with the office before flying
- Driving and listening to voice-mail messages or talking with someone in the office

Cell phones can also be used to check stock quotes, access websites, or provide other financial services.

GENERAL TIPS FOR SAVING TIME IN THE OFFICE

- When scheduling for the day or week, remember that things generally take longer to accomplish than originally thought.
- Empower planned giving staff to answer questions and deal with problems. Tell others in the office which planned giving staff member handles which area so that colleagues know where to go with questions.
- Discourage colleagues and staff from dropping by the office to chat by establishing "open office" hours or encouraging correspondence by e-mail.
- Get enough sleep. Things always take longer when one is overtired.
- Actively schedule some time each day to get out of the office. Breathing fresh air each workday helps employees wake up and be more alert.
- Drink a lot of water during the day to keep refreshed and hydrated. This is especially important if one works in an airtight building. Keep a large bottle of water nearby.
- Bring healthful snacks for midafternoon, when one's blood sugar is low. Consider nutritious, portable foods like yogurt and fruit.
- Exercise.
- Balance workdays to accomplish a variety of activities each day. Spend some time in the office and outside of the office, seeing donors. Keep the day stimulating.

CONCLUSION

With all that is required of planned giving officers, it is important to try to make the most of all available work time. Explore how to organize the day, week, and year; control the office environment; and manage meetings, travel time, working from home, and technology to help increase productivity. Work to incorporate many of the specific time-saving measures suggested in this chapter to focus time on where it is most needed to make the planned giving program the best that it can be.

PART THREE

Planned Gifts

CHAPTER 7

Bequests and the Bequest Society

INTRODUCTION

Bequests are the foundation of a planned giving program at a small charity. Nationally, approximately 80 percent of all money raised through planned giving comes from bequests. Many donors who wish to make a gift, but do not wish to part with current assets, find bequests the most attractive way to make charitable gifts. Many donors who make bequests to nonprofit organizations are childless couples or individuals who view the charity as a substitute for their heirs. Their gifts can be substantial. Even though there may not be a formal bequest or planned giving program in place, most small nonprofit organizations have received bequests. A small nonprofit can take the first step in starting a planned giving program simply by marketing and promoting bequests directly to donors and indirectly to attorneys specializing in estate planning and to certified public accountants with large tax planning practices. This chapter focuses on issues related to bequests and what is needed to attract more bequests to a small charity.

HOW A BEQUEST WORKS

Through a bequest (a clause in a will), a donor can make a gift of a specific dollar amount ($100,000), a fraction (one quarter), a percentage (25 percent), or an entire estate to a charity. Fractions or percentages are advantageous because they allow donors to allocate their estates equitably among beneficiaries, including family, friends, and charities. For example, a donor may leave 15 percent of his estate to each of his four siblings and distribute 20 percent each to two charities. Because the donor will never know the exact dollar amount of his estate at the time of his death, using fractions or percentages is the most efficient and effective method to distribute the proceeds. However, donors also can make a specific gift of $25,000 to a charity and then distribute the rest of their estates to heirs using fractions or percentages. In this case, the $25,000 is paid first and the balance of the estate is allocated thereafter.

TAX LAW AND CHARITABLE GIFT PLANNING

Taxation, both federal and state, is an important consideration for most donors. The old adage that "You can give it to the IRS or your favorite charity" is true. Taxation can serve as an incentive when it comes to charitable gift planning and can motivate philanthropically minded donors to benefit charities. Donors sometimes view charitable gift planning as the last tax shelter through which income, estate, gift, and capital gains taxes can be diminished or avoided entirely. The U.S. system of taxation permits and encourages taxpayers to make gifts to charities, since without private support to our nation's charities, many educational, health, social service, environmental, and cultural programs would go unfunded. Charities remove some of the pressure that the federal government would feel if it were obligated to deliver these charitable services.

Charitable giving is a very effective way to reduce the size of a donor's estate. Reducing the estate diminishes the impact of federal estate and gift taxes. Donors can make charitable gifts so that their net taxable estate is less than the individual exemption of $1,000,000 in 2002. This amount will increase gradually to reach $3,500,000 in 2010. (See Chapter 20 for more information.) Charitable gift planning should be incorporated into the donor's overall estate planning objectives rather than be treated as a separate activity.

Many donors wish to benefit a charity during their lifetime, but cannot afford to part with current assets. Bequests provide major benefits to charities, yet allow donors to retain the use of their assets during their lifetime.

THE WILL

Perhaps surprisingly, over half of all Americans die without a will. The reasons why are varied. Sometimes it is due to a lack of knowledge or a failure to understand the need for a will. Sometimes the reasons are more complex, involving emotional and psychological factors that keep individuals from drafting a will. Whatever the reason, the result is the same—intestacy. People who die without a will are considered to have died intestate, and the state where they were domiciled shall, in effect, make a will for them. (Domicile is the state that the deceased intended to have as a permanent residence). Laws on intestacy vary considerably from state to state. Intestacy has been described as a fate worse than death. Rather than people making their own decisions about distributing assets, the state determines the formula for distributing assets and sometimes adds extensive, expensive, and cumbersome legal formalities. There is no consideration for people's needs or wishes. One can avoid intestacy simply by making a valid will.

Formalities

A will enables people to make a charitable bequest. A revocable trust often is drafted at the same time as the will, and a charitable gift may be included in the revocable trust. The formal requirements for drafting wills are simple. Most states require that the testator—the person making the will—be 18 years of age or older, of sound mind, and sign or execute the will in the presence of two or more competent witnesses. Most donors meet these requirements easily.

To make a charitable gift to a nonprofit organization, donors must either include the bequest to the charity in the body of the will or have a codicil drafted to include the bequest. A codicil (amendment to a will) is a written document, often one or two pages, that is physically attached to the donor's existing will. A codicil may confirm the validity of the existing will and also include new provisions and/or exclude old provisions from the existing will. Many donors make bequests through a codicil because doing so is less expensive and time consuming than drafting a new will.

Updating a Will

People should update their wills at least every five years. Wills five years old or more may be stale. Changes in family situations or in the tax law can make a will obsolete practically overnight. Some changes in circumstances that may prompt people to update a will include:

- Marriage, divorce, birth, adoption, or death.
  - Marriage revokes a will in its entirety in most states, unless it is expressly contemplated in the will.
  - Divorce or annulment generally revokes the disposition of property to a former spouse.
- Changes in the nature and value of property, such as a substantial increase in the appreciation of a stock portfolio.
- Changes in state and federal laws and in the interpretation of those laws.
- Moving from one state to another, although a will validly executed in one state should be valid in all other states. People who move to or from a community property state may need to amend their wills.

PARTS OF A WILL

A properly executed will transfers property from the testator (maker of the will) to beneficiaries. Will requirements vary by state, but most wills contain a number of standard provisions or clauses. These include:

- A clause revoking all previously drafted wills or codicils
- A clause that directs the payment of all debts, taxes, funeral expenses, and administrative costs by one or more beneficiaries
- A clause naming an executor or a personal representative of the estate
- A clause appointing a guardian to act on behalf of minor children of the decedent
- Distribution clauses, which permit personal and real property to be distributed to specific beneficiaries, including charities
- A residuary clause that directs the distribution of the remainder or residue of the estate to individual beneficiaries or charities

SUGGESTED LANGUAGE FOR CHARITABLE BEQUESTS

Charities should provide sample bequest language to donors who wish to make a gift through a bequest to the organization. The donor's attorney will incorporate some or all of the language into the donor's will. Sample bequest language follows. Donors are most likely to make a gift to a charity in one of two ways—through a specific bequest or as a percentage of the donor's estate.

Specific Bequest

Through a specific bequest, a donor leaves a certain sum of cash, securities, or property to the nonprofit organization. For example, the following language is appropriate for a bequest of a specific dollar amount:

> I bequeath the sum of _____ dollars ($_____) to [specific name] charity, <CITY, STATE ZIP>, to be used or disposed of for _____ [or as its Board of Directors in its sole discretion deems appropriate].

Percentage of Estate

A bequest also can provide for a percentage of a donor's estate to benefit the nonprofit organization, and donors can make gifts through the residuary clause of their wills. The residuary estate consists of everything that is not specifically given away and permits a donor to distribute a portion of the estate to be split among individual beneficiaries or to a nonprofit organization. The residuary clause is sometimes called the "remainder" or "residue" of the estate. As discussed, because donors do not know the exact size of their estates at death, using a percentage or fraction is a more

---

NOTE

Rather than provide an unrestricted bequest, donors also can designate that the bequest be used to support an endowed fund or other specified project.

equitable way to divide their estates. Donors can benefit organizations and individuals in relative proportion. Example: A donor wants to leave money to two charities, but does not know the value of her estate. By leaving 10 percent of her estate to the Salvation Army and 5 percent to the American Red Cross, the donor is demonstrating a desire to leave twice as much to the Salvation Army as the American Red Cross.

The following is sample bequest language for a donor who wishes to leave an unrestricted gift of a percentage of an estate to a charity:

> I devise and bequeath [all or (_____ percent)] of the remainder of my property to [specific name] charity, <CITY, STATE ZIP> to be used or disposed of for ___ [or as its Board of Directors in its sole discretion deems appropriate].

BEQUESTS TO CHARITY/SAMPLE PROVISIONS

A bequest to charity is a way of perpetuating support for the role the charity plays in the donor's life. It also enables the donor to make a major gift that might not otherwise be possible.

Suggested Forms of Bequests

When making or revising a will, a donor should obtain the assistance of an attorney. At most charities, members of the development staff will work with donors and their attorneys to design an estate plan specifically tailored to each donor's wishes. The following are suggested forms for making various types of bequests. Donors' attorneys will draft appropriate clauses in the will to accomplish the donors' goals.

Outright Bequest in Will
Specific dollar amount:

> I bequeath the sum of ___ dollars ($_____) to [name of charity], <CITY, STATE ZIP>, to be used or disposed of for ___ [or as its Board of Directors in its sole discretion deems appropriate].

Specific property (personal property):

> I bequeath <DESCRIPTION OF PROPERTY> to [name of charity], <CITY, STATE ZIP>, to be used or disposed of for ___ [or as its Board of Directors in its sole discretion deems appropriate].

Specific property (real estate):

> I devise all of my right, title and interest in and to the real estate located at <DESCRIPTION OF PROPERTY> to [name of charity], <CITY, STATE ZIP>, to be used or disposed of for ___ [or as its Board of Directors in its sole discretion deems appropriate].

Share of, or entire residue of, estate:

> I devise and bequeath (all/or ___ percent [___%]) of the remainder of my property to [name of charity], <CITY, STATE ZIP>, to be used or disposed of for ___ [or as its Board of Directors in its sole discretion deems appropriate].

Conditional Bequest in Will Insert conditional language in one or more of the above provisions. For example:

> If my husband/wife does not survive me, I bequeath the sum of ___ dollars ($_____) to [name of charity], <CITY, STATE ZIP>, to be used or disposed of for ___ [or as its Board of Directors in its sole discretion deems appropriate].

Restricted Bequest If the gift to the charity is restricted, insert the restriction in place of the words "to be used or disposed of as its Board of Directors in its sole discretion deems appropriate." For example:

> I bequeath the sum of $_____ to [name of charity], <CITY, STATE ZIP>, for the following use and purpose: <DESCRIPTION OF PURPOSE>.

In the event of a gift subject to a restriction, include the following provision:

> If in the judgment of the Board of Directors of <charity>, it becomes impossible to accomplish the purposes of this gift, the income or principal may be used for such related purposes and in such manner as determined by its Board of Directors.

STANDARD BEQUEST FORMS

Many charities wish to see donors sign some type of bequest form that confirms in writing their intention to leave a gift by will to the nonprofit. Like bequest intentions themselves, these forms are not binding.

Why use them? An organization may wish to have a donor sign a bequest form if the organization has a policy for crediting bequests. Another reason is to impress upon donors the seriousness of the intention; the organization views the gift seriously and will be counting on the donors' future support. Perhaps equally important, a signed bequest form satisfies the nonprofit's accounting procedures to credit a gift upon a donor's death.

However, few donors are willing to sign bequest forms. The most common reason for not signing a standard bequest form is that donors are unable to estimate the size of their estates at death and therefore have no way of estimating the size of the gift. Donors also may say that their lawyer, financial advisor, or trust officer advised them not to sign anything for fear that the standard bequest form will be viewed as a binding contract. Donors should be told that bequest intentions are revocable and that the organization wants the form on file to help determine future cash flow and to stay informed of a donor's intention so that once the bequest is received, the funds will be used to benefit the program designated by the donor. Despite the benefits of having donors complete a bequest form, do not be overly aggressive in asking them to sign a standard bequest form. The risk is that donors will be alienated and the nonprofit will lose the gifts altogether. Raise the issue once with a donor; if the donor does not follow through with a signature, set the issue aside.

LEGALLY BINDING DOCUMENTS FOR BEQUESTS

Courts in several states have upheld pledge documents, which place an obligation on a donor to carry through with an intention to make a gift through a bequest. To have a legally binding obligation, there has to be "consideration." Consideration, a legal term, is provided by the charity if it performs an act, such as erecting a building in exchange for and in reliance on a donor's promise to provide funding. If consideration is provided by the charity, a charitable pledge agreement becomes binding. Even without consideration, a charitable pledge agreement may state that it is a binding obligation on the donor's personal representative (executor) to transfer a certain amount of money to the charity. A contract to make a will places an obligation on the donor to execute a valid will, which honors the donor's obligations to make a bequest to the charity. Once the binding legal pledge or contract to make a will is signed, the donor's will should be amended if it does not currently provide for the gift to the charity.

TARGETING DONORS FOR BEQUESTS

Like other gift vehicles, bequests need to be marketed to an organization's constituents; most donors and prospects should be solicited for a bequest, especially donors who have made a planned gift to the organization. Conversely, donors who already have made a bequest should then be solicited for a life income gift. Donors who make annual gifts and have consistent giving records are also excellent prospects for making a bequest. A series of annual gifts shows loyalty to the nonprofit, and loyalty is what a bequest is all about.

MARKETING BEQUESTS

In order to attract bequests to a planned giving program, it is necessary to market the benefits of bequests. Use the following marketing techniques to promote the value of bequests.

Bequest Ad

Include an ad in all publications that outlines the benefits of making a bequest to the organization. Some bequest benefits to include follow:

- Make a gift without depleting current income
- Support a program/department/project of choice
- Honor or memorialize a loved one through a bequest
- Reduce estate taxes
- Provide support to the nonprofit organization

Exhibit 7.1 is an ad to attract gifts through an estate.

"Thank-You" Bequest Ad

Include an ad in organizational publications that thanks donors who have already remembered the organization in their wills. Ask donors to identify

EXHIBIT 7.1	AD: GIFTS THROUGH AN ESTATE

Gifts through Your Estate Benefit ‹ORGANIZATION›

Gifts through your estate provide important benefits to you and ‹ORGANIZATION›. Gifts may be made by will or trust, through which you may direct either a specific dollar amount ($25,000) or a percentage (25%). In addition, you may designate your gift to support a particular program or department of interest to you. Through your gift you can:

- Preserve current assets.
- Reduce or eliminate federal estate taxes.
- Make an enduring contribution to ‹ORGANIZATION›.
- Become a member of the ‹PLANNED GIVING SOCIETY›.

The Office of Planned Giving will be pleased to discuss ways to make a gift through your estate to benefit ‹ORGANIZATION›. Contact ‹NAME›, ‹TITLE›, ‹ADDRESS›, ‹CITY, STATE ZIP›; ‹TELEPHONE›.

themselves to the planned giving office so that the organization can recognize and acknowledge their gift. Include in the ad a response form to mail back with a prospect's name and address. Many bequests are made by donors without children. These donors need to be identified, recognized, cultivated, and included in planned giving activities. Surviving spouses who may not be as close to the organization also need to be cultivated. In all cases, a "thank-you" ad opens up an effective line of communication to those who have most generously supported the nonprofit through bequests.

Financial Column or Newsletter

Include in a planned giving newsletter or other nonprofit publication a column that discusses the importance of a will and the benefits of making a gift through one's estate. Alert readers to specific programs or projects at the organization that can benefit from bequests. Exhibit 7.2 is a newsletter about estate planning.

Donor Profile — Testimonial Ad

Everyone enjoys reading a story about a donor who left her entire estate or a significant portion of her estate to a nonprofit organization. Profile a

EXHIBIT 7.2 NEWSLETTER: ESTATE PLANNING

Gifts through Your Estate Benefit ‹ORGANIZATION›

Vol. ‹ # ›   ‹PUBLICATION DATE›

‹ORGANIZATION›
Newsletter

‹PLANNED GIVING SOCIETY›:
Making Leadership Gifts through Estate Planning

The ‹PLANNED GIVING SOCIETY› was established to honor donors who make gifts in special ways. ‹PLANNED GIVING SOCIETY› members are recognized for their support of ‹ORGANIZATION› through planned giving. The many vehicles of planned giving include bequests, pooled income funds, charitable gift annuities, charitable remainder trusts, and insurance programs. They provide a way of planning for ‹ORGANIZATION›'s future along with your own.

‹PLANNED GIVING SOCIETY› members are recognized in honor of ‹NAME OF FOUNDER›. ‹FOUNDER'S NAME› is thought of as the ultimate planner for ‹ORGANIZATION›.

YOUR BEQUEST

Bequests have always played an important role in supporting ‹ORGANIZATION›. For many donors, a gift made through a will is the most realistic way to provide a substantial contribution to ‹ORGANIZATION›. Property, including cash, securities, jewelry, works of art, and real estate, may be given through your will. A will is a legal document that allows you to decide to whom your assets are to be distributed and in what amounts or proportions.

Summary of Benefits

The federal estate tax rate is 37% to 50%, and it declines gradually in future years. The unified credit increases until 2009.

Estate and Gift Tax Rates
and Credit Exemption Amount

Calendar Year	Estate and GST Tax Deathtime Transfer Exemption	Gift Tax Credit Exemption	Highest Estate and Gift Tax Rates
2002	$1 million	$1 million	50%
2003	$1 million	$1 million	49%
2004	$1.5 million	$1 million	48%
2005	$1.5 million	$1 million	47%
2006	$2 million	$1 million	46%
2007	$2 million	$1 million	45%
2008	$2 million	$1 million	45%
2009	$3.5 million	$1 million	45%
2010	N/A (taxes repealed)	$1 million	Maximum gift tax rate equal to maximum income tax rate (35%)

EXHIBIT 7.2   NEWSLETTER: ESTATE PLANNING (CONTINUED)

- A charitable bequest reduces or may eliminate federal estate taxes.
- Most states provide estate or inheritance tax benefits for bequests to charitable organizations.
- Your bequest enables you to make a substantial gift to <ORGANIZATION>.
- Your bequest may be used for a purpose of special interest to you.

TYPES OF BEQUESTS

Specific Bequest
<ORGANIZATION> receives a specific dollar amount, a specific piece of property, or a stated percentage of the estate. This is one of the most popular forms of bequests.

Residuary Bequest
<ORGANIZATION> will receive all or a stated percentage of an estate after distribution of specific bequests and payment of debts, taxes, and expenses.

Contingent Bequest
<ORGANIZATION> will receive part or all of the estate under certain specified circumstances.

Trust Established Under a Will
A trust may be established that provides for both <ORGANIZATION> and other beneficiaries.

FUNDING SCHOLARSHIPS THROUGH YOUR ESTATE

Endowed scholarship funds provide financial assistance to worthy and needy students at <ORGANIZATION>. Scholarship funds can be tailored to meet your specific goals. First, you must decide whom you wish to benefit. You may choose to provide assistance to a student studying a specific major at a particular college at <ORGANIZATION>. You may decide whether the recipient should be a graduate or an undergraduate, and whether the candidate must be financially needy and academically worthy to receive the award.

You must also consider how to fund the scholarship. The minimum level at <ORGANIZATION> is < $ > to establish a named endowed scholarship fund. You may fund it now with cash, or fund it partially or completely through a planned gift or through a bequest from your estate.

Your named fund can grow with the help of family and friends. You can make additional gifts at any time. Often, relatives and friends make gifts to the fund in lieu of birthday or holiday presents.

ENDOWED NAMING OPPORTUNITIES

There are many ways to establish a permanently endowed fund. Through your estate you can make a leadership gift to provide funding for one of the following:

Endowed Naming Opportunities

Distinguished University Chair	< $ >
<ORGANIZATION> Chair	< $ >

EXHIBIT 7.2   NEWSLETTER: ESTATE PLANNING (CONTINUED)

Professorship	‹ $ ›
Lectureship	‹ $ ›
Scholar-in-Residence	‹ $ ›
Full Tuition Scholarship	
Room and Board	‹ $ ›
Fellowship	‹ $ ›
Full Tuition Scholarship	
(In-State)	‹ $ ›
Endowed Fund	‹ $ ›

We want to thank you . . . so let us know . . .

‹PLANNED GIVING SOCIETY› MEMBERSHIP APPLICATION

If you have made a planned gift or included ‹ORGANIZATION› in your will or trust, you are eligible for membership in the ‹ORGANIZATION›'s ‹PLANNED GIVING SOCIETY›. The ‹PLANNED GIVING SOCIETY› recognizes the valuable contributions of friends who include ‹ORGANIZATION› in their estate plans. Most important, you will become a member of an organization that is committed to furthering the goals of ‹ORGANIZATION›. Please complete the membership application below:

Name _____

Address _____

Type of Provision	Estimated Amount
1. Outright bequest in will:	
(a) Specific dollar amount	$_____
(b) Specific property (please describe)	$_____
_____	
(c) Share of entire residue of estate (____%)	$_____
2. Conditional bequest or will (please describe conditions)	$_____
_____	
3. Trust under will or to be funded by will (please describe)	
(a) Charitable remainder trust	$_____
(b) Other	$_____
4. As beneficiary of a life insurance policy	$_____
5. Other (please describe)	$_____
_____	

If your gift to ‹ORGANIZATION› is for other than ‹ORGANIZATION›'s general purposes, please describe any restrictions on a separate sheet. For accounting purposes, please provide a copy of the relevant section of your will or trust that makes provisions for ‹ORGANIZATION›.

_____   _____

    Date   Signature

Please return this form to:
   ‹NAME›, ‹TITLE›, ‹ADDRESS›, ‹CITY, STATE ZIP›; ‹TELEPHONE›.

EXHIBIT 7.2   NEWSLETTER: ESTATE PLANNING (CONTINUED)

‹ORGANIZATION› Life Income Gifts

Your life income gifts to ‹ORGANIZATION› pay dividends. There are several options to choose from, depending on your age, your needs, and the way you fund your gift. A life income gift provides the following benefits:

- A stream of income for the lifetime of the donor and/or the donor's spouse
- A charitable income tax deduction
- An opportunity to establish an endowed fund in your name or in the name of a loved one
- Avoidance or a reduction of capital gains taxes on gifts of appreciated property
- Membership in an ‹ORGANIZATION› leadership club
- A reduction in federal estate taxes

Please send me more information about
Life Income Gifts

_____ Your Age _____ Spouse's Age

Name _____
Address _____
City _____State _____Zip _____
Telephone _____

Mail this coupon to:
‹ORGANIZATION›, ‹ADDRESS›, ‹CITY, STATE ZIP›

This newsletter is designed to offer ‹ORGANIZATION› alumni and friends information on financial planning, estate planning, and charitable giving. ‹ORGANIZATION›, Office of Development, ‹ADDRESS›, ‹CITY, STATE ZIP›; ‹TELEPHONE›.

donor in an organizational publication who feels strongly about the organization and has made a financial commitment through a bequest. Donor profiles show role models and can be very persuasive in demonstrating to other donors that they, too, can make a gift.

CREDITING BEQUESTS

No organization seems to have solved the problem of how best to credit bequests promised in a living donor's will. Such bequests are inherently difficult to deal with because wills can be changed or revoked by donors. However, most donors honor their bequest intentions. Different nonprofits offer the following suggestions for crediting bequest intentions:

- Recognize donors who make bequest intentions as members of a bequest society. Add to the campaign totals only the money received once the bequest materializes.

- Provide full credit for promised bequests that are accompanied by a signed bequest form from the donor.

- Credit unrealized bequest intentions if certain requirements are met, such as:
  - The donor must be a certain minimum age, often 65 or 70.
  - The amount of the gift must be a certain amount or percentage, based on a conservative estimate of the future value of the donor's estate.
  - The bequest intention must be in writing on the organization's approved bequest form and must be accompanied by a copy of the relevant portion of the donor's will.
  - The donor must have a preexisting relationship with the organization, such as service as a past or current trustee, dean, staff physician, administrator, or employee.

- Count the bequest at full value minus a discount to arrive at a "present value" of the gift. The discount should reflect delay in receipt of the bequest based on the donor's life expectancy, inflation, or other factors. Example: Assume a donor makes a bequest of $1,000,000 and the bequest is discounted at an annual rate of 5 percent. If the donor's life expectancy is five years, the value of the bequest is $783,526; if 10 years, the value of the bequest is $613,913; if 15 years, the value of the bequest is $481,017.

- Give full credit for a bequest intention if the donor already has made a substantial current gift to the nonprofit. Decide what the minimum amount is for a "substantial" gift.

Once an organization adopts a policy, it should be adhered to consistently. Check the crediting guidelines developed by the Council for the Advancement and Support of Education (CASE) for additional information.

RECOGNITION EVENTS

A well-run recognition event can be one of the best sources of new and repeat business for a planned giving program. When hosting an event to recognize donors who have made a bequest to the organization, include all donors who have made a planned gift. The key is inclusion, not exclusion, especially at a small organization. To have a successful event, there should be sufficient attendance to provide credibility to the program. Ten to 12 people are not enough for a formal luncheon, but could be appropriate for an informal reception. Expand the number of potential invitees to make those who attend feel that they are part of an elite group that makes special gifts. Consider using the event also as a cultivation event; invite prospects who may make a gift to the organization. Hosting the event facilitates communication, and donors are likely to discuss business and future gifts at the event. Consider the following issues when planning a recognition event:

Bequest Society

If the nonprofit organization does not have a formal bequest society in place, establish one. Select a name for the society, perhaps naming it after one of the organization's founders or one of the first donors who made a bequest to the organization or in honor of a donor who made a significant gift to the nonprofit. Next send out a letter to planned giving donors, prospects, annual fund donors, and anyone else who may qualify for potential bequest society membership, including trustees, administrators, and longtime volunteers. Inform them that the nonprofit is establishing a recognition program for all donors who indicate an intention to make a bequest or planned gift to the organization. Consider including a survey asking potential bequest donors for a time preference in attending a recognition event and for subject topics they would like to learn more about. Inform them of the benefits that bequest society membership provides, such as a newsletter, annual luncheon, and membership pin or plaque. Follow up with telephone calls to donors if they do not respond. Responses should indicate how soon to have a second recognition event. If the numbers are not sufficient to host an event in the near future, continue to market the bequest society regularly and repeat this approach a year later.

Timing

Consider having the function during the daytime. Most older donors do not want to drive at night and will turn down an evening invitation no matter how compelling. Choose a time of year when donors are at home, not during the summer or winter seasons when they may be away.

Location

When selecting the location for the event, remember that many donors are elderly and will not want to climb flights of stairs. Wheelchair accessibility is also important, so a first-floor location is ideal. Mark the location well, and have volunteers available to direct attendees. Ensure that parking is readily available and proximate; otherwise provide shuttle buses or other transportation from the parking location to the event.

Marketing the Event

Donors like to feel part of a successful organization. Market the event to donors in publications in the same way planned giving vehicles are marketed; remember that each event builds on preceding ones. Every year, as new donors are added, the attendance should increase. Start the marketing process by sending a letter to all planned giving donors and anyone else who is considered a planned giving prospect. Approximately three and a half months before the event, notify potential attendees of the date, location, and purpose of this year's event. Inform donors and prospects that they will receive an invitation shortly, which should be mailed approximately six weeks before the event. Include in newsletters and publications the date of the event and time, location, and any other relevant information. Also call invitees to confirm attendance.

Guest Speaker(s)

Select a speaker for the event who is a present or prospective donor who has had a positive experience with the planned giving office. Speakers who have been directly involved with the planned giving program are in an excellent position to promote planned giving as well as offer an interesting presentation. Most donors attend the event because they enjoy and appreciate the recognition and the feeling that comes from being a part of a special group. Identify roles for staff in the program, roles that provide an opportunity to reinforce to the donors the staff's experience, the benefits of the program, and the needs of the organization. Consider sharing with attendees information about the highlights of the year's planned giving program.

Donor Recognition

Most recognition events include the actual honoring of participants. Presenting a bequest pin is one possibility. Donors will be delighted to receive the attention, and it encourages goodwill and future support.

Bequest Event Checklist

Exhibit 7.3 is a function checklist to be used for a bequest event or for any other special event. The following areas should be considered:

- *Food.* Providing attendees with food is an important draw for every event. Keep in mind that many people do not eat red meat so consider serving chicken, fish, or a vegetarian meal.

- *Bar Service.* Offer beer, wine, mixed drinks, fruit juice, and non-alcoholic beverages to donors, unless the organization prefers that liquor not be served.

- *Promotional Materials.* Have available the recognition society's latest newsletter along with a basic planned giving brochure and any materials about the program or organization that donors should see.

- *Staffing.* Be free to greet and meet prospects and to talk with a donor who wishes to discuss making a new gift. Add additional staff to assist attendees at the event. Place staff members at a reception table to answer questions, distribute name tags, and help with coats.

- *Audiovisual Needs.* Ask if the speaker has particular audiovisual needs. Arrange for a podium, microphone, lighting, overheads, and the like.

- *Photographer.* A photographer should be available to take pictures of donors at the recognition event. Use these photographs in the next planned giving newsletter to highlight the event. Send photographs to special donors to have as keepsakes.

EXHIBIT 7.3   FORM: FUNCTION CHECKLIST

NEEDED	ORDERED	CONFIRMED

EXHIBIT 7.3   FORM: FUNCTION CHECKLIST (CONTINUED)

VOLUNTEERS

Enlist chairperson

Appoint committee

Thank committee

EVENT PRELIMINARIES

Enlist speaker

Book and confirm function space

Requisition for labels

Invitation copy

Food ☐   Beverage ☐   Hotel ☐

Requisition for food service

Menu ☐   Guarantee ☐   Entree ☐

Bar ☐   Liquor ☐   Wine ☐   Beer ☐

Nonalcoholic drinks

Hotel space

Rooms ☐   Suites ☐

Singles ☐   Doubles ☐

Reception rooms

Parking permits ☐ Passes ☐

PUBLIC RELATIONS

Brochure copy

Posters

Handouts/press kits

Press releases/calendar announcements

Media announcements

Live coverage

Biographies for introductions

Photographer (Hours needed) from: to:

STAFFING

Bartenders

Coat-check attendants

Staff

EXHIBIT 7.3   FORM: FUNCTION CHECKLIST (CONTINUED)

ROOM SET-UP

Flag ☐	Banner ☐

Flowers

Rugs installed ☐	Floor installed ☐

Head table

Chairs ☐	Tables ☐

Water pitcher and glasses

Display tables

Coat rack

AUDIOVISUAL

Microphones ☐		P/A system ☐
Podium ☐	Projector ☐	Screen ☐
Overhead ☐	Flipchart ☐	

Tape recorder ☐

SUPPLIES

Name tags ☐

Registration materials ☐ Desk supplies ☐

Brochures ☐ Newsletters ☐

- *Miscellaneous.* Do not forget flowers for tables, parking arrangements, coat checks, and name tags.

- *Follow-up.* When the event is over, send attendees a letter thanking them for participating. Thank them again for their continued support of the organization. Follow up immediately with donors who discussed making additional gifts. Send a note to donors and prospects who did not attend the event. Let them know how successful the event was, what they missed, and that they will be able to attend next year's program.

CONCLUSION

Bequests are the first and primary building block of a planned giving program. Every small nonprofit organization can and should promote bequests as a way to make gifts to the organization; the largest of all charitable gifts come in the form of bequests. Raising the awareness of bequests among donors and staff members greatly increases the opportunity to expand the charity's financial support. Marketing programs, including ads, testimonials, and brochures promoting bequests, attract donors and prospects. Bequest societies enable charities to recognize donors who have made gifts through their estates.

CHAPTER 8

Endowed Funds and Current Use Awards

INTRODUCTION

Endowed funds and current use awards are essential gifts that help finance the work of small nonprofit organizations. These gifts may be funded outright through a gift of cash or stock or through a planned gift. At most small nonprofit organizations, the planned giving staff member handles these gifts and often prepares gift agreements (fund descriptions).

Planned gifts help charities offer programs, deliver services, conduct their business, and fulfill their missions. A planned gift can be used to meet the needs of the charity in a variety of ways. Nonprofit organizations should educate donors about the ways that gifts could be used to help donors understand their needs. What are the charity's priorities? What is the charity's greatest need? Which programs or activities need funds? Planned gifts can be used to accomplish almost any charitable purpose that is important to the donor.

This chapter outlines the way that donors can make gifts through funds that fulfill the nonprofit's needs. Included are descriptions of the types of programs donors might support and the ways to provide support through current use awards and endowed funds. The chapter also explores the way current use and endowed funds can be used, either immediately through a current use account or distributed as income through a donor's endowed fund. The following are definitions that will be used throughout the chapter:

Unrestricted gift   Nondesignated gift used by the charity at its discretion.

Restricted gift   Gift specifically designated by the donor for a purpose.

Endowed fund   Fund permanently managed in perpetuity with earnings distributed annually.

Current use awards   One-time restricted gifts that provide immediate support to the charity for the purpose designated by the donor.

Both current use and endowed funds can be unrestricted or restricted.

UNRESTRICTED GIFTS

Unrestricted gifts come with no strings attached. A gift is made for the use of the charity at the charity's discretion by its board of directors or president. The gift can be expended for any purpose that fulfills the charity's mission. Unrestricted gifts are the most valuable to nonprofit organizations because they can be used for any purpose. These gifts are sometimes difficult to obtain because many donors wish to designate their gifts, not wanting to give charities broad discretion in their utilization. Unrestricted gifts also enable the charity to respond to changes that could not be foreseen at the time of the gift. For example, a permanently endowed fund that allows the president to use the income at his or her discretion enables presidents over the years to use the income in support of a variety of projects. At a small nonprofit organization, it is possible for a donor to get to know the charity's staff and programs. As a result, small nonprofits may actually receive a larger percentage of unrestricted gifts than their larger counterparts.

RESTRICTED GIFTS

Restricted gifts are gifts where the donor includes criteria limiting use for a particular purpose (scholarships), program (cardiac care), or department (19th-century art). Criteria or guidelines are developed governing use of the gift. A gift agreement prepared by the charity defines the restrictions and limitations of the gift and is discussed later in this chapter. Most large gifts are restricted because the donors have specific purposes in mind when the gifts are made.

ENDOWED FUNDS

An endowed fund is like an investment account or bank account. The principal is invested and the endowed fund distributes income from the earnings of the fund. With an endowed fund, only a portion of the earnings are spent, preserving the principal intact. Endowed funds are managed in perpetuity and usually make distributions that are based on a percentage of the principal value of the endowment. After deducting management fees, most charities distribute approximately 4 to 5 percent of the market value of the endowed fund, depending on the restriction included in the gift agreement and the charity's investment policy. For example, if the market value of the fund is $10,000 and the payout is set at 5 percent, then $500 will be distributed this year. The distribution can be used immediately, or it may be returned to the principal or reserved for future use. In most cases, endowed funds are restricted in that their income is designated to benefit a specific department, program, or project at the charity. The charity depends on income from individuals' endowed funds to continue programs from year to year, and endowed funds provide stability to a charity. The earnings from these funds can be used for scholarships, operating support, program support, or any other purpose consistent with the intent of the donor and the needs of the charity. A donor can allocate the distribution by providing that, for example, 50 percent be used for scholarships for chemistry majors and 50 percent be used for the chemistry department in support of departmental objectives.

Endowed funds also can be established in honor of individuals who are/were important to the donor. People make gifts because of people, and donors may wish to make gifts in honor or memory of a parent, mentor, friend, child, or distinguished individual at the charity, such as a professor, doctor, curator, staff member, or department head.

Generally, when donors establish an endowed fund, other donors can make gifts to it. Donors also can make additional annual gifts, planned gifts, and bequests in support of their endowed fund. Donors can add to their endowed funds at any time, and they also can make affordable multiyear pledges to provide significant financial support over time.

CREATING AN ENDOWED FUND

When donors create an endowed fund, they make a lasting contribution to the charity's future. An endowed fund provides annual support in

GIFT TIP

Below is a marketing piece to help families increase the size of their endowed family funds. This information may be placed in an ad or sent to donors at year-end.

BUILDING YOUR ENDOWED FAMILY FUND

- Make an annual gift to the fund. Over time these annual gifts may double the size of your family fund.
- Honor family members' birthdays, anniversaries, and weddings by making gifts to the fund in their names.
- Some families, in lieu of exchanging birthday or holiday presents, make a gift to the family fund.
- Make a planned gift and designate your gift to benefit your family fund.
- Through your will, leave a percentage of your estate or a specific dollar amount to your fund.
- Let friends, colleagues, and relatives know about your fund and invite their support. Charities usually send a thank-you letter to each donor and let you know the names and addresses of contributors to your fund.
- For memorial services, suggest that in lieu of flowers, fruit, baskets, or other items, gifts be made to your family fund.

perpetuity. Endowed funds help support faculty projects, research, scholarships, professorships, exhibits, lecture series, academic programs, facility operations, and much more. Donors may honor the memory of a loved one and establish a memorial-endowed fund. A named memorial gift fund becomes a lasting symbol of the bond between the charity and those who are forever honored and their families. The next sections provide an overview of the types of endowed funds donors can create.

SCHOLARSHIP/FELLOWSHIP FUNDS

At educational institutions, teaching hospitals, and other organizations that have a formal teaching component, endowed scholarship/fellowship funds provide much-needed financial assistance to worthy and financially needy students. Scholarships usually are awarded to undergraduate students and fellowships are awarded to graduate students. Donors may choose to provide assistance to a student studying a specific major in a certain department or studying a particular subject. A graduate or an undergraduate student majoring in a specific department may be selected, and donors can decide whether the candidate must be financially needy and/or academically worthy to receive the award. Donors may require that recipients maintain a minimum grade point average or require other criteria, such as participation in extracurricular activities.

OTHER ENDOWED FUNDS

Endowed funds can be established for almost any purpose that helps the charity fulfill its mission. Each of the endowed funds listed in Exhibit 8.1 may bear the donor's name or may be named in honor or in memory of someone important to the donor. At a small nonprofit organization, it is unlikely that most of these funds would be in place.

EXHIBIT 8.1   DIFFERENT FUNDS

OBJECTIVE:	PURPOSE:
STUDENT SUPPORT	Financial aid, room and board, book funds
Scholarships	Financial support for students to offset tuition
Fellowships	Support for graduate students, teaching or research stipend
Awards	Merit awards for student performance, book awards
SEMINARS	For students, faculty, staff, and the public
Lecture Series	Underwrites honorarium of speaker and expense of series
Scholars in Residence	Brings to the charity a distinguished scholar for 4 to 6 weeks
Visiting Scholar	Brings to the charity a scholar for a semester or half a year
Guest Speaker	Underwrites a single speaker for a one-time event
Speaker Series	Underwrites annual series of two or more speakers
EQUIPMENT	Software and hardware
Computers	Provides support to secure, replace, and upgrade software, hardware, Internet access, connectivity, and networking capabilities
Technology	Software, servers, Internet access
Scientific Equipment	Telescopes, microscopes, medical supplies

EXHIBIT 8.1   DIFFERENT FUNDS (CONTINUED)

OBJECTIVE:	PURPOSE:
PROJECTS	Special events
Display	Underwrites the cost of a display or exhibit, presentation or performance at a theater, museum, opera, symphony, hospital, or university
Exhibitions	Underwrites an exhibition at a charity
Presentations	Provides resources to make presentations at public forums or community functions
Performances	Underwrites plays, experimental and traditional theater companies, or charities involved in music
Curation	Funds research and cataloging activities
Restoration	Funds restoration and cleaning of collections and displays
Faculty/Staff	Funds for achievement and incentive
Awards	Recognize achievement
Release Time	Pays for the cost of a faculty member's salary so that research or special projects can be conducted
Faculty Support	Supplements faculty salaries, attendance at conferences
Program Support	Funds for the charity's units.
Departments	Underwrites the charity's departments or programs
Services	Supplements the cost to deliver charity's services to those who need them
Screenings	Medical evaluations, public education, clinics
Facilities	Bricks and mortar
Capital Projects	Add wing, addition, or new facility
Naming Opportunities	Naming an existing or new building
Operations	Supplements the charity's budget
Maintenance	Pays for upgrades and improvements
Entrepreneurial Funds	Funds for entrepreneurial activities and for exploring new programs
Innovation	Spawn innovation, creativity and exploration
Entrepreneur Funds	Provides seed money or research for start-up projects
Resources	All charities, but especially libraries, need scholarly journals, research books, and online resources
Books	Scholarly works for research and study
Periodicals	Research publications
Online Publications	Technology based research promoting web-based research

CURRENT USE AWARDS

Through a current use award, a donor makes a gift and the charity either immediately or within the year distributes the amount of the award consistent with the donor's wishes. The contribution provides immediate financial assistance to purchase books or supplies, covers operational expenses, or funds specific projects. Most current use awards are relatively small, but there is no reason why they should be. At many organizations a donor can create a named current use fund for as little as $1,000. Donors can make gifts as large as they want, as long as they realize that with a current use gift the money will be spent at once or within a year.

FINANCING AN ENDOWED FUND

Most small nonprofit organizations offer a variety of endowed fund options with different minimum amounts. Many charities have minimums of $10,000 but the minimum can be as high as $50,000 to $100,000 or more. The minimums usually are related to the scope of the endowed fund and its cost. For example, at a large university establishing a chair might cost $2,000,000; a professorship might cost $500,000; whereas a scholarship would be $25,000. Small charities can establish minimums consistent with the nonprofit's traditions and donors' giving capacity. The fund may be supported financially with gifts of cash, through a planned gift, or through a bequest from a donor's estate. If the planned gift is a life income gift, the charity must wait until the death of the donor to use the remainder. This is an important point; many donors mistakenly believe that a life income gift provides resources to the charity at the time the gift is made. However, with most planned gifts, the income is paid to the donor for life and only upon the death of the donor or other beneficiary is the remainder available to the charity. Depending on the vehicle selected, the payout rate, and the life span of the beneficiaries, the remainder value may be 35 to 70 percent of the initial gift.

FUND DESCRIPTION

When an endowed fund is established, the charity prepares a personalized fund description (gift agreement) that describes the purposes of the endowed fund. The donor's input is very important because the agreement should reflect the donor's intentions. The donor should be involved in the process from the beginning, and planned giving staff members should explain how the donor's money will be used and review any restrictions about the use of the gift. Each donor should receive an agreement that includes a statement about the fund's purpose, a brief biographical sketch about the donor, criteria for making the award and selecting recipients, and a distribution clause for paying income to designated purposes. The fund description also should name a successor department or program in case the initial program ceases to exist.

Selection of Recipient

Donors sometimes wish to be involved in the selection of recipients for endowed scholarship funds. A donor who claims a charitable income tax deduction cannot be the sole decision maker in the selection of the recipient; otherwise the donor's charitable income tax deduction could be jeopardized. The donor may, however, serve as a member of a selection committee composed of the charity's representatives.

For scholarship funds, donors and charities also should avoid using overly restrictive criteria that prevent the development of an adequate pool of candidates. Basic criteria should be established and restrictions should be expressed in the form of preferences.

MECHANICS OF A FUND DESCRIPTION

Most fund descriptions are no more than one or two pages long and include an explanation of the fund and have signature and date lines at the bottom. The following information should be included:

- Name of the fund: The Diana Smith Endowed Scholarship Fund at (XYZ Charity).

- Names of the parties creating the fund. Generally this includes one or more donors and the name of the organization. "XYZ University and Miss Diana Smith hereby propose to establish The Diana Smith Endowed Scholarship Fund at XYZ University."

- Description of how the fund shall be financed, such as through a bequest, outright gift, planned gift, or a combination. Most charities permit and encourage additional gifts to be made to funds. These gifts may be made by the donor or by friends, family, and colleagues: "This endowed fund shall be supported by a gift in the amount of $10,000 from Mrs. Smith. Family members, friends, and colleagues may make additional gifts. The fund may also serve as a memorial to Mrs. Smith and memorial gifts may also be made to the fund."

- Biographical sketch about the donor(s) outlining their relationship with the charity. This information helps recipients know about the individual who created the fund and serves as a permanent memorial to the donor at the donor's death.

- Definition of the fund's purpose reflecting the donor's wishes: "The income of the fund shall be awarded to a graduate student at The School of Medicine who wishes to study gerontology."

- Administration of the fund. Will the income be awarded on an annual basis? Will some of the income be returned to principal? If the income is not awarded, should it be returned to principal or accumulated for future use?

- Restrictions. If the fund is for a scholarship, must the recipient be financially needy, academically worthy, or have attained a particular grade point average? Are there geographical requirements for recipients (resident of New York)? Should the recipient be focusing on a particular area of study? The restrictions should reflect the donor's interests. Donors also may express their wishes as a preference rather than an absolute requirement: "The income shall be awarded annually to students who have maintained a Grade Point Average of 3.5 or better who are majoring in Foreign Languages."

- How the recipient will be selected. Will a committee composed of representatives from the charity be used? "Selection of candidates shall be made by the Office of Financial Aid in consultation with the Dean of the College of Liberal Arts." Should candidates submit a 1- to 2-page essay outlining their achievements to help the selection committee evaluate candidates?

- Standard default clause. Include such a clause to protect the donor if in the future the charity is unable to fulfill the terms of the fund: "If it becomes impossible to accomplish the purposes of this gift, the income or principal, or both, shall be used for scholarships in the department of XYZ."

Exhibit 8.2 is a sample multipurpose fund description. Exhibit 8.3 is a sample current use gift agreement.

EXHIBIT 8.2   MULTIPLE-PURPOSE ENDOWED FUND DESCRIPTION

The Meriam Wilson Endowed Fund
at
Charity

Charity and Meriam Wilson hereby propose to establish the Meriam Wilson Endowed Scholarship Fund at Charity in accordance with the wishes of the donor, Meriam Wilson. Meriam Wilson is an alumna of the College of Art, Class of 1938. The fund shall be established through current gifts and the donor's estate.

The fund is defined and administered as follows:

The title of the fund shall be the Meriam Wilson Endowed Scholarship Fund. The fund shall be established in two parts:

Part I Financial Aid for Students

Three fourths of the income shall be used to make an annual award to one or more full-time undergraduate or graduate students majoring in science or engineering. Eligible candidates for the fund must have a demonstrated financial need and solid academic standing. Selection of candidates shall be made by the Office of Financial Aid in consultation with the College of Art.

Part II Faculty Support

One-fourth of the income from the fund shall be used to make an annual award to a full-time member of the faculty at the College of Art for research and study of Alzheimer's disease and related disorders.

For both Part I and Part II, in any year in which there is no student or faculty member eligible to receive the award, any income not distributed shall be added to principal or accumulated for future use.

If in the judgment of the Executive Committee of the XYZ Charity it becomes impossible to accomplish the purposes of this gift, the income or principal, or both, may be used for scholarships in such manner as determined by the charity.

_____   _____
      Date   Meriam Wilson

_____   _____
      Date   For charity:
                                    <NAME>, <TITLE>

EXHIBIT 8.3	THE DENISE ANDREWS CURRENT USE AWARD

Denise Andrews and XYZ charity hereby propose to establish The Denise Andrews Current Use Award at XYZ charity in accordance with the wishes of the donor. The award shall be supported by a gift of $3,000.

The Award is defined and administered as follows:

The title of the award shall be The Denise Andrews Current Use Award. The current use award shall be used to provide an annual exhibition of local artists' works of art at XYZ Charity. The artists must live or work in city of ‹CITY›, and the work shall exemplify the traditions, values, and history of the region.

The award shall be made at the discretion of the Department Head of Art History. The Denise Andrews Current Use Scholarship Award shall be awarded in future years contingent upon the donor making additional gifts to fund the award.

_____   _____
Date   Denise Andrews

_____   _____
Date   [NAME]
                         [TITLE]

CONCLUSION

The donor, in consultation with the nonprofit organization, makes decisions about the way the fund will be established and used. The gift may be restricted or unrestricted and may be a current use gift or an endowed fund. It may be funded through an outright gift, a planned gift, or a gift through the donor's estate. Be sure the description or gift agreement reflects the donor's wishes.

CHAPTER 9

Basic Life Income Gifts: Charitable Gift Annuities, Deferred Gift Annuities, and Pooled Income Funds

INTRODUCTION

Life income gifts provide mutual benefits to both the donor and the charity. These gifts provide income streams and tax advantages to donors and needed resources to nonprofit organizations. Life income gifts help donors leverage gifts by enabling them to make larger gifts because of the income stream. In addition, the charity receives the remainder of the gift, which is the amount that is left over upon the donor's death after the life income has been paid to the donor. In general, the charity receives about 50 percent of the gift amount at the donor's death. This chapter explores the three most common life income vehicles: charitable gift annuities, deferred gift annuities, and pooled income fund gifts. These options are appropriate vehicles for most small charities. They can be managed in house or by an outside manager such as a financial institution.

CHARITABLE GIFT ANNUITIES

Charitable gift annuities are among the most common and popular of the planned gift, life income-producing vehicles. If a small nonprofit organization must choose to offer a single life income gift option, it should select the charitable gift annuity. Through a charitable gift annuity a donor makes a gift to a charity and receives an income for life and, if desired, an income for a second beneficiary. Spouses can make a joint gift providing income streams for their joint lifetimes. Unmarried individuals also may make gifts that provide income to two or more individuals and to the survivor. Upon the death of the survivor beneficiary, the charity receives the remainder of the gift. A portion of the income is tax free, and the donor claims a charitable income tax deduction that is affected by the beneficiary's age(s), discount rate, and frequency of payment. Charitable gift annuities are age sensitive—higher rates are paid to older donors. They provide the greatest financial benefit to donors over age 70, who receive the highest income rates.

Benefits to donors for charitable gift annuities include

- Income for life paid annually, semiannually, quarterly, or monthly
- A fixed rate that is often greater than money market rates
- A immediate charitable income tax deduction for 35 to 50 percent of the gift amount
- The opportunity to support a charity

The charitable gift annuity is a contract between the donor and the charity. The charity is legally obligated to pay a fixed rate of income for the lifetime of the beneficiary that is locked in at the time the gift is made. However, if a new gift is made a year or two later, the rate likely will be a little higher for that gift annuity because the donor is a little older. The transaction is, in reality, a bargain sale—part sale and part gift, because the donor is giving an amount to the charity that exceeds the annuity promised by it. The annuity is backed by the general assets of the charity but is an unsecured obligation of the charity.

If the charity ceases to exist, suffers financial setbacks, or becomes bankrupt, the donor will need to line up with other creditors to receive payments depending on the reason the charity failed and whether the charity holds insurance to cover that type of failure. In the event of a financial calamity, to be certain that payments are met, some charities purchase insurance to protect their charitable gift annuities, called reinsurance. Many states require a nonprofit to register with the state if it offers charitable gift annuities in that state. If a donor requires the charity to purchase a commercial annuity contract to insure that payments will be made, the charitable income tax deduction may be affected by the premium paid to the commercial carrier. Work with experienced legal counsel to establish a charitable gift annuity program.

Gift Annuity Rates and the American Council on Gift Annuities

The number and age of the beneficiaries affect a gift annuity rate. Many charities follow the suggested rates of the American Council on Gift Annuities, an organization that suggests rates that charities pay to annuitants. The rates are the same for both sexes at the same ages, encouraging donors to make gifts to the charity they truly wish to support rather than selecting a charity because it offers a higher rate. Occasionally charities deviate from the suggested rates. If a donor requests a rate that is greater than the recommended rate, the charity's remainder may be diminished or depleted. A charitable gift annuity is just that: a charitable gift that provides resources to charities. These options are not designed to compete with commercial annuities or other forms of financial investments. The American Council on Gift Annuities revises its suggested gift annuity rates periodically. See Exhibit 9.1.

EXHIBIT 9.I	FINANCIAL BENEFITS FROM A $10,000 CHARITABLE GIFT ANNUITY

A Gift Option for Donors over Age 65

Age	Payout Rate	Annual Income	Tax Deduction*
65	6.7%	$670	$3,346
70	7.2%	$720	$3,745
75	7.9%	$790	$4,157
75/73	6.9%	$690	$3,314
80/78	7.5%	$750	$3,816

*Based on a discount rate of 6.0%

Tax Consequences of Charitable Gift Annuities

When donors make a charitable gift annuity, there can be various tax consequences. The following subsections discuss donors' charitable income tax deductions and gift, capital gains, and estate tax consequences.

Valuation of the Charitable Income Tax Deduction   Depending on the donor's age and other factors, the donor will likely receive a charitable income tax deduction of approximately 35 to 50 percent of the gift. Most charities use planned giving software to calculate charitable income tax deductions and other financial consequences. The exact value of the deduction is determined by subtracting the present value of the annuity (life income interest) from the present value of the gift to determine the remainder interest to the charity, which is equal to the donor's charitable income tax deduction. The value of the annuity is determined by applying the IRS discount rate to the stream of payments over the donor's life expectancy and that of any other beneficiary. (The IRS discount rate is 120 percent of the federal midterm rate, which changes monthly.) When calculating the charitable income tax deduction, the nonprofit organization can use the rate for the month in which the gift is made or the rate from either of the two preceding months. Usually the highest discount rate is selected to ensure the highest charitable income tax deduction. The donor obtains a charitable income tax deduction in the year the gift is made; if the deduction cannot be used completely in the first year, it is carried forward for up to five additional years.

> **TIP**
>
> For gifts of cash, the charitable income tax deduction may be used to offset up to 50 percent of the donor's adjusted gross income. If the gift is funded with appreciated property (which would produce long-term capital gains on sale), the charitable income tax deduction may be used to offset up to 30 percent of the donor's adjusted gross income.

Gift Taxes   A charitable gift annuity established for the benefit of someone other than the donor's spouse is potentially a taxable gift, and the donor may owe a gift tax on the value of the charitable gift annuity. The taxable gift is not based on the stream of income paid

TIP

Donors can reduce the size of their estates through the use of the annual exclusion. Donors can make tax-free gifts of up to $10,000 per year to any number of beneficiaries. Married couples may combine their annual exclusions to make tax-free gifts of $20,000 per year.

to the beneficiary, but on the total value of the charitable gift annuity at the time the gift is made. If payments to the third party begin within the year, the donor can use the $10,000 annual gift tax exclusion to eliminate or reduce the gift tax due on the charitable gift annuity. If the donor is the first annuitant and reserves the right to revoke the interest of the second beneficiary, no gift is made until the donor's death. The donor's estate will pay tax on the value of the second beneficiary's annuity at that time.

Capital Gains Taxes and Income Taxation
Donors who fund a charitable gift annuity with appreciated property held for more than a year and a day will have to pay capital gains taxes, currently assessed at a maximum rate of 20 percent on most investment property, such as stock or real estate. The tax is assessed on that portion of the property that is used to purchase the charitable gift annuity. If the donor is the sole beneficiary or the first beneficiary, the gain can be spread out by reporting it over his or her life expectancy. If the spouse is younger, the donor may prefer to report the gain over the spouse's lifetime. If so, outright gifts to the spouse of the appreciated property can be accomplished without tax consequences by using the unlimited marital deduction. The unlimited marital deduction allows spouses to freely transfer unlimited amounts of property, cash, or other assets to each other without paying gift or estate taxes on the transfer. The spouse can then make the gift to fund the charitable gift annuity. A portion of the stream of income received by the beneficiary will be excluded from gross income because it is considered a tax-free return of capital. The rest is taxed as ordinary income and as capital gain income, if appreciated property is used to fund the gift. Once a donor

TIP

Spouses who are U.S. citizens can transfer any amount of property to each other tax free using the unlimited marital deduction.

reaches his or her life expectancy (calculated at the date of the gift), the entire amount of the annuity is taxable.

Estate Taxes   For donors who are the only annuitant, the income stream ceases on their deaths and the value of the annuity is excluded from their estates. If a spouse is the sole remaining annuitant, the spouse's interest may qualify for the estate tax marital deduction. If a third person is the sole remaining annuitant and the donor has retained, but not exercised, the right to revoke that person's annuity, the value of the third party's annuity will be taxed in the donor's estate.

Acceptable Assets to Fund a Charitable Gift Annuity

The most common and the easiest way to fund a charitable gift annuity is to use cash. Donors also can fund charitable gift annuities with securities, but if the securities have appreciated, donors will have to pay capital gains taxes on the gain in the sale part of the transaction. For many donors, the capital gains tax rate (20 percent for most investment assets such as stock) is less than their marginal income tax rate. Tax-free securities are also acceptable to fund a charitable gift annuity, but the annuity will be taxed as if the assets transferred were not tax exempt.

Occasionally real estate is used to fund a charitable gift annuity, if the real estate can be sold and converted to cash quickly. Because the charitable gift annuity payment is an immediate obligation of the charity, non–income-producing assets, such as real estate, need to be sold and converted to income-producing assets so that the payment can be made. The donor and the charity need to be realistic about the likelihood of resale in case the real estate sale is delayed or the property sells for less than anticipated. Keep in mind that other costs associated with real estate, such as brokers' commissions and attorneys' fees, will reduce the amount of sale proceeds below the appraised fair market value of the contributed real estate. The nonprofit organization and the donor should share the responsibility for these costs, or they should be negotiated.

Gift Annuity Contract

Because charitable gift annuities are contractual agreements, the only document needed is a one-page gift annuity contract, prepared by the nonprofit organization, which includes the annuity rate, amount of payment, and the payment schedule, which is most often monthly but may be quarterly or annually. Many charitable gift annuities are managed in house by the charity, although they can be administered outside the charity, usually by a bank, trust company, or investment firm.

Exhibit 9.2 is an example of a two-beneficiary gift annuity agreement. All agreements should be reviewed by the nonprofit's attorney.

DEFERRED GIFT ANNUITIES

Like the charitable gift annuity, the deferred gift annuity pays an income stream, but it begins at a point in the future. The deferred gift annuity is a very appropriate option for younger to middle-age donors, ages 25 to 60. When a donor makes a gift, the charity agrees to pay the donor and, if the donor wishes, a second beneficiary a stream of income for life, beginning

---

EXHIBIT 9.2   TWO-BENEFICIARY CHARITABLE GIFT ANNUITY AGREEMENT

‹CHARITY›, a charitable corporation located in ‹CITY, STATE›, agrees to pay to ‹DONOR›, of ‹CITY, STATE› (hereinafter called the "Donor"), for the Donor's life and thereafter to the Donor's spouse, ‹SPOUSE'S NAME›, for (HIS/HER) life if (HE/SHE) survives the Donor, an annuity in the annual sum of ‹AMOUNT IN WORDS›, (‹DOLLAR AMOUNT›) from the date hereof, in equal quarterly installments of ‹ $ › on the last day of March, June, September and December; provided, however, that the Donor may by the Donor's last will revoke the annuity to be paid to the Donor's said spouse. The first installment shall be payable on ‹DATE›. This annuity shall be nonassignable, except in the case of a voluntary transfer of part or all of such annuity to Charity.

The obligation of Charity to make annuity payments shall terminate with the payment preceding the death of the survivor of the Donor and the Donor's said spouse, unless the Donor revokes the annuity payable to the Donor's said spouse, in which case ‹ORGANIZATION'S› obligation shall terminate with the payment preceding the death of the Donor.

Charity certifies that the Donor, as an evidence of the Donor's desire to support the work of Charity and to make a charitable gift, has this day contributed to Charity $____, receipt of which is acknowledged for its general charitable purposes.

The annuity agreement has been entered into in (State of Charity's primary office) and is governed by the law of the ‹STATE› (Charity's primary office).

IN WITNESS WHEREOF, Charity has executed this instrument this ____ day of _____, 20____.

For Charity:
By: ‹NAME›, ‹TITLE›

at a point in the future. The income stream must be deferred for at least one year after the gift is made. Upon the donor's death, the charity receives the remainder of the gift. Many donors choose age 65 or older to receive the income stream because they will have retired and expect to be in a lower tax bracket. Used this way, the deferred gift annuity is similar to an individual retirement account (IRA). Unlike the charitable gift annuity, the deferred gift annuity pays the highest rate to the youngest donors because there is a longer period of time between the date of the gift and the drawing of income. The charity invests the principal of the gift for years, anticipating the time when income payments must be made.

Older donors also may use a deferred gift annuity and defer income for several years. Doing so may be especially useful for a donor who wants to defer receiving income until sometime after age 70 or later. Exhibit 9.3 presents the benefits of deferred gift annuities.

In summary, the benefits of deferred gift annuities are

- Immediate charitable income tax deduction
- Guaranteed income in the future, often at retirement
- Excellent yield

Charitable Income Tax Deduction

The charitable income tax deduction is used in the year the gift is made, not in the year the donor begins receiving the income. The charitable

EXHIBIT 9.3   FINANCIAL BENEFITS FROM A $10,000 DEFERRED GIFT ANNUITY DEFERRED TO AGE 65

Gift Options for Donors Age 25–60

Age	Payout Rate	Annual Income	Tax Deduction*
40	26.4%	$2,640	$4,906
45	20.2%	$2,020	$4,717
50	15.3%	$1,530	$4,542
55	11.6%	$1,160	$4,294
60	8.7%	$ 870	$3,998

*Based on a discount rate of 6.0%

income tax deduction is typically quite high, approximating about 40 to 50 percent of the gift. For example, a 55-year-old donor who makes a $10,000 deferred gift annuity to a charity and begins receiving payments at age 65 obtains approximately $4,294 as a charitable income tax deduction. The charitable income tax deduction is based on the donor's age, current discount rate, and frequency and timing of payments. More frequent payments will reduce the charitable income tax deduction, as will receiving a payment at the beginning of the payment period rather than at the end of the payment period.

Gift Taxes

Currently it is unclear whether a donor is assessed a gift tax when creating a deferred gift annuity to benefit another. The annual exclusion, discussed in Chapter 20, allows a donor to give up to $10,000 to any number of beneficiaries each year free of gift tax. However, the annual exclusion does not protect gifts of a future interest, which may include the deferred gift annuity because payments to a beneficiary do not begin immediately. If a donor makes a deferred gift annuity to benefit someone other than his or her spouse, the donor may be required to pay a gift tax. If a donor makes a deferred gift annuity and benefits a spouse, no gift tax is due because of the unlimited marital deduction.

Income Taxes

A portion of the income from a deferred gift annuity, like that from a charitable gift annuity, is treated as both a return of one's investment and taxable income from an investment. Therefore, a donor generally receives some tax-free income because part of the income is considered a return of the initial principal, which was already taxed. The part considered investment income is taxed as ordinary income; it is taxed as capital gain income if appreciated property is used to fund the deferred gift annuity.

POOLED INCOME FUNDS

Recognized in 1969 when they were included in the Internal Revenue Code, pooled income funds are another important gift option for donors and small nonprofit organizations. The concept is simple: The donor makes a gift to a pooled income fund that works like a mutual fund. The donor receives a variable income based on market performance for life and perhaps for another beneficiary's lifetime. Unlike the charitable gift annuity, which is age sensitive, the pooled income fund rate is market sensitive and the rate may increase or decrease depending on the investment performance and earnings of the fund. The income stream must run for the lives of the beneficiaries; an income stream for a specified number of years is not allowed. The donor obtains a charitable income tax deduction in the year the gift is made; upon the death of the last beneficiary, the charity receives the remainder interest—the amount that remains after payment of the income stream. The amount may be more or less than the original amount of the gift depending on investment performance and market conditions. The remainder interest cannot be split among unrelated charities; it can go only to the charity that established and managed the fund.

The fund is considered pooled because the gift is commingled with other donors' gifts; the larger amount of smaller gifts in the fund produces the opportunity for a higher rate of return than a single donor's gift could achieve independently. Most charities require a minimum gift of $5,000 to a pooled income fund; additional gifts can be made, often at $1,000 or more. A donor can make a gift of appreciated securities to a pooled income fund and avoid paying capital gains taxes on the appreciation. Donors obtain a current charitable income tax deduction for the present value of the remainder after the death of the last beneficiary.

Pooled income funds define income as income from earnings on investments such as interest, certificates of deposit, bonds, and dividends from stock, net of investment expenses and management fees. Capital gains from the sale of assets are considered principal rather than income. No capital gain or any portion of the portfolio can be distributed as income for the beneficiaries. Instead, the actual net income produced by the fund, less expenses, is distributed proportionately to the beneficiaries.

Exhibit 9.4 presents the benefits of pooled income funds.

Capital Gains Taxes

A donor can make a gift to a pooled income fund and completely avoid capital gains taxes on the gift. This is a significant incentive to make a gift to a pooled income fund, especially for donors who own highly appreciated securities; if the asset was sold, the donor would incur a capital gains

EXHIBIT 9.4   BENEFITS OF POOLED INCOME FUNDS

- Increase current yield
- Avoid capital gains tax on gifts of appreciated securities
- Receive an income for life
- Receive an immediate charitable income tax deduction
- Membership in a leadership club

Example: Financial Benefits from a $10,000 Gift to the Pooled Income Fund*
Gift Options for Middle-Age to Older Donors

Age	Payout Rate	Annual Income	Tax Deduction*
60	6.0%	$600	$3,503
65	6.0%	$600	$4,170
70	6.0%	$600	$4,900
70/68	6.0%	$600	$3,536
75/73	6.0%	$600	$4,312

*Based on a discount rate of 6.0%

tax rate of 20 percent for most investment assets. Example: If a donor sold securities for $11,000 that were purchased years ago for $1,000, she would be taxed at a maximum rate of 20 percent on the gain of $10,000 for a total capital gains tax of $2,000. If the donor instead made a gift of the appreciated securities to a charity, she avoids capital gains tax and preserves the principal for charity.

Gift Taxes

If a donor makes a gift to a pooled income fund and either the donor or the spouse is the beneficiary of the income stream, no taxable gift is made. If the income interest is given to the donor's spouse, it may qualify for the gift tax marital deduction if a QTIP election is made. The assets are included in the donee spouse's estate, but the donee spouse will receive a charitable income tax deduction for the amount going to the charity.

If, however, a donor makes a gift to a pooled income fund for the benefit of a third party other than himself or his spouse, a taxable gift is made. The rate of the gift tax charged is the same as the estate tax, and all gifts made during one's lifetime or at death are ultimately aggregated. The gift/estate tax increases progressively from 37 to 50 percent in 2002 with the rates falling gradually over the next several years. If the third party has the right to receive income currently from the pooled income fund, the gift may qualify for the $10,000 annual gift tax exclusion. See Chapter 20 for a full discussion of taxes.

Income Tax to Beneficiary

The income distributed by the pooled income fund is taxed to the beneficiary (whether the donor, spouse, or a third party) as ordinary income. If the donor is the first beneficiary, the income is taxable to the donor, while alive, and the value of any interest passing to a survivor beneficiary is included in the donor's taxable estate at its value at that time. Alternatively, a donor who does not want to be taxed on the income may make a taxable gift of the income interest to the designated beneficiary during his or her lifetime without reserving the right to revoke the beneficiary's income interest.

Charitable Income Tax Deduction

A donor who makes a gift to a pooled income fund obtains a charitable income tax deduction in the year the gift is made. Planned giving software calculates the charitable income tax deduction by determining the value of the income stream over the life expectancy of the income beneficiary under IRS actuarial tables. The deduction is based on the highest return earned by the fund in the three preceding years. If the pooled income fund is less than three years old, the IRS preselects a rate based on current treasury bill rates.

Estate Taxes

Once a donor makes a gift to the pooled income fund, the value of the gift passes outside the donor's estate for estate tax purposes except for the value of any life interest passing to a beneficiary other than the donor's spouse at death. Additionally, the asset used to fund the pooled income fund is removed from probate.

Acceptable Assets for a Pooled Income Fund

A pooled income fund is unique, and not all types of assets can be used to fund a pooled income fund gift. Because each beneficiary's income is affected by all of the other donors' gifts, a donor cannot make a gift to the fund that will not immediately generate an income. Otherwise, the total amount of income in the pool would stay the same while the number of beneficiaries would increase, reducing all beneficiaries' income streams. Most gifts to a pooled income fund are made in the form of cash or readily marketable securities, which generate income immediately. Closely held securities are not usually accepted into a pooled income fund because they can be difficult to value, the transaction is time consuming, and a buyer is not always readily available. The self-dealing rules also may prohibit a sale to the donor or his or her family. Tax-exempt securities are not permitted as gifts to a pooled income fund. Donors who want to give tax-exempt securities, which typically do not appreciate significantly, may sell the securities, and then contribute the cash proceeds. While theoretically gifts of real estate can be transferred to a pooled income fund, they are inappropriate and are not permitted by most charities.

Creating a Pooled Income Gift

Creating a pooled income gift requires involvement from an attorney and some costs, including the drafting of pooled income fund documents. Most small charities choose not to administer their own pooled income fund and prefer to use a bank or trust company that manages pooled income funds. Check with a planned giving provider to learn where this option exists.

Making a Pooled Income Fund Gift through a Community Foundation

Many community-based foundations offer pooled income funds under the name of the foundation. Area charities are permitted to participate in their funds. Donors to the organization can make a gift to the community foundation and designate the remainder of the gift (the amount that is left after the death of the donor) to support the charity.

CONCLUSION

Life income gifts, such as charitable gift annuities, deferred gift annuities, and gifts to a pooled income fund, provide incentives to donors and benefits to charities. Most charities offer these options; many smaller nonprof-its will be offering some or all of them soon. These vehicles provide mutual benefits because both the donor and the charity benefit. Nonprofit organ-izations and donors appreciate the mutual benefits that charitable gift annuities, deferred gift annuities, and gifts to a pooled income fund pro-vide. These gift options also make it easier for individuals to become major donors.

CHAPTER 10

Trusts

INTRODUCTION

Trusts are comprehensive, personalized asset management vehicles that can be used to accomplish specific purposes for both donors' families and favored nonprofit organizations. Because trusts can be administered easily by outside managers, gifts through trusts should be promoted by all small nonprofit organizations. Contact financial institutions to learn what trust administration services they offer. Trusts usually are combined with wills, a durable power of attorney, and a healthcare proxy to create an estate plan. Several types of trusts exist, including revocable trusts, charitable remainder annuity trusts, and charitable lead trusts. This chapter begins with an overview of trusts—terms, types, funding, and distribution—and then focuses on charitable trusts and how they are used to accomplish charitable gift planning objectives.

PARTIES TO A TRUST

There are a number of parties to a trust. They include the grantor of the trust, the trustee, and the beneficiaries. A trust is established by a written agreement between the maker of the trust and the trustee.

Maker, Grantor, or Settlor

The maker of a trust, often called the grantor, donor, or settlor, is the one who creates the trust. If the trust is created by more than one person (e.g., by spouses), those individuals usually are considered joint grantors. The grantor transfers his or her assets to a trustee. The trustee then holds and manages the trust.

Trustee

Depending on a donor's preferences, the trustee may be the grantor, another individual, or an institution, such as a bank, trust company, or investment firm. The trustee manages assets for the benefit of one or more beneficiaries. The trustee is held to a standard of prudence as defined by state law.

Current vs. Remainder Beneficiaries

Broadly speaking, there are two types of beneficiaries: current beneficiaries and remainder beneficiaries. Current beneficiaries are those beneficiaries who may receive income or principal from the trust, either automatically or at the discretion of the trustee. Remainder beneficiaries receive the remaining principal or corpus of the trust upon its termination. Depending on the type of trust, a charity may be the beneficiary of either a remainder interest (charitable remainder trust) or an income interest (lead trust).

THE REVOCABLE INTER VIVOS TRUST (LIVING TRUST)

A properly drafted revocable (one that can be revoked or changed) inter vivos (established during life) trust can be a very effective tool for managing assets during life and after death. It is revocable in that the grantor may revoke or amend all or part of the trust. The grantor can transfer assets to the trust during his or her life. Any assets that are transferred to the trust during the grantor's life will not be subject to probate, which is one advantage of an inter vivos trust. In addition, any asset owned in a state other than the state in which the grantor is domiciled and in which the grantor will be subject to probate may be held in the trust, thereby avoiding the extra burden of a separate probate proceeding (known as ancillary administration) in the other state. A revocable inter vivos trust may continue past the lifetime of the grantor for the benefit of the grantor's spouse, children, grandchildren, or other beneficiaries. A successor trustee, such as a bank or trust company, often is appointed to serve as trustee after the grantor's death.

In most states, all noncharitable trusts, including revocable inter vivos trusts, must provide for a termination of the trust to comply with what is known as the Rule Against Perpetuities, which prevents trusts from operating in perpetuity. A trust may terminate upon the occurrence of a specific event, such as when the youngest beneficiary of the trust reaches the age of 21.

Usually it is not possible or practical to transfer all assets owned by the grantor to the trust during the grantor's lifetime. Any assets not transferred during life may be transferred at death through a "pourover" provision in the grantor's will. This provision transfers any remaining assets to the trustee of the trust. These assets then are managed as part of the corpus of the trust. Any asset that is transferred through a pourover provision is subject to probate.

Tax Implications

Because donors have all the elements of ownership and control over a revocable inter vivos trust, including the right to revoke and amend the trust, they are taxed on any income that the trust earns and on any capital gains that the trust produces. For gift tax purposes, an individual has not made a completed gift through a transfer to a revocable trust, but has retained ownership and control over the trust. Therefore, there is no gift tax due on any asset transferred to a revocable inter vivos trust. For federal estate tax purposes, all assets in a revocable inter vivos trust are includible in one's estate.

Exhibit 10.1 compares the payout formulas for charitable remainder trusts and charitable lead trusts.

CHARITABLE REMAINDER TRUSTS

Charitable remainder trusts are important gift planning vehicles. They can produce substantial financial and tax benefits for donors as well as gifts to charitable organizations. These trusts may be established either during life, through an inter vivos trust, or at death, through a testamentary trust. Charitable remainder trusts are established for the life of one or more beneficiaries or a period of years not exceeding 20 years. Like other life income gift options, charitable remainder trusts provide income to beneficiaries. Upon the death of the beneficiaries or the termination of the trust term, the remainder is transferred to benefit one or more nonprofits. The Internal

EXHIBIT 10.1 **PAYOUT FORMULAS FOR CHARITABLE REMAINDER TRUSTS AND CHARITABLE LEAD TRUSTS**

TYPES OF CHARITABLE TRUSTS	PAYOUT
Charitable Remainder Annuity Trust	Pays donor fixed payout dollar amount representing percentages of the trusts assets on date established
Charitable Remainder Unitrust	Pays income to donor for life or term of years, remainder goes to charity
1. Fixed percentage trust	Pays donor fixed percentage of value of trust assets as valued annually
2. Net income trust	Pays lesser of stated percentage or actual net income
3. Net income trust with makeup	Pays lesser of stated percentage or actual net income and makes up difference between actual net income and stated percentage when income exceeds stated percentage
Flip trust	Pays donor actual net income until trust "flips" to pay stated percentage
Lead Trust	Pays income to charity, remainder to grantor or heirs
1. Grantor trust	Pays income to charity, remainder to grantor
2. Nongrantor trust	Pays income to charity, remainder to heirs
3. Annuity form	Pays charity fixed dollar amount
4. Unitrust form	Pays charity stated percentage of trust's assets as valued annually

Revenue Service defines a charitable remainder trust as "a trust which provides for a specified distribution, at least annually, to one or more beneficiaries, at least one of which is not a charity, for life or for a term of years, with an irrevocable remainder interest to be held for the benefit of, or paid over to, charity." Charitable remainder trusts include charitable remainder annuity trusts and charitable remainder unitrusts. They are discussed later in detail. Benefits of charitable remainder trusts include:

- Income to beneficiary for life or for a term of years; remainder to charity
- Avoid capital gains tax on the contribution of appreciated assets

- A significant charitable income tax deduction for the donor
- Customization to meet a donor's needs

Historical Tier System and the Taxation of Trust Income

Distributions from a charitable remainder trust paid to a beneficiary are taxed to the beneficiary. Regardless of whether all income produced by the trust is distributed, the trust itself does not pay income taxes on its earnings so long as it has no unrelated business income, such as debt-financed income. Distributions from a charitable remainder trust are characterized for purposes of the beneficiary's tax liability according to the historical income of the trust. Distributions from the trust are characterized in the following order:

1. Ordinary income
2. Capital gain income
3. Tax-exempt income
4. Return of principal/corpus

For example, all ordinary income earned by the trust in prior years or during the current taxable year must be distributed to the beneficiaries prior to any capital gain income.

Common Features of Charitable Remainder Trusts

There are a number of features common to charitable remainder trusts.

Income Stream   As the grantor of a charitable remainder trust, the donor selects a payout rate that will provide a stream of income to beneficiaries for life or for a term of years. By law the rate may not be less than 5 percent nor more than 50 percent, but the appropriate range of rates in any particular case (usually 5 to 7 percent) could be more limited due to the age of the beneficiaries, prevailing interest rates, and other requirements imposed by law. As the payout rate increases, a donor's charitable income tax deduction decreases, and vice versa. The payout rate is established at the time of the creation of the trust and should be selected to provide the donor with an appropriate income stream and the greatest tax benefits, while still protecting the remainder value for the nonprofit.

Charitable Income Tax Deduction   Donors who transfer assets to a charitable remainder trust are likely to receive a charitable income tax deduction, which could produce significant tax savings. The amount of the charitable income tax deduction is the present value of the remainder interest passing to charity and is greatly affected by the number of beneficiaries and their ages. The charitable income tax deduction is often 35 to 50 percent of the amount used to fund the trust; of course, the exact figure depends on the terms of a particular trust.

Capital Gains Taxes   If assets such as appreciated securities are transferred to a charitable remainder trust, neither the transferor nor the charity will have to pay capital gains taxes on the gain when the trustee sells the securities. Distributions to beneficiaries, however, can be characterized as capital gains to the full extent of the trust's total capital gains.

Gift Taxes   Transfers to a charitable remainder trust are eligible for a gift tax deduction to the extent of the present value of the nonprofit organization's remainder interest, but to claim this deduction, the donor will need to file a gift tax return. If the trust provides income only to the donor, the income payout does not have gift tax consequences. If the donor's spouse receives a present stream of income from the charitable remainder trust, the donor has made a gift to her spouse of the present value (measured at the time the trust is established) of the total income stream, but the gift qualifies for the unlimited gift tax marital deduction for federal tax purposes, thereby creating no gift tax consequences. If a donor provides a present income stream from a charitable remainder trust to a person other than a spouse, the donor has made a taxable gift of the present value of the income interest, with gift tax consequences. Donors who provide a future income stream to anyone also have made a taxable gift, unless they specify in the trust documents that they are retaining the right to revoke the future income interest through their wills. If the gift is a present interest, the $10,000 annual exclusion (which is indexed for inflation but only in $1,000 increments) may offset some or all of the gift; if the value of the gift exceeds the exclusion, then the donor's $1,000,000 lifetime exemption (in 2002) may be used to eliminate or reduce any gift tax due. The annual exclusion will increase gradually over time.

The lifetime exclusion allows a donor to transfer property at death up to $1,000,000 without having to pay any gift tax or estate tax in 2002. The estate tax exemption amount increases gradually until 2010, when the estate tax is to be repealed. The gift tax exemption is set at $1,000,000. Exhibit 10.2 illustrates estate, generation skipping, and gift tax rates and their exemptions.

Estate Taxes   Assets transferred to a charitable remainder trust could have estate tax consequences at a grantor's death depending on whether the interest to the beneficiary flows for life or for a number of years and whether the beneficiary is the donor, a spouse, or other beneficiary. Assets transferred to a charitable remainder trust that provide income to the grantor will be included in the grantor's gross estate, but the grantor's estate will receive an estate tax charitable deduction for the value of the remainder interest earmarked for the charity. An income interest shared by the grantor and the grantor's spouse that continues for the spouse after the grantor's death will escape estate tax due to the federal estate tax marital deduction, provided that the surviving spouse is a U.S. citizen. If the trust provides for income to anyone other than the grantor and/or the grantor's spouse, then there may be gift or estate tax consequences. See Exhibit 10.2 for more information on gift and estate taxes.

EXHIBIT 10.2 ESTATE AND GIFT TAX RATES AND CREDIT EXEMPTION AMOUNTS

Calendar Year	Estate and GST Tax Credit Exemption	Gift Tax Credit Exemption	Highest Estate and Gift Tax Rates
2002	$1 million	$1 million	50%
2003	$1 million	$1 million	49%
2004	$1.5 million	$1 million	48%
2005	$1.5 million	$1 million	47%
2006	$2 million	$1 million	46%
2007	$2 million	$1 million	45%
2008	$2 million	$1 million	45%
2009	$3.5 million	$1 million	45%
2010	N/A (taxes repealed)	$1 million	Maximum gift tax rate equal to maximum income tax rate (35%)

Probate Assets transferred through an inter vivos charitable remainder trust avoid probate. Assets transferred at death through a will must pass through probate. Some states, such as Florida and Virginia, have limitations on out-of-state trustees of trusts that receive assets at death.

Drafting a Charitable Remainder Trust

The donor's attorney can draft a charitable remainder trust. If a donor does not have an attorney, the charity's planned giving officer should refer him or her to attorneys who specialize in estate or charitable gift planning. The Internal Revenue Service has provided model forms for drafting charitable remainder trusts.

Naming the Trustee For many charitable remainder trusts, the trustee may be an institution such as a bank, trust company, or investment firm, although the nonprofit organization remainderman may serve as trustee or co-trustee of a charitable remainder trust. As co-trustee, the nonprofit is most often paired with an institutional trustee. The donor and the nonprofit should be aware that a charity serving as trustee could present a potential conflict of interest. The conflict occurs in the selection of the investment assets of the trust. The income beneficiary might want maximum income while the nonprofit wants to preserve the remainder; however, the nonprofit also wants to maintain the donor's goodwill and cannot afford to ignore the income beneficiary's wishes.

Naming the Charitable Remainderman To qualify as a charitable remainder trust, the trust must designate a charity having 501(c)(3) status to receive the remainder. The designation 501(c)(3) refers to a section of the Internal Revenue Code. The donor can reserve the right to change the charitable remainderman without jeopardizing the charitable nature of the trust; however, there can be no noncharitable remainder interest created by the trust. A donor also can name more than one charitable remainderman. To deduct the charitable gift for income tax purposes to the maximum extent (up to 50 percent of adjusted gross income for gifts of cash and up to 30 percent for most gifts of appreciated capital gain property), precise language must be used to limit the remainderman not only to a 501(c)(3) charity but also to one having public charity status.

Types of Charitable Remainder Trusts

The two basic categories of charitable remainder trusts are the charitable remainder annuity trust and the charitable remainder unitrust. While these trusts share many characteristics, they also have some differences. The type of trust selected will most likely be based on the donor's risk tolerance, desire to secure a larger income, and desire to make additional gifts. We look first at the charitable remainder annuity trust (see Exhibit 10.3), followed by a discussion of the charitable remainder unitrust.

The charitable remainder annuity trust provides a fixed, guaranteed dollar amount paid to a donor or a beneficiary, which is not less than 5 percent of the value of the trust's assets at the time the trust is established. The distribution is paid at least once per year regardless of the trust's investment performance, and the trustee must invade the principal of the trust, if necessary, to make the distribution to the beneficiaries. The distribution may be obtained from income from fixed income investments or from the sale of capital assets. If the trust's investments fail to perform, the trust principal can be diminished or depleted by the trustee making the fixed, guaranteed dollar distribution to the beneficiaries. Depletion of trust assets further strains the ability of the trust to grow, resulting in further depletion of assets to make distributions in future years while reducing the value of the remainder to the charity. In many cases, if the amount selected represents more than approximately 8 percent of the trust's assets, the donor and the charity risk depleting the principal of the trust. Once the trust is established, no additional contributions can be made to a charitable remainder annuity trust, although more than one charitable remainder annuity trust

EXHIBIT 10.3 BENEFITS OF A $250,000 CHARITABLE REMAINDER ANNUITY

Trust and Unitrust for a Donor Age 70*

Payout Rate	Annual Income**	Charitable Income Tax Deduction Annuity Trust	Unitrust
5%	$12,500	$141,405	$134,867
6%	$15,000	$119,687	$120,800
7%	$17,000	$98,040	$108,665

*Based on discount rate of 6.0%.
**For a unitrust this is only first year income; future years will vary.

may be established. Because of the legal expenses involved in drafting a trust, most donors do not establish more than one.

Characteristics of a charitable remainder annuity trust include the following:

- Income is a fixed dollar amount.

- Trustee may invade principal, if necessary, to make payment.

- The trust is unded one time only; no additional gifts can be made to the trust.

EXAMPLE Mr. Jackson ages 70, makes a gift to a charitable organization by establishing a charitable remainder annuity trust. The trustee is obligated to pay Mr. Jackson a fixed dollar amount regardless of the trust's investment performance. If Mr. Jackson's charitable remainder annuity trust is funded with $250,000 and pays out a 5 percent annuity, it will provide a fixed annual income of $12,500 a year for his lifetime. The charitable income tax deduction for a $250,000 charitable remainder annuity trust is $141,405. As a comparison, if the rate were set at 7 percent, the annual income would be $17,500 with a charitable income tax deduction of $98,040. ■

Five Percent Exhaustion Test for Charitable Remainder Annuity Trusts Charitable remainder annuity trusts have a special requirement. The 5-percent exhaustion test provides that if there is more than a 5-percent chance that the trust assets will be depleted so that the charitable remainderman will receive nothing, the donor is not entitled to a charitable income tax deduction. This provision does not apply to charitable remainder unitrusts. Planned giving offices in many charities use software to model proposed gifts. Planned giving computer software programs will indicate if there is more than a 5-percent chance of asset depletion.

Funding Charitable Remainder Annuity Trust/Tuition Trust Parents of students at preparatory schools, secondary schools, colleges, and universities often ask for information about how to provide for their children's education. The cost of tuition represents a major financial burden for many families, and some early financial planning can help. Parents and grandparents often are surprised to find that charitable giving can provide attractive financial benefits and tax savings and can greatly assist in offsetting the expense of tuition.

Parents may consider establishing a charitable remainder trust for a term of years to help cover the cost of a child's tuition. A charitable remainder trust, when used to pay for tuition, is sometimes called a charitable tuition trust. It can be a good choice for parents who would like to make a gift to an educational institution, provide income to their children for tuition, and realize substantial tax savings. Parents usually establish a charitable tuition trust for four to six years, during which time the prescribed payout from the trust is paid to the student and is taxed at the student's income tax rate. Upon the termination of the trust, the trust property passes to the charity. The parent can designate the purpose for which the remaining trust property should be used.

A $250,000 charitable remainder annuity tuition trust established for a four-year period paying 7 percent generates an income of $17,500 annually and produces a charitable income tax deduction of $188,015. In addition to the charitable income tax deduction, additional benefits and further tax savings are possible by funding the tuition trust with appreciated securities, which enables donors to avoid the capital gains taxes they would have owed had they sold the securities. All gifts to a charitable remainder trust are irrevocable. Donors should consult with a lawyer, accountant, or financial advisor to ensure that the trust is structured to meet their particular tax needs. A charitable remainder trust for a term of years may be more broadly used to provide an income stream for a longer duration, 20 years maximum, so as to provide income for an extended period to offset educational costs for graduate work or to cover the cost of tuition for other children.

Charitable Remainder Unitrust

There are three types of charitable remainder unitrusts, each of which is used for different purposes and affects a beneficiary's payout differently.

Charitable Remainder Unitrust 1: Straight Fixed Percentage   For the straight fixed percentage charitable remainder unitrust, the amount paid is not dependent on the income produced by the trust but is determined by multiplying the percentage payout rate by the fair market value of the trust's assets as determined annually, usually on the first business day of the year. As with the annuity trust, the trustee is obligated to make the distribution and must invade the principal of the trust, if necessary, to make the payment. Unlike the annuity trust, the payment is variable and is affected by the increase or decrease in the market value of the trust's assets. Depletion of principal is a concern to both the beneficiaries and the charity, as a reduction in principal jeopardizes the production of income and the remainder value. Nonprofit organizations do have some protection because the distribution is a function of the market value, calculated by multiplying the fixed percentage by the annual market value of the fund. Depending on the needs of the lifetime beneficiaries, trustees can invest in equity and fixed income assets to promote growth and generate income.

Characteristics of a charitable remainder unitrust include the following:

- Stated percentage of the value of the corpus as valued annually
- Principal may be invaded to make payment
- Lifetime management tool
- Additional gifts to a charitable remainder unitrust may be made

EXAMPLE Mr. Jackson, age 70, chooses to make a gift through a charitable remainder unitrust of $250,000. The charitable remainder unitrust will pay him a predetermined percentage of the fair market value of the trust's assets, but not less than 5 percent, as revalued annually. If the payout rate is established for the Jacksons at 5 percent, they receive an annual income of $12,500 in the first year and a 5 percent payout each succeeding year based on the annual valuation of the trust. However, if the rate were set at 7 percent, the annual income would be $17,500. This type of trust can provide a hedge against inflation because as the assets of the trust increase in value, so does the income. Additional contributions can be made to a unitrust. The Jacksons also receive a charitable income tax deduction. If they cannot use the full amount in the first year, it may be carried over for five additional years. The charitable income tax deduction for the Jacksons' charitable remainder unitrust with the rate set at 5 percent is $134,867; at a 7 percent rate, the income tax charitable deduction is $108,665. ◾

Charitable Remainder Unitrust 2: Net Income Unitrust The net income unitrust pays the lesser of actual net income or the stated percentage unitrust amount. Income is defined under state and local law, and most states follow the income-only rule, defining income as interest income, bond income, and dividends from stocks, excluding long- or short-term capital gains. In most states, capital gains are considered to be principal, not income. If no income is produced, then nothing is distributed. The trustee may not invade the principal to make the distribution since the distribution is measured as the lesser of actual net income or a fixed percentage. The trustee must fully understand the donor's wishes when this type of trust is established. For example, investments in growth stock will produce little or no income, although, if market conditions are favorable, the portfolio may grow in value. This type of trust may be appropriate for a beneficiary who is younger and who would like to receive income in the future.

Benefits of a net income unitrust include the following:

- Pays lesser of net income or stated percentage
- May not invade principal to make payment

■ **EXAMPLE**   A couple in their 50s who wish to retire at age 65 could fund the trust with growth stock. Over time the growth stock will likely increase the value of the corpus. As the couple approaches retirement, the trustee can gradually convert the growth assets to income investments, enabling the beneficiaries to receive net income from an asset pool that has greatly increased in value during the investment period. ■

Charitable Remainder Unitrust 3: Net Income Unitrust with a Makeup Provision   The charitable remainder unitrust with a makeup provision is similar to a net income unitrust except that, under certain circumstances, the donor can receive payments in excess of the percentage unitrust amount in order to "make up" for prior payments of net income that were less than the percentage unitrust amount. With this type of unitrust, a donor receives the stated percentage of the trust or net income, whichever is less. However, if in one year the donor received net income only (because net income was less than the stated percentage amount), the donor can recover part or all of the shortfall between that year's net income and the percentage amount in future years when the trust has net income that exceeds the stated percentage. In a year when a makeup payment is possible, such a payment is limited to the lesser of the donor's total shortfall for all prior years and the amount for which the trust's net income for the current year exceeds the percentage amount. This vehicle typically is funded with growth stock or real estate. As discussed, net income may be defined in the trust to include realized capital gains.

Characteristics of a net income unitrust with a makeup provision include the following:

- Pays lesser of net income or stated percentage, but can make up shortfall if net income is less than the stated percentage
- No invasion of principal
- Best for gifts of real estate

For an illustration of a net income unitrust with a makeup provision for a gift of real estate, see pp. 200–201.

Flip Trusts Flip trusts combine the benefits of a net income unitrust with a regular unitrust. Donors who wish to make gifts of assets that are likely to take some time to sell, such as real estate or stock of a closely held corporation, can transfer those assets to a net income unitrust. Through the net income unitrust, the donor receives the stated percentage or net income, whichever is less, and since the assets transferred are non–income-producing ones, no income is produced. However, following the sale of these assets (or some triggering event), the trust "flips" to a regular unitrust, enabling the trustee to invest for total return. Return is measured by income (interest and dividends) and capital appreciation, such as gains on the value of the trust's corpus. For example, if the income is earned at a rate of 3 percent of fair market value and the trust calls for a payout of 5 percent, then the additional 2 percent is obtained from the principal. If the trust assets have appreciated, then the payout is made from capital appreciation of the assets. A flip trust can work well for beneficiaries who are relatively young and likely to have a fairly long life expectancy. For these donors, capital appreciation is an important part of the plan and investing for total return enables capital appreciation to occur.

Treatment of Capital Gains The IRS has suggested that in some cases, a net income unitrust might be allowed to define income to include capital gains. The ability of a trust to include capital gains in income depends on whether local law permits such treatment. Furthermore, any inclusion of capital gains in income is limited to the gains that occur *after* the property is donated to the trust. As discussed earlier, historically trustees have selected investments that produced income by investing in bonds or stocks that paid interest and dividends equal to or as nearly equal as possible to the percentage amount. Most trustees would prefer to invest for total return by selecting investments based on their potential for performance rather than whether their return would be considered income or capital gain. A net income unitrust that can be structured to include postcontribution capital gains in income would allow trustees to invest for total return, thereby enabling beneficiaries to receive capital gain earnings from the investments

QUALIFIED TERMINABLE INTEREST PROPERTY (QTIP) WITH REMAINDER TO A NONPROFIT

Through the use of a qualified terminable interest trust (QTIP trust), donors can provide for their spouses and also benefit a nonprofit organization. A QTIP trust enables donors to take full advantage of the unlimited marital gift and estate tax deduction by transferring assets to the trust. Donors' spouses have a right to income for life. Also, donors may give their spouses some degree of access to the principal. Upon the death of the spouse, the remainder of the trust is distributed to remainder beneficiaries of the donor's choosing. These remainder beneficiaries may include a charity.

Unlike a charitable remainder trust, where a donor receives a charitable income tax deduction, a QTIP trust with a charitable remainder beneficiary provides no income tax deduction to a donor. The transfer of assets to a QTIP trust qualifies for the estate and gift tax marital deduction, thus preventing the decedent spouse from having those assets actually taxed in his or her estate. The QTIP property is includible in the estate of the surviving spouse, but that estate receives an estate tax charitable deduction for any portion distributed to a qualified charity. Any income distributed to surviving spouses during their lifetime is taxable to them, and the QTIP trust itself is taxable although it may deduct income paid to the surviving spouse. The trust will be taxed on capital gains that are realized in the trust.

CHARITABLE LEAD TRUSTS

A lead trust is frequently described as the opposite of a charitable remainder trust. The "lead" income interest is paid to the charity, and after a number of years (based on a term of years or a lifetime) the remainder is distributed either to the grantor (a grantor lead trust) or to someone other than the grantor, such as the grantor's heirs or other beneficiaries (a nongrantor lead trust). Unlike a charitable remainder trust, a charitable lead trust is not subject to a minimum payout of 5 percent. In addition, a charitable lead trust (other than a grantor lead trust) is a fully taxable trust. The lead trust pays taxes on its income and capital gains, unlike the charitable remainder trust, which is a tax-exempt trust. The lead trust may deduct amounts paid to the charitable beneficiary pursuant to the terms of the governing instrument. Lower interest rates coupled with high estate gift tax rates make for a potentially advantageous environment for using charitable lead trusts as part of an estate plan. Grantor lead trusts have limited usage, so we focus on nongrantor charitable lead trusts.

Characteristics of charitable lead trusts include the following:

- Income to charity for a period of years
- Remainder to grantor or heirs
- Potential tax benefits
- Estate tax savings for nongrantor lead trust

NONGRANTOR CHARITABLE LEAD TRUSTS

A nongrantor charitable lead trust provides income to the nonprofit for a period of years. At the end of the term of years, the remainder is transferred to someone other than the grantor, often the grantor's children. As the grantor, a donor does not receive a charitable income tax deduction but instead receives estate and gift tax benefits, and the trust income is not taxed to the grantor. If the nongrantor charitable lead trust is an inter vivos trust (established during life), a donor obtains a gift tax charitable deduction on the present value of the stream of income passing to charity. If the nongrantor trust is a testamentary trust (established upon the donor's death), the donor's estate obtains an estate tax charitable deduction for that value. The donor does pay gift or estate tax on the present value of the remainder passing to heirs or other individual beneficiaries. Under some circumstances, grantors are able to use nongrantor lead trusts to help transfer assets to their heirs with reduced federal estate, gift, or generation-skipping transfer tax consequences; grantors may be able to pass a considerable amount of property to their offspring while substantially reducing taxes and benefiting a charity.

NONGRANTOR CHARITABLE LEAD ANNUITY TRUSTS

Through a nongrantor charitable lead annuity trust, donors irrevocably transfer assets, usually cash or securities, to a trustee. During the charitable lead annuity trust's term, the trustee invests the trust's assets and provides a fixed dollar amount each year to the nonprofit. These payments continue until the trust term ends. The trust's term may be for a specific number of years, one or more lifetimes, or a combination of the two. When the charitable lead annuity trust term ends, the trust distributes all of its accumulated assets to the remainder beneficiaries, who are often the donors' family members. Any asset appreciation that occurs within the trust will be distributed to the trust's beneficiaries, free of additional gift or estate taxes.

NONGRANTOR CHARITABLE LEAD UNITRUST

During the lead unitrust's term, the trustee invests the unitrust's assets and pays a fixed percentage of the unitrust's value, as valued annually, to the nonprofit. The lead unitrust's term may be for a specific number of years, one or more lifetimes, or a combination of the two. When the lead unitrust term ends, the unitrust distributes the accumulated assets to family members or other beneficiaries.

CONCLUSION

Trusts provide a variety of flexible alternatives to donors who want to make gifts to a charity. In particular, charitable remainder trusts and charitable lead trusts offer customized options that can meet the needs of the donor and support the charity. The charity should provide information to donors on the types of trusts that are appropriate for their situations. Always suggest that donors consult with their financial and legal advisors about any large gifts, especially one that involves a trust.

PART FOUR

Gifts of Assets Other Than Cash

CHAPTER 11

Gifts of Securities

INTRODUCTION

Other than gifts of cash, the most popular way for donors to make gifts to a small nonprofit organization is through gifts of securities. All nonprofit organizations, including small nonprofits, can and should accept gifts of securities. Gifts of securities include not only publicly traded stocks like IBM, Microsoft, and GE but gifts of mutual funds, treasury bills, corporate and municipal bonds, and closely held stock. Calculate the value of gifts of securities as a percentage of the organization's gift revenue. If the percentage is low, then take extra effort to promote gifts of stock and mutual fund shares to all constituents.

Most organizations do not retain small blocks of stock given by donors, but sell the stock upon receipt. Make sure donors know that, in all likelihood, their securities will be sold. Because timing can be important in the trade or subsequent sale of a security, the nonprofit organization should have policies in place for handling gifts of securities prior to promoting such gifts. Typically, donors hold the securities in a "street account" with a stockbroker or bank, or some physically hold the securities (stock certificates) in their possession. A transfer of securities to the charity differs depending on the way the securities are held. The following are some of the issues involved in making a gift of securities.

SECURITIES HELD BY THE DONOR'S STOCKBROKER OR BANKER

When making a gift of securities, donors should be instructed to call the charity to let it know that a gift of securities is being made. Provide donors with the organization's tax identification number, which enables the securities to be transferred to the charity. In most cases, the charity has an outside broker handle gifts of securities. Once the securities are in the charity's account, they are typically sold, and the charity's broker receives a commission. If donors want their brokers to receive the commission, the charity can establish an account and donors may then transfer the stock to that account. Sometimes it takes time for the nonprofit organization's account to be established, so ask in advance. The stock can be sold directly from that account, resulting in a check mailed to the nonprofit organization for the proceeds, minus a broker's commission. Donors or their brokers should not sell appreciated securities until they are in the nonprofit organization's account, or the donor will incur a capital gains tax on any appreciation. As a charitable organization, the nonprofit is not liable for any capital gains taxes upon its sale of appreciated securities.

SECURITIES GIFTED VIA THE DEPOSITORY TRUST COMPANY

A depository trust company (DTC) transfer is the most efficient way for a donor to make a gift of securities to a charity. This electronic system allows easy transfer of securities from the donor's account to the nonprofit's account at a brokerage firm or to an outside manager administering charitable gifts. Instruct donors to call the charity to let it know that a gift is being made of securities via DTC transfer and record the number of shares and name of the stock. The donor's name is not attached to the transfer, so when the securities arrive, the nonprofit does not know who sent them unless the donor has first alerted the nonprofit. Small nonprofits that are local in scope should contact brokerage houses in their area to promote gifts of securities through the use of DTC Instructions. Exhibit 11.1 can be widely distributed to both donors and brokerage companies.

EXHIBIT 11.1	FORM: ASSET TRANSFER INSTRUCTIONS

To Transfer Stocks, Corporate Bonds, and Municipal Bonds—DTC Eligible:

‹FINANCIAL INSTITUTION›
Attention: ‹NAME›, ‹TITLE›
‹ADDRESS›
‹CITY›, ‹STATE› ‹ZIP›
DTC ID ‹ # ›
For Account ‹ # ›
Account Name: ‹NAME OF ACCOUNT›

To Transfer Stocks, Corporate Bonds, and Municipal Bonds—Physical Delivery:

‹FINANCIAL INSTITUTION›
Attention: ‹NAME›, ‹TITLE›
‹ADDRESS›
‹CITY›, ‹STATE› ‹ZIP›
DTC ID ‹ # ›
For Account ‹ # ›
Account Name: ‹NAME OF ACCOUNT›

To Transfer Cash:

By wire: ‹FINANCIAL INSTITUTION›
           Attention: ‹NAME›, ‹TITLE›
           ‹ADDRESS›
           ‹CITY›, ‹STATE› ‹ZIP›
           DTC ID ‹ # ›
           For Account ‹ # ›
           Account Name: ‹NAME OF ACCOUNT›

By mail: ‹FINANCIAL INSTITUTION›
           Attention: ‹NAME›, ‹TITLE›
           ‹ADDRESS›
           ‹CITY›, ‹STATE› ‹ZIP›
           DTC ID ‹ # ›
           For Account ‹ # ›
           Account Name: ‹NAME OF ACCOUNT›

To Transfer U.S. Treasuries and Agencies:

Federal Reserve Wire
‹NAME OF ACCOUNT/CUSTOMER #/ACCOUNT #›
Account Name: ‹NAME OF ACCOUNT›
Routing ‹ # ›

SECURITIES HELD IN THE DONOR'S POSSESSION

If donors have physical possession of stock certificates, they should sign a stock power for each stock certificate that will be transferred to the charity. A stock power is a document that allows the charity to sell the securities. For example, if donors have a certificate for IBM stock, they need to sign a stock power for the IBM certificate with signature guarantees. A signature guarantee proves that the donor's signature is valid and that the person guaranteeing the signature knows him or her. Stock powers can be obtained from a broker, bank, or business stationery store, and signature guarantees can be obtained from a bank or brokerage company.

If delivered by mail, the stock powers should be sent to the charity in a separate envelope, apart from the stock certificates. If the stock certificates and powers are sent in the same envelope and the envelope is lost or stolen, they could be negotiated by anyone. By sending them separately, the securities and stock powers cannot be negotiated until both are together, because one is not negotiable without the other.

Alternatively, donors can endorse the back of a stock certificate signing their name exactly as it appears on the stock certificate. Use this method to transfer securities only if the certificates can be hand carried immediately to the charity or to an outside financial manager because, once they are signed, the certificates are immediately negotiable. If the company issuing the stock is a small corporation, it may be convenient to ask it to transfer the stock by issuing a new certificate in the nonprofit's name.

DONOR WISHES TO GIVE PART OF A STOCK CERTIFICATE

Sometimes donors wish to give to a charity a stock certificate that represents more shares than they wish to transfer. It is easy for donors to give only a portion of the shares owned. Donors should instruct their brokers or the charity's broker, usually in writing, to transfer a specific number of shares to the charity while retaining the remaining shares in the donors' accounts. Donors must enclose a signed stock power with instructions as to when and where to send the gift. The broker then requests that two new stock certificates be issued, one to the charity for a specific number of shares and one to the donor for the remaining shares.

VALUE OF THE GIFT

If the securities have been held by a donor "long term" (described more fully later), the value of the securities for tax purposes is the average of the high and the low value of the security ("the mean value") on the date the gift is made. If the gift is made on a Saturday, Sunday, or holiday, or if no trades occurred on the date of gift, a weighted average of the mean values on the preceding and succeeding business days must be used. If no high- and low-value information is available (which is sometimes the case with bonds), bid and ask prices must be averaged. The charity or donor's broker can determine the value of the gift for tax purposes by looking in the *Wall Street Journal* the day after the gift is made. The *Wall Street Journal* quotes prices for the close of business from the prior day.

To calculate the value of the gift, take the daily average of the high and the low, and multiply it by the number of shares the nonprofit received. For example, if a donor transfers 100 shares of stock that traded that day between $10 and $11 per share on the date the stock was delivered to the charity, the mean is $10.50 and the value of the gift (100 x $10.50) is $1,050. The charity should issue a receipt for the donor's charitable income tax deduction.

DATE OF THE GIFT

If a donor makes an outright gift (not a gift to a trust or a pooled income fund) of securities through the mail either to the nonprofit or the non-profit's broker or outside financial manager, the date on which the envelope is postmarked is the date of the gift. Thus, if a donor wishes to make a year-end gift of securities and the envelope is postmarked in one year but received the following year, the donor is credited as making the gift in the year the envelope was postmarked. If a donor personally delivers the stock certificate(s) and power(s) to the charity, the day of delivery is the date of the gift. If a donor makes a gift of securities by telling the broker to trans-fer shares of stock from his account to the nonprofit, the date the stock is actually delivered to the charity's account in the name of the charity (even if the account is with its broker) is the date of the gift. If a donor sends securities by special courier, such as Federal Express, the date the charity receives the securities is the date of the gift.

DONOR'S CHARITABLE INCOME TAX DEDUCTION

If donors have held the gifted securities for more than one year (long term), they may claim the mean value of the securities on the date of the gift as a charitable income tax deduction in the year the gift is made. Donors may deduct up to 30 percent of their adjusted gross income (assuming they have not made cash gifts to public charities in excess of 20 percent of their adjusted gross income) and any excess may be carried forward for up to five additional years. If they have held the securities for one year or less (short term), the deduction is limited to the cost basis of the securities. If donors wish to make a gift of securities that have decreased in value, they will find it more advantageous to sell the shares of stock, deduct the capital loss from any capital gains they have incurred for that year, and contribute the proceeds to the charity. Exhibit 11.2 presents the tax consequences of gifts of securities.

EXHIBIT II.2   GIFTS OF SECURITIES

SECURITY	TAX CONSEQUENCE or STRATEGY
Publicly traded stock held long term*	Deduction equal to mean value on date of gift
Publicly traded stock held short term	Deduction equal to cost basis
Stock with a built-in loss*	Sell stock, take loss, and give proceeds in cash
Closely held stock*	Deduction equal to appraisal value
S corporation stock*	Deduction equal to shareholder's cost basis; creates unfavorable tax consequences for the charity
Dividend reinvestment plans*	Deduction for fair market value of full shares; then receive deduction for gift of partial shares
Series EE bonds*	Pay tax on ordinary income from bond interest; then give proceeds
Preferred stock	Deduction equal to cost basis
Series HH bonds*	Pay tax on ordinary income from bond interest; then give proceeds
Zero coupon bonds*	Deduction equal to market value of bond
Mutual funds*	Deduction equal to market value of fund

*Held long-term

Donors can make a gift of stock and purchase similar shares without triggering the so-called wash-sale rules. Under the wash-sale rules, a loss sustained upon a sale or disposition of stock is disallowed if the taxpayer acquires substantially identical stock within 30 days prior to or after the sale. However, a gift is not a sale or disposition, so the wash-sale rules do not apply.

SERIES EE AND HH BONDS

Series EE savings bonds are discount bonds purchased for 50 percent of their face value. The difference between their value at maturity and their purchase price is interest, which is taxed at the donor's ordinary income tax rate. The interest can be reported annually or deferred until maturity. At maturity, Series EE bonds also can be traded for HH bonds that postpone the payment of income tax.

Series HH bonds can be purchased at face value only through the exchange of Series EE bonds. These bonds pay interest semiannually until they reach maturity in five years. The donor cannot make a gift of Series EE and HH bonds directly to a charity without first being taxed on any accumulated income. The income from the bond is considered ordinary income, and the IRS does not allow a donor to avoid the taxation of ordinary income by transfer to a charity. To transfer the bond, the donor must redeem the bond at a Federal Reserve Bank or an appropriate national bank. Income taxes will be payable on the accumulated interest earned on the bond. The donor may then transfer the proceeds of the bond to a charity and receive a charitable income tax deduction equal to the value of the proceeds.

ZERO COUPON BONDS

Zero coupon bonds are sold by corporations and governments at a discount. The bond reaches its full value when it matures. The holder of a zero coupon bond must pay taxes each year on the accrued interest even though the holder does not actually receive the interest. The holder may defer paying taxes on the accrued interest when the zero coupon bonds are in a tax-deferred retirement account or may avoid such taxes on the interest component on tax-free municipal zero coupon bonds. If the bonds are sold before reaching full value, the owner will not receive the maturity value and may pay a penalty for selling before maturity. Donors who sell a zero coupon bond receive the value of the bond on the date of the sale. If they wish to make a charitable gift of a zero coupon bond, they will receive a charitable income tax deduction for the market value of the bond on the date of gift, but income tax will still be payable on any interest accumulated through the date of the gift.

GIFTS OF SHARES OF A MUTUAL FUND

As discussed, a donor can make a gift of shares in a mutual fund to a charity. The fair market value of a mutual fund is its public redemption price (net asset value) on the valuation date, which is quoted daily in the business section of most newspapers and the *Wall Street Journal*. It is not as easy or fast to transfer shares of a mutual fund as it is to transfer shares of stock. Mutual fund companies usually require written authorization to transfer shares, and the authorization must be mailed to the mutual fund company, which further delays the transfer. Be prepared for some delay (especially if timing is important, as with year-end gifts), and be careful of market fluctuations that can affect the value of the gift during the transfer process and the amount of the donor's charitable income tax deduction. Once the shares are transferred to an account in the name of the charity, the charity can sell the mutual fund shares.

GIFTS FROM DIVIDEND REINVESTMENT PLANS

Increasingly, donors are making gifts of securities that have been purchased through a dividend reinvestment program. Mutual funds and blue-chip corporations are especially likely to offer dividend reinvestment programs. With such programs, the dividend or other income earned on the securities is reinvested rather than paid to the donor.

Donors who wish to make a gift of shares in a mutual fund or corporation with a dividend reinvestment program should send a letter instructing the agent holding the shares (whether the mutual fund or corporation itself, the broker, or another party) to stop the automatic reinvestment immediately. In addition, donors must send a signed stock power with their signature guaranteed for their original shares and any shares acquired through reinvestment.

The agent will need to issue a new stock certificate in the charity's name or credit the charity's account for any full shares; depending on the program, fractional shares may be transferred as well or liquidated instead. Completion of this transaction sometimes can require a significant amount of time. A gift through a dividend reinvestment plan is also challenging because it can be difficult to determine donors' total cost basis. Each month or quarter as the dividend is reinvested, donors own a greater overall number of securities and the monthly price of the stock is likely to change. Fortunately, the company will usually be able to provide cost basis information.

Gifts of reinvested stock often turn into two separate gifts, one gift of the originally owned shares, which will be delivered to the charity promptly, and the second gift of shares acquired through reinvestment (which may include fractional shares), which may be delivered several months later. Most donors prefer to treat this as one gift, with a charitable income tax deduction that can be taken in one year. However, if this transaction is done at year-end and any of the shares are not issued by the company until the new year, donors will obtain a deduction for those additional shares only in the later year. Any shares bought through the dividend reinvestment plan within one year of the gift are "short-term" shares, and no deduction will be available for any appreciation over the cost basis.

CLOSELY HELD STOCK

One of the most significant assets of a small business owner is likely to be the value of the company's closely held stock. Closely held stock, unlike publicly traded stock, is not freely marketable, nor is its value as apparent or as easily determined. Closely held stock is held mostly by individuals who started family-run businesses or private businesses with relatively few stockholders. It is private because it is not publicly traded, and there are usually restrictions on the transfer of the stock to third parties. If permitted, the owner of closely held stock can give the stock to a charity and deduct its appraised value. Donors who wish to make gifts of closely held stock should consult with their attorneys or tax advisors because there are a number of important issues to consider in handling this type of gift.

VALUATION OF CLOSELY HELD STOCK

Closely held stock is not traded on an exchange. Therefore, it is not easy to determine its value. To ascertain the value of closely held stock, an appraiser who is knowledgeable about corporate valuation must determine its value. To approximate the value of the closely held stock, contact the treasurer of the closely held corporation or business. Donors cannot deduct a gift of closely held stock having a value of $10,000 or more unless they obtain a qualified appraisal and attach IRS Form 8283, summarizing the appraisal, to their federal income tax returns for the year of the gift.

RESTRICTIONS ON TRANSFER

Most closely held stock is subject to restrictions on the transfer of the stock to a third party. Many closely held corporations are family businesses or were started by friends or close associates who intended to keep the stock controlled by the original shareholders. As such, shareholders usually have repurchase agreements that forbid the stock from being sold to a third-party purchaser without first being offered to the corporation or other shareholders. Restrictions on transfer usually are located on the face of the stock certificate, but all of the corporate documents, including the articles of incorporation, bylaws, and stock transfer agreements, should be read carefully for any restrictions on transfer. These restrictions may prevent the transfer of the stock to a charity or may reduce its value.

GIFT OF CLOSELY HELD STOCK MUST BE AN ARM'S-LENGTH TRANSACTION

Donors who make gifts of closely held stock and charities that receive it must do so with no strings attached, even though the nonprofit organizations may be eager to sell the stock promptly. Be cautious about donors who place conditions on the transfer of closely held stock by trying to control the timing of the resale or redemption, or by directing the sale of the stock to a specific third-party purchaser. Be especially careful not to enter into a prior written agreement with either the closely held corporation or a potential third-party purchaser. So long as the transfer is an arm's-length, independent transaction and the charity is free to accept or reject any offer to purchase or redeem the stock, the donor will not be taxed on the charity's gain on sale.

In a typical case, a donor makes a gift of closely held stock to a charity. A donor must have the stock appraised to obtain a charitable income tax deduction equal to the value of the stock. An appraiser who is knowledgeable in establishing the value of closely held stock must conduct the appraisal. The nonprofit organization then typically asks the issuing corporation to redeem the stock and receives a check for the redemption price. It is important that the appraised price bear some relation to the redemption price, although it need not be identical. If the stock is sold within two years of the gift, the charity is required to notify the Internal Revenue Service on Form 8282. Determine who within the nonprofit is responsible for issuing Form 8282.

CLOSELY HELD STOCK AND DEBT

Be careful if a donor is personally liable for debt on gifted stock. Sometimes a donor may attempt to make a gift of stock of a closely held company to a charity where the stock was subject to debt for which the donor was personally liable. Relief from debt is a taxable event, and a nonprofit organization that unwittingly assumes debt of a donor or accepts property that is subject to a mortgage, even if the donor was not personally liable (as in the case of a nonrecourse obligation), has conferred a benefit. This gift creates a gain and the donor is taxed accordingly.

TRANSFER TO A CHARITABLE REMAINDER UNITRUST

In theory, a holder of closely held stock also may gift the stock to a charitable remainder unitrust, paying the lesser of net income or the percentage amount. As the owner of the stock, the donor transfers the stock to the trustee of the charitable remainder trust, who may ask the corporation to redeem the stock or sell it to an Employee Stock Ownership Plan (ESOP) or a third-party purchaser.

However, a redemption of closely held stock by a charitable remainder trust invokes the self-dealing rules. Self-dealing rules prohibit donors and their families from buying, selling, or dealing with a trust that has been the recipient of donors' property. If a donor transfers shares of closely held stock to a charitable remainder trust and the donor and his or her family have more than a 35 percent interest in the corporation immediately prior to the transfer, a redemption of those shares to the corporation violates the self-dealing rules unless a special procedure is followed. This special procedure involves an offer to redeem being made to all holders of the class of stock being redeemed. If it appears that the self-dealing rules will be violated if a charitable remainder trust is used, the donor may consider the use of a charitable gift annuity, which is not subject to those rules. In addition, as a fiduciary, the trustee of a charitable remainder trust is expected to make prudent investments. It may not be considered a prudent investment for a trustee to hold indefinitely a single asset with limited marketability, such as closely held stock. Donors should consult with their attorneys before making gifts of closely held stock.

S CORPORATION STOCK

Before proceeding with any gift of closely held stock, it is important to determine if the stock is issued by a C corporation or by an S corporation. C and S corporations are also discussed in Chapter 20, "Tax Consequences of Charitable Gifts." Like C corporations, S corporations offer their shareholders protection from personal liability, but for tax purposes, S corporations are similar to partnerships. An S corporation's gains and losses are allocated proportionately to each shareholder and are includible in the individual shareholder's tax return, which avoids the double taxation that occurs when a C corporation pays tax and then issues an after-tax dividend to its shareholders, who must then pay tax on the dividends. Shareholders of an S corporation must be no more than 75 in number, and the corporation may have only one class of stock.

A change in the law now allows a charity to be a holder of S corporation stock. The donee charity must be a 501(c)(3) charity. Prior to this change, S corporation status would be lost if any stock in the corporation were transferred to a charity. A gift of S corporation stock is deductible by the individual shareholder, subject to the regular 30 to 50 percent limitation, so long as the gift is made to a public charity, not a private foundation. However, the income tax deduction must be reduced by any gain other than long-term capital gain that would be realized if the assets of the S corporation were sold. Moreover, if the gift is made to a private foundation, it is deductible only to the extent of the donor's basis in the S corporation stock. Although the new law permits the transfer of S corporation stock to a nonprofit organization, all income or loss flows through to the charity as unrelated business taxable income, which can substantially diminish the value of the gift to the charity. In addition, any capital gains on the nonprofit's sale of appreciated S corporation stock also will be treated as unrelated business taxable income. All nonprofit organizations should seek competent legal counsel before accepting a gift of S corporation stock.

The change in the law does not extend to transfers to a charitable remainder trust. A transfer of stock to a charitable remainder trust will result in a loss of S corporation status, and if the charitable remainder trust had unrelated business taxable income by virtue of the S corporation stock, it would not be tax exempt for that year. Private foundations may have their own difficulties in holding S corporation stock, as doing so for certain periods will violate the excess business holding rules applicable to private foundations. S corporations can make gifts of their assets to charities. Doing so may produce income tax deductions for the S corporation shareholders.

PREFERRED STOCK—SECTION 306 STOCK

Section 306 of the Internal Revenue Code provides that certain preferred stock received as a tax-free stock dividend shall be treated as ordinary income property, if sold. (Otherwise, this stock would be treated as capital gain property and its sale taxed accordingly.) The rule that ordinary income property that is contributed to charitable organizations may be deducted only to the extent of the cost basis (rather than the fair market value of the stock) thus applies to Section 306 stock and diminishes the benefit of making a gift of such stock.

CONCLUSION

Encourage donors who want to make a charitable gift to look at their investment portfolios for securities that can be used to fund a gift. Talk with area stockbrokers about the advantages available to donors who make gifts of securities. Hold a seminar or workshop on charitable giving for financial planners, stockbrokers, trust officers, and others likely to advise donors about their investment portfolios. Appreciated securities provide tremendous benefits to donors through the avoidance of tax on capital gains and a charitable income tax deduction equal to the value of the securities if the securities have been held long term. Mutual funds also provide similar attractive benefits. For some donors whose primary asset is a closely held corporation, the value of their closely held stock may provide a valuable asset for gift purposes, although various considerations warrant caution.

The nonprofit organization's planned giving staff member should advise donors about how best to accomplish their goals. Ask donors to consult with their personal advisors.

CHAPTER 12

Gifts of Real Estate

INTRODUCTION

Real estate is one of the most valuable assets that a donor can use to make a charitable gift. Depending on how the gift is structured, the real estate could be a personal residence, vacant land, a farm, a second home, a vacation home, or just about any other type of real property. Donors may also make gifts of rental property that can provide income streams to the charity. Real estate can be given outright or can be used to fund a variety of charitable gift-planning vehicles. This chapter discusses the ways that real estate can be used to make a gift to small nonprofit organizations. Small charities should be extremely careful when accepting a gift of real estate. Some individuals and firms promote gifts of real estate in cases where the real estate is environmentally damaged. In other cases, the gift is gift brokered—the agent is seeking a fee to disclose the name of a prospective seller. Some of these individuals prey on smaller nonprofit organizations, which they perceive to be less experienced in these matters. Work closely with competent legal counsel to determine if a particular real estate gift is right for the nonprofit organization.

FACTORS TO CONSIDER

There are a number of issues to consider when a donor makes a gift of real estate (see Exhibit 12.1).

EXHIBIT 12.1   BENEFITS TO DONORS OF GIFTS OF REAL ESTATE

Type	Benefit
Outright Gift	Income tax deduction equal to appraised value
Gift of Fractional Interest	Income tax deduction equal to appraised value
Retained Life Estate	Partial tax deduction—an option only if property can be sold quickly
Charitable Gift Annuity	Income stream and deduction
Deferred Gift Annuity	Income stream and deduction
Charitable Remainder Trust • Net Income • Net Income with Makeup	Income stream and deduction • Lesser of net income or percentage • Makes up income later
Conservation Easement	Income tax deduction, estate deduction, and property tax deduction

- *Title to real estate.*   The title to the real estate should be free and clear of defects and liens, and held in the donor's name. Restrictions on the use of the property or easements that affect the use and enjoyment of the property also can reduce the value and the ability of the charity to sell it.

- *Mortgage.*   Most charities do not accept gifts of real estate with mortgages attached. Even if the property is desirable, these charities do not wish to spend cash to pay off the mortgage or deal with other related legal issues. In addition, the donor's charitable income tax deduction for the gift of real estate is reduced by the amount of the mortgage, and the donor also may realize some income subject to taxation through the transfer. The best plan, for both the donor and the charity, is to make gifts of mortgage-free property.

- *Marketability.*   Unless the property will be held by the charity and maintained as part of its real estate holdings, the property most likely will be sold and the proceeds used to support the charity as directed by the donor. If the donor has had the property up for sale for some time and there has been little interest, a gift of this property is likely to be of little immediate value to the charity. If donors really want to help the charity, they should make gifts of a valuable and marketable piece of real estate.

- *Environmental risk.* A number of environmental risks are involved in gifts of real estate. Farm or agricultural property may be contaminated through the overuse of pesticides or herbicides or may contain buried tanks, oil drums, or fertilizer. Residential property may have been the former site of a landfill or the property may be adjacent to a landfill resulting in damage to well systems. Commercial businesses may pollute groundwater or release dangerous emissions into the air. Charities have become increasingly aware of the need to check properties for environmental hazards. Typically, a member of the charity's staff who is knowledgeable in real estate should conduct a physical site inspection, walking the property to detect discoloration in the soil, depressions in the land, foul or noxious odors, or other evidence of environmental hazards.

OUTRIGHT GIFTS OF ENTIRE PROPERTY OR FRACTIONAL INTEREST

Through a deed, donors can make a gift of real estate by giving full ownership interest in the property to a charity. The most typical gifts include an outright gift of vacant land, a farm, a second home, or a vacation home. A donor may also make a gift of an undivided fractional interest in property, such as one quarter, two thirds, or one half.

To determine the property's value, in most cases a qualified appraisal must be conducted on the property. To meet IRS requirements, the appraisal must be conducted no more than 60 days prior to the transfer; it may be conducted after that date as long as donors receive the appraisal report before the due date of the tax return on which they first claim a charitable income tax deduction for the real estate.

> **TIP**
>
> Donors sometimes want to make a gift of use of their real estate for a period of time such as a week or a month. Donors may do so, but will not receive a charitable income tax deduction for a gift of the use of the property.

GIFT OF A PERSONAL RESIDENCE OR FARM WITH A RETAINED LIFE ESTATE

Donors can make a gift of a personal residence or farm, retain the right to live in it for their lifetime, and obtain a charitable income tax deduction.

Charitable gift annuities require that payments begin to be made to the annuitant within one year of the gift to charity. Because there is often a delay in the sale of real estate, a charitable gift annuity is not always an appropriate gift option for real estate.

Retained life estates are most appropriate for donors who intend to give the property to a charity at their deaths. By doing so during life, through a retained life estate, donors receive a current charitable income tax deduction and still have the use and enjoyment of the property. Donors are still responsible for maintenance, insurance, and real estate taxes, but the gift produces a charitable income tax deduction that can be used on donors' tax returns for the year in which the gift is made, subject to the limits on charitable deductions imposed by the IRS. The property will be included in donors' estates, but the estates will receive an estate tax charitable deduction for the value of the charitable interest. Small nonprofits should promote the benefits of gifts of real estate through a retained life estate. Many small charities have generous donors who are committed to the charity. Through a retained life estate, donors may make a generous gift without sustaining any changes in their style of living.

To be eligible for treatment as a gift to charity with a retained life estate, the donated property must be a personal residence or farm, a houseboat, yacht, or other property that serves as a personal residence.

Benefits of a retained life estate include the following:

- Donor retains the right to live in the property for life.
- Donor receives a charitable income tax deduction.
- Donor is still obligated to pay for maintenance, insurance, and taxes.

EXAMPLE   If a husband and wife, ages 70 and 72, make a gift of a retained life estate for their personal residence, they receive a charitable income tax deduction of $133,333 if their home was valued at $200,000. The donor's charitable income tax deduction is less than the fair market value of the home because the donor has retained the right to live in the home for his or her lifetime.

Real estate can be used to fund life income gifts such as charitable gift annuities, deferred gift annuities, and some types of charitable remainder trusts. The following sections describe ways to make gifts of real estate using planned gift or life income gift options.

GIFTS OF REAL ESTATE TO FUND CHARITABLE GIFT ANNUITIES

If it is likely that the property can be sold relatively quickly, real estate can be used to fund a charitable gift annuity. As described in Chapter 9, through a charitable gift annuity, a donor makes a gift to a charity and receives an income stream for life and a charitable income tax deduction. (The income stream also may be paid to a beneficiary other than the donor.) The rate is fixed and the annuity must begin to be paid within one year, if not sooner, according to the terms of the annuity contract. The charitable gift annuity rates are generally rates suggested by the American Council on Gift Annuities, based on the ages of the donors at the time the gift is made. Because there is frequently a delay in the sale of real estate, a charitable gift annuity funded with real estate is often not the most attractive option for either the donor or the charity.

Why, then, use real estate to fund a charitable gift annuity? In most cases, it is not advisable unless the charity can sell the property immediately or within one year. The charity also may accept property to fund a charitable gift annuity if it is interested in keeping the property for its own use.

> **EXAMPLE** Assume that Mr. and Mrs. Jackson, ages 83 and 79, wish to give their home and surrounding property valued at $600,000 to a charity. In return they wish to receive a guaranteed fixed income for their lifetimes through a charitable gift annuity. For donors ages 83 and 79 making a $600,000 gift, the annuity rate is currently 7.8 percent, which produces an annual payment of $46,800. Additionally, the donors receive a charitable income tax deduction of approximately $240,120, which they can use for up to 30 percent of their adjusted gross income. Any excess can be carried over for up to five years. When real estate is transferred to fund a charitable gift annuity, an irrevocable gift is made that precludes the donors from occupying their property. ▪

CHARITABLE DEFERRED GIFT ANNUITY

Unlike a charitable gift annuity, which requires payments to begin within a year after the transfer of property to charity, the charitable deferred gift annuity allows payments to the annuitant to be delayed to an agreed-upon date of at least one year after the gift is made. This option is a more acceptable life income gift option for a gift of real estate. The deferred charitable gift annuity postpones the payment to the annuitant until a time, perhaps one to three years, when it is likely that the property can be sold and can generate an income. Like a charitable gift annuity, the deferred charitable gift annuity is a contract between the donor and the charity that provides a stream of income to the annuitant for life, beginning at a predetermined date in the future. A gift made through a deferred charitable gift annuity is irrevocable, and the donor is prohibited from occupying property once it has been transferred. A deferred gift annuity is a very appropriate gift option for real estate since its very nature contemplates beginning payments at a point in the future, which can coincide with the sale of the property.

TIP

Donors should consider using real estate to fund a deferred gift annuity. The payment of the annuity can be delayed until it is likely that the property is sold.

■ **EXAMPLE**   Mr. and Mrs. Jackson, at ages 60 and 56, wish to give their home and surrounding property valued at $600,000 to a charity and in return wish to receive a guaranteed fixed income for their lifetimes. The deferred gift annuity rate is based on the donors' ages at the time the gift is made. For donors ages 60 and 56 making a $600,000 gift and deferring payments five years, until age 65 and 61, the annuity rate is 8.1 percent, which produces an annual income payment of $48,600 to begin in five years. The Jacksons also receive a charitable income tax deduction of $158,664 in the year the gift is made (which they can use to offset up to 30 percent of their adjusted gross income). ■

GIFT OF REAL ESTATE TO A CHARITABLE REMAINDER UNITRUST

Like other life income gift options, a charitable remainder trust provides a stream of income and a charitable income tax deduction. In addition, a charitable remainder trust avoids any capital gains taxes on the transfer of appreciated real estate that the donor might incur had the donor sold the real estate to a private party. A charitable remainder unitrust pays a beneficiary a predetermined percentage, but not less than 5 percent, of the fair market value of the trust's assets, as revalued annually. The higher the payout rate, the lower the donor's charitable income tax deduction.

Net Income Unitrust

The net income unitrust can be well suited for gifts of real estate in situations where the donor wishes to receive a life income and there is likely to be a delay in the sale of the property. Most parcels of real estate are usually non–income-producing assets, meaning that there is no stream of income available to pay the unitrust amount to the trust's beneficiary. A net income unitrust is a solution that enables a donor to make a gift yet protects the charity from the obligation to pay the beneficiary a stream of income until the property is sold. Through a net income unitrust, a beneficiary receives the lesser of the stated percentage of the trust's value or the actual net income. Upon the eventual sale of the property, the proceeds received by the trust are invested, producing a stream of income for the donor's lifetime. In this way, a charity can accept a gift of real estate without having to pay the income before the property is sold. The donor still receives a charitable income tax deduction in the year the gift is made. The trust must receive from the donor sufficient cash or marketable securities to enable it to meet expenses, such as real estate taxes, insurance, and maintenance costs, until the property is sold.

> **TIP**
>
> Donors in their 50s may wish to consider funding a net income unitrust with appreciated securities and, when they are in their 60s, ask the trustee to invest in a growth and income portfolio to provide income to donors during their retirement.

EXAMPLE If a donor, age 68, makes a gift of $100,000 in real estate to a 5 percent net income unitrust, she will receive a charitable income tax deduction of $51,064. If the property eventually is sold at the end of two years for $120,000, during the first year the donor receives the lesser of the stated percentage or actual net

TIP

Donors should consider using a net income unitrust with a makeup provision for gifts of real estate where there is likely to be a delay in the sale of the property. This option pays the lesser of the net income or stated percentage, but offers the possibility of eventually making up the amount by which the net income has fallen short of the stated percentage.

income. In this case, the actual net income was less than the stated percentage and so the donor will receive the actual net income, which is likely zero. The same is true for the second year. Eventually, in the third year, after the property is sold, the donor would receive the lesser of the stated percentage (5 percent) or the actual net income based on the value of the assets of $120,000. ▨

Net Income Unitrust with a Makeup Provision

Donors who wish to enable the trust's beneficiaries to make up lost income in years when the net income of the trust is less than the stated percentage amount should consider a net income unitrust with a makeup provision. A net income unitrust with makeup provision, like a net income unitrust, permits a beneficiary to receive the lesser of the stated percentage or the net income, but provides for the possibility of the shortfall in years when the net income is less than the stated percentage. Such "lost income" may be recouped in any later year in which the trust's income exceeds the stated percentage.

▨ **EXAMPLE**   Assume that real estate worth $600,000 is transferred to a net income unitrust with a makeup provision. Assume that the donors (the income beneficiaries) are ages 75 and 77 and that they select a payment rate of 6 percent. Assume further that the property sells for $600,000 in year 1 and earns 8 percent in year 2. With a net income unitrust with a makeup provision, the donors receive the stated percentage of the trust's value or the net income, whichever is less; if no income is produced in the first year, the donors receive nothing. In year 2, the property produces 8 percent.

The donors receive the lesser of the net income and the percentage amount, which in this case is the percentage amount (6 percent of $600,000, or $36,000). However, they also can receive a distribution from the makeup balance so that the aggregate payment for the year (in this case, 8 percent of $600,000, or $48,000). The donors thus would receive $12,000 from the makeup balance in addition to the regular payment of $36,000. This process can continue each year until the deficit is completely recouped. ■

Donors will also receive a charitable income tax deduction in the year the trust is established, limited to 30 percent of their adjusted gross income. In this example, the charitable income tax deduction for a $600,000 charitable remainder unitrust is $274,134, and with the rate of 6 percent, the percentage amount would be $36,000. If the entire tax deduction is not used in the first year, it can be carried over for five years.

Flip Unitrusts

The flip unitrust, described in Chapter 10, often is the best type of unitrust to use for gifts of real estate. A flip unitrust starts out as a net income unitrust, but in the year following a triggering event, it flips into a unitrust that pays a fixed percentage amount. In the context of a gift of real estate, the sale of the real estate is generally the triggering event. Thus, if a donor contributes real estate to a flip unitrust where the triggering event is the sale of the real estate, in the years up through and including the year of the sale, the donor will receive the lesser of the net income and unitrust amount. Net income is likely to be zero in this situation, so the donor would receive nothing. In each year following the year of sale, however, the donor will receive the unitrust amount. Through a flip trust, donors have greater certainty regarding the amount of annual payments they will receive in the years following the triggering event. Furthermore, after the triggering event, the trustee can invest for total return and need not feel hampered by a perceived need to generate high levels of income.

CONSERVATION EASEMENTS

Donors who are interested in land preservation or wish to preserve certain attributes of real property, such as open space, and own real estate that they want protected from development should explore the use of a conservation easement. Conservation easements help charities preserve and conserve open space and, at the same time, offer significant income and estate tax benefits to donors if a variety of conditions are met. Small charities that are involved in land preservation and in conservation of open space and related issues should market the attractive features of conservation easements. Exhibit 12.2 is an ad that can be included in a charity's newsletters and other publications.

Income tax and estate tax deductions for conservation easements have been available for years, and a tax change in 1997 increased the possibility of obtaining significant estate tax deductions for a conservation easement. Through a conservation easement, a donor grants to a qualified organization a permanent restriction on the use, which may be made of real property owned by the donor. A conservation easement can, for example, restrict development of a landowner's property, preserving views and open space. The restrictions on the property must be transferred to a charity or governmental unit. In turn, the landowner receives favorable tax benefits and preserves and conserves desirable aspects of the real estate. The ease-

EXHIBIT 12.2 AD: CONSERVATION EASEMENTS

‹ORGANIZATION›

Conservation Easements

Landowners, are you interested in preserving open space, scenic views, or historical buildings? If you are a landowner interested in preservation issues, a conservation easement may be helpful to you. A conservation easement preserves land in perpetuity and provides donors with significant tax benefits.

Your conservation easement to ‹ORGANIZATION› can provide the following benefits:

- Preservation of open space
- Preservation of wildlife habitat
- Land preservation
- Protection of scenic views
- Income tax benefits
- Estate tax benefits
- Local property tax reductions

The Office of Planned Giving will send you information on ways a conservation easement can benefit both you and ‹ORGANIZATION›. Please complete the form on the back of this card.

ment then prevents or limits development of the property except that which is specifically allowed by the easement. Provided that the easement meets numerous requirements under tax laws, the donor receives a charitable income tax deduction equal to the difference between the value of the property without the easement and the value of the property with the easement. The amount of the decrease in the property's value due to the easements also is excluded from the donor's estate, thus reducing federal estate taxes, which range from 37 to 50 percent of a donor's taxable estate. The top rate will gradually decrease in the future.

Benefits of conservation easements include the following:

- Preservation of open space
- Preservation of wildlife habitat
- Land preservation
- Protection of scenic views
- Income tax benefits
- Estate tax benefits
- Local property tax reductions

TAX CONSEQUENCES

As discussed, donors obtain favorable tax treatment for the contribution of a conservation easement that meets tax law requirements.

Charitable Income Tax Benefits

Donors receive a charitable income tax deduction for the value of the conservation easement. The value of the conservation easement is generally equal to the difference between the value of the land before the granting of the easement and the fair market value of the land afterward. The fair market value of the land is determined by its "highest and best use." In many cases, development rights are an important part of the land's highest and best use. For example, a five-acre tract of land with an ocean view has multiple values depending on the land use. To determine the highest and best use, an appraiser examines the possible purposes of the property.

Like other gifts of property, the donor's charitable income tax deduction is limited to 30 percent of adjusted gross income, and any excess may be carried forward for up to five additional years. The cost of the apprais-al is typically an expense paid by the donor and is reported for tax pur-poses as a miscellaneous itemized deduction.

Estate Tax Benefits

For wealthy donors, federal estate taxes remain a formidable obstacle. Tax rates range from 37 to 50 percent (decreasing gradually in the future), and for many donors the value of real property represents a significant portion of their estates. Through a conservation easement, donors reduce the value of their estates by an amount equal to the value of the relinquished prop-erty rights. This technique allows donors to substantially decrease the value of their estates while enjoying the use of the property.

The Economic Growth and Tax Relief Reconciliation Act of 2001 has expanded the use of conservation easements. The act removes the restric-tion that required the property to be located in certain areas. The estates of donors who make such gifts are eligible to receive estate tax benefits for up to 40 percent of the value of the property, up to $500,000 in 2002. In addition, this tax treatment can be obtained through the creation of a post-mortem conservation easement. The rules regarding conservation ease-ments are very complex, so it is important to obtain advice from a competent professional.

Property Tax Consequences

Local real estate property taxes are assessed on the property's value. The taxes are assessed by a municipality, county, or other governmental unit. For tax purposes, the property is allocated into two parts: the value of the buildings and improvements to the land, and the value of the land itself. Since the value of the land can be diminished substantially by a conserva-tion easement, the donor's property tax bill also can be reduced.

Because the donee charity or governmental unit that received the ease-ment is a tax-exempt organization, and since holding the development right is a part of the donee's charitable purpose, the value of the develop-ment right generally escapes local property taxes.

CONCLUSION

Gifts of real estate provide options to donors who own various types of real estate including personal residences, vacation property, vacant land, or other types of property. Regardless of the type of property, it should be mortgage free, be marketable, have a clear title, and should not be environmentally damaged.

There are a number of very attractive planned giving options for real estate, such as a gift with a retained life estate, charitable remainder trust, charitable gift annuity, and deferred gift annuity. In addition, for property owners interested in preservation or conservation, a gift of a conservation easement may be most attractive. Encourage donors to evaluate the choices and suggest that they consult with their professional advisors.

CHAPTER 13

Gifts of Tangible Personal Property

INTRODUCTION

A donor may hold a variety of valuable and unique assets that can be used to make charitable gifts. These assets include tangible personal property such as artwork, antiques, and collections. Moving, displaying, managing, and storing tangible personal property, especially collections, can be an expensive undertaking. Before accepting such a gift, small charities should evaluate the potential costs carefully. This chapter provides an overview of the unique requirements involved in transferring these assets to small nonprofit organizations and examines the tax treatment for each type of noncash asset. The chapter ends with a section on the importance of establishing gift review committees to evaluate and approve gifts of tangible personal property and other noncash assets.

TANGIBLE PERSONAL PROPERTY

Tangible personal property includes art, antiques, collections, collectibles, and many other assets that can be used to enhance existing collections at a charity or start new ones. The rules for making gifts of tangible personal property are different from the rules for making gifts of other assets, such as securities or real estate. Generally, for a gift of tangible personal property, the IRS requires that the property be related to the tax-exempt purposes of the charity for the donor to receive the largest charitable income tax deduction. Gifts of farm implements to an agricultural college or museum satisfy this requirement, as do gifts of art to a museum.

DEFINITION OF TANGIBLE PERSONAL PROPERTY

Tangible personal property is property that can be held physically, as distinguished from intangible property, such as cash or securities. A variety of tangible personal property can be used to make a gift including:

- Furniture
- Art
- Antiques
- Coin and stamp collections
- Livestock (cattle, thoroughbred horses, breeding stock)
- Jewelry
- Equipment
- Collections/collectibles
- Boats, yachts, recreational vehicles
- Automobiles
- Aircraft
- Books
- Clothing
- Computers, hardware and software

TRANSFER OF PERSONAL PROPERTY

To transfer ownership or legal title to a charity, the property must be physically transferred and the charity should formally accept the property. In many cases, a simple deed of gift drafted by the nonprofit organization is sufficient. A deed of gift is a document that identifies or inventories the property being transferred and includes a statement signed by the donor demonstrating an intent to transfer. Exhibit 13.1 is a sample of a deed for a gift.

Titles to certain types of tangible personal property are transferred more formally. For example, automobiles and recreational vehicles must be

EXHIBIT 13.1   DEED OF GIFT

‹Name of Charity›

DONOR: _____
Name(s)

ADDRESS: _____
Street

_____
City, State Zip

I/We, ‹NAME OF DONOR(S)›, represent and guarantee that I/we am/are the lawful owner(s) of the property described below, that it is free of all encumbrances and that I/we have the right to give or transfer the property to ‹Name of Charity›, legal title to the following property:

‹DESCRIPTION OF PROPERTY›

I (We) declare the appraised value of the above listed property(s) on this date as $_____.

_____   _____
Donor Signature   Date   Donor Signature   Date

STATE OF _____, COUNTY OF _____

The foregoing instrument was acknowledged before me this ___ day of _____, 20__

My commission expires: _____   _____
NOTARY PUBLIC

ACCEPTANCE OF GIFT

_____, on behalf of ‹Name of Charity›, accept the Legal title of the gift from ‹NAME OF DONOR(S)›, donor(s), of the above-described property.

_____   _____   _____
Signature   Title   Date

STATE OF _____, COUNTY OF _____

The foregoing instrument was acknowledged before me this ___ day of _____, 20__

My commission expires: _____
NOTARY PUBLIC

_____

transferred at a registry of motor vehicles; yachts and boats are transferred at the appropriate state agency or registry.

RELATED USE

For a donor to obtain the maximum charitable income tax deduction benefits, the property given to the charity must be related to the nonprofit organization's exempt purposes. For example, a gift of art is almost always related to the exempt purpose of the charity if it is placed on display. A gift of a painting to a museum clearly satisfies the related use rule. In most cases, a gift of artwork to be displayed at a university or hospital passes the related use test. Other examples that pass the test include books donated to a school library and medical equipment given to a hospital. Property that is given to a charity for auction will not pass the related use test.

Donors who are considering making a gift of tangible personal property should inquire whether the property will be used or sold by the charity. Donors also may want to obtain a written statement from the charity indicating the anticipated use of the property. If the property has a use related to the exempt purposes of the charity, the donor can claim a charitable income tax deduction equal to the full fair market value of the property if the donor has held the property for at least a year and a day to qualify as a long-term capital asset. To have a related use, it must be "reasonable to anticipate" that the charity will use the property in a way related to the mission of the charity for its exempt purposes. The related use rule limits the charitable income tax deduction only. Donors may make a gift of tangible personal property through their wills even if it is unrelated to the exempt purposes of the charity and still obtain an estate tax charitable deduction or the gift tax charitable deduction, or for gifts during life equal to the property's fair market value.

GIFT OF A FUTURE INTEREST IN TANGIBLE PERSONAL PROPERTY

Sometimes donors want to make a gift of a future interest in tangible personal property. This situation occurs when a donor transfers ownership of the tangible personal property, such as a painting, by deed of gift to a charity but retains the right to the possession of the property. A similar situation occurs when a donor lends the property to the charity retaining ownership and his or her will transfers the property by bequest to the charity. In both situations, the donors will not receive a charitable income tax deduction until they have given up all rights to the use and enjoyment of the property.

However, a donor can make a gift of an undivided fractional interest in tangible personal property. In this case, the donor may give, for example, a one half interest in a painting to a museum that is able to display it. The donor must allow the charity to have physical possession of the painting for that fraction of the year. The donor then will be entitled to a charitable income tax deduction for that one-half interest of the value of the artwork.

UNRELATED USE

Small charities often rely on the use of auctions, silent auctions, and other events in which donors contribute items for resale by the charity. If donors make a gift of property to a charity that has an unrelated use or is sold by the charity at auction or other event, they obtain a charitable income tax deduction equal to the cost basis of the property limited to 50 percent of their adjusted gross income with some adjustments. If donors are the makers or creators of the tangible personal property, they are entitled only to a charitable income tax deduction equal to the cost basis of the materials used to construct the property. For example, if a painter makes a gift of her painting to a charity, she may deduct only the cost of the raw materials. If there is no related use, the donor may be better off selling the property and making a gift of the proceeds to obtain a charitable income tax deduction for the fair market value of the property. When selling the property, the donor will pay any capital gains taxes due on the appreciation of the property.

TAX CONSIDERATIONS FOR GIFTS OF NONCASH ASSETS

Noncash assets may be either ordinary income property or capital gain property. There is different tax treatment depending on the classification of the property (see Exhibit 13.2). Donors who hold tangible personal property that, if sold, would produce ordinary income or short-term capital gain receive a charitable income tax deduction equal to the cost basis of the

EXHIBIT 13.2 GIFTS OF NONCASH ASSETS

Asset	Tax Consequences
Tangible personal property	If "related-use," held long term, deduction equal to appraisal value
Tangible personal property created by donor	Deduction equal to cost basis
Tangible personal property donated for resale by charity	Deduction equal to cost basis
Ordinary income property	Deduction equal to cost basis
Capital gain property with related use	If held long term, deduction equal to appraisal value; If held short term, deduction equal to cost basis

property. Donors who hold capital gain property long term (for at least a year and a day) may be able to deduct the appraised value of the property.

For example, a breeder of thoroughbreds may own horses for breeding and for sale. The horses for breeding are considered capital assets; a gift of these horses to a college of agriculture entitles a donor to a charitable income tax deduction equal to the fair market value of the horses so long as the horses have been held long term. If, on the other hand, a donor makes his living selling yearlings, a gift of these horses produces ordinary income and entitles the donor to obtain a charitable income tax deduction equal to the cost basis.

Artists, authors, and playwrights who donate their own creations are limited to a charitable income tax deduction equal to the cost basis of their work unless those costs have already been deducted as business expenses; in such cases, no deduction is permitted. The charitable income tax deduction is equal to the cost of materials used by the artist, such as paint and canvas. If the artist were to sell the work, ordinary income would be produced; hence the charitable income tax deduction is equal to the cost basis.

SUBSTANTIATION REQUIREMENTS

When a noncash gift is made to a charity, the IRS requires strict reporting. The donor has the burden of substantiating a noncash gift. Both the donor and the charity can be penalized if the reporting requirements are not followed.

Form 8283

IRS Form 8283, the Appraisal Summary, must be filed by donors including individuals, partnerships, and S corporations that make noncash charitable contributions in certain circumstances. The need to file Form 8283 depends on the status of the taxpayer and the size and type of gift. The following summarizes Form 8283 requirements:

- *Gifts valued at $500 or less.*   If gifts are valued at $500 or less, donors do not have to complete Form 8283. However, if the gift to a charity is one of a number of similar gifts donated to one or more charitable organizations, donors should total the value of the gifts and follow the guidelines for a gift of the total amount. For example, a donor may donate five paintings worth $300 each to five different charities, bringing the total gift to $1,500. She is required to complete Form 8283, Part A, for a gift of $1,500 value. The nonprofit organizations should have a statement of the value of the gift(s) for internal accounting purposes.

- *Gifts valued between $501 and $5,000.*   If a gift is valued between $501 and $5,000, the donation must be reported on Part A of IRS Form 8283, which should be attached to the donor's income tax return. An appraisal is not required. However, the organization should have a copy of Form 8283 for its records.

- *Gifts valued over $5,000.*   If the amount claimed as a charitable income tax deduction exceeds $5,000, the IRS requires that the donor complete Part B of Form 8283, along with a signature from a qualified appraiser.

- *Gifts of nonpublicly traded stock.*   Nonpublicly traded stock is stock not listed on an exchange or not regularly traded. If a donor makes a gift of nonpublicly traded stock, Part B of Form 8283 must be completed regardless of the value of the stock. A qualified appraisal is required if the value of the stock exceeds $10,000. For more information see Chapter 11.

APPRAISALS

Donors must have a qualified appraisal when the amount of the noncash gift reported as a charitable income tax deduction exceeds $5,000. They do not need a written appraisal if the donated property consists of:

- Publicly traded securities
- Nonpublicly traded stock worth $10,000 or less

ART WORTH $20,000 OR MORE

A qualified appraisal must be made for art worth $5,000 or more. A qualified appraiser is a professional who is in the business of making appraisals and knowledgeable about the type of property involved. Donors must attach a completed appraisal summary to their tax returns. If a donor's total deduction for a gift of art is $20,000 or more, he or she must attach a completed copy of the signed appraisal (plus an appraisal summary on Form 8283); if a single piece of art is valued at $20,000 or more, the donor may be required to supply an 8 × 20 inch color photograph or a 4 × 5 inch, or larger ,color transparency of the item. In cases where the value is less than $5,000, the donor is encouraged, but not required, to submit an appraisal.

TAX DEDUCTIBILITY OF APPRAISAL

The donor is responsible for the cost of the appraisal, and it is a miscellaneous itemized deduction. Current tax provisions limit tax benefits from miscellaneous deductions. Only aggregate miscellaneous deductions in excess of two percent of a donor's adjusted gross income are deductible.

FORM 8282

If the charity sells, exchanges, or disposes of contributed property other than cash or marketable securities for which a Form 8283 was required within two years of the date of the gift, the charity must complete and file Form 8282 with the IRS and send a copy to the donor. Form 8282 allows the IRS to monitor potential fraud. The appraisal must be realistic and approximate the value of the item in case the charity eventually sells the property for substantially less than the appraised value.

GIFT REVIEW COMMITTEE

Many nonprofit organizations create a gift review committee to approve all gifts of tangible personal property, property other than cash or marketable securities, including gifts of real estate, as well as all restricted gifts before they are accepted by the organization. A gift review committee also should be consulted on complex, unusual, or potentially controversial gifts.

The committee may decide to delegate certain decisions to an appropriate officer at the organization. The gift review committee should be empowered to accept only gifts that can be sold, are of real value to the organization, or can be used by the organization without burdensome management.

The existence of a gift review committee is particularly important in a number of instances. For example, when a donor who is well connected with the nonprofit wishes to make a gift of art to the organization, a number of issues need to be considered. Is the gift of real value to the nonprofit? If not, is the relationship with the donor important enough for the organization to accept the gift? Does the donor insist that the artwork be displayed rather than sold? If so, do liability issues arise? Will the artwork be safe and properly cared for? Will it cost the nonprofit more money to protect the gift? Where will the artwork be displayed in the organization? Who will make this decision? These types of questions need to be explored and answered before the gift should be accepted.

A gift review committee plays an important role with gifts of real estate. In some situations, a donor may wish to make a gift of real estate but may require that the nonprofit use the property for a specific purpose. The gift review committee would be asked to explore the relationship the donor has with the organization; whether the organization could actually use the property; whether maintenance, taxes, and insurance are prohibitively expensive to accepting the gift; and if the nonprofit has the capacity to manage the property.

Suggested Composition

A gift review committee should be composed of several key nonprofit officers. The following individuals or representatives from their office should be considered for membership in the committee:

- Vice president for development
- Director of development
- Director of planned giving
- Vice president for business affairs
- Comptroller/treasurer
- General counsel

PROCEDURES

A gift-in-kind description form should be completed by the development officer working on the gift and submitted to the committee with supporting documentation that can help the committee evaluate the gift. A gift description form should summarize information about the donor who is making the gift, describe the gift being made to the organization including its value and potential use, and list the name of the program or department that may use the gift.

Once the gift review committee gives written approval of a gift, the gift can be accepted. When a gift is received by a certain department or office, the office should provide proof to the vice president of development. Proof can be established by a shipping invoice or letter that the gift is available for pickup. After a gift is received, the vice president for development or the director of planned giving should send an acknowledgment of the gift to the donor and ask the president of the organization or a representative from the appropriate department to acknowledge the gift as well as the staff member involved. Any acknowledgment of a gift may include its description but should not include its value.

RESTRICTED GIFTS

The gift review committee also should review and approve all restricted gifts to the organization. A restricted gift is any gift where a donor places special, out-of-the-ordinary restrictions as to the gift's use. For example, real estate donated to a hospital by an individual who requires that the property be used to house physicians from other countries is a restricted gift. The gift review committee also should review a donor who imposes or places a restriction on the use of a gift or establishes criteria for eligibility in the case of an endowed fund or scholarship.

Donors sometimes wish to be involved in the selection of scholarship recipients for endowed funds, as discussed in Chapter 7. A donor who makes a gift and claims a charitable income tax deduction cannot be the sole decision maker in selecting the recipient. If the donor were to select the recipient, the donor's charitable income tax deduction would be jeopardized since the donor would in effect be paying tuition or providing medical care or another type of service to a specific individual designated by the donor. The donor can, however, serve as a member of a selection committee. Nonprofits should be cautious and avoid accepting gifts that place discriminatory restrictions excluding members of an ethnic or racial group from benefiting from that gift. These discriminatory restrictions potentially could cause the nonprofit to lose its tax-exempt status or the donor to lose the charitable income tax deduction for the gift. Businesses that make gifts also may confuse charitable giving with employee benefits. A corporate donor may offer to make a gift to establish a scholarship fund that limits the pool of potential recipients to employees of the corporation. Restricting the recipient to a pool of candidates limited to employees of the corporation will again place the charitable income tax deduction in jeopardy.

GIFTS OF REAL ESTATE

Before a gift of real estate is accepted by an organization, the gift review committee should approve and recommend acceptance of the property. The development officer responsible for the gift of real esate should complete a real estate review form and submit it to the committee. A gift of real estate involves many factors that can affect the decision to recommend acceptance of the property. These factors are discussed more fully in Chapter 12, but generally include concerns about existing mortgages, ownership, zoning, environmental hazards, and marketability.

CONCLUSION

Noncash assets include a wide variety of tangible personal property. The rules for gifts of these types of assets vary considerably from gifts of more traditional assets such as securities or real estate. Once staff members become familiar with these rules, these assets may offer options that previously had not been considered. Place ads or information about gifts of tangible personal property in organizational publications to help stimulate interest in this type of gift. To further promote the gifts, small nonprofit organizations can hold open houses or other events featuring gifts of tangible personal property contributed by donors or displays of the nonprofit's own collections. Gift review committees also will ensure that appropriate assets are accepted by the nonprofit organization.

CHAPTER 14

Gifts of Life Insurance and Retirement Plan Assets

INTRODUCTION

This chapter covers gifts of two types of assets that donors may use to make charitable gifts. Gifts of life insurance and retirement plan assets can be of significant value to a small nonprofit organization, but for a variety of reasons they also can be a challenge to handle for both the donor and the charity. In the case of gifts of life insurance, small nonprofit organizations should tread carefully and, in general, should not embark on a program that exclusively promotes life insurance as the focal point of its development efforts. Some life insurance agents and companies target nonprofit organization, especially smaller ones, offering spectacular returns while trying to gain access to the nonprofit's database of potential new clients. Because most insurance products pay only upon the death of the insured, there is a considerable lag time before the charity receives any benefit. Be cautious and seek advice before embarking on a life insurance program that is mass marketed to the nonprofit's constituents. View life insurance as just one option that can be used to build a diversified development program.

In the case of gifts of retirement plan assets, tax considerations limit the effectiveness of these gifts. New legislation might make these gifts more attractive in the future. Nevertheless, these assets can be used to benefit a nonprofit. Nonprofit organizations and donors should consult with professionals knowledgeable in the field of retirement planning before a gift is made.

GIFTS OF LIFE INSURANCE

Life insurance is a potentially valuable gift option for charitable gifts. Life insurance is a leveraged gift, meaning that for a relatively small sum of money (the premium), a donor can produce a substantial death benefit for charity. However, it may take years or decades before the charity receives the death benefit.

Specific terms are used with regard to life insurance.

Subscriber   The individual who takes out a life insurance policy.

Insurer   The company or carrier of the life insurance policy.

Beneficiary   The one who receives the death benefit upon the death of the insured. A charity is the beneficiary for charitable gifts of life insurance.

Premium   The cost of the policy paid to secure coverage. It may be paid monthly, quarterly, or annually, depending on the terms of the policy.

Owner of the policy   The one who has the right to deal with the policy or select the beneficiary. The charity is the owner of a gifted life insurance policy.

Death benefit or face value   The amount of money that is paid upon the death of the insured to the beneficiary.

Insured   Generally the individual on whose life the policy is issued; this term also can be used to describe the policy's owner.

Cash surrender value   The amount the subscriber or insured would receive if the policy were cashed in to the insurance company. The cash surrender value reflects the value of premiums paid and any investment growth, minus administrative expenses.

WAYS TO USE LIFE INSURANCE

Often life insurance is used like a bequest. A donor, usually older, transfers an insurance policy to a charity and, as with a bequest, the charity receives a lump sum payment upon the death of the insured. A donor can make a gift of a fully or partially paid-up policy. There are different tax consequences for full or partially paid-up policies, which are explored in Exhibit 14.1. Note that in some states a charity might not be allowed to hold a policy on a donor's life. It is important to check with a professional who is familiar with the state's insurance laws before promoting gifts of life insurance.

CHARITABLE INCOME TAX DEDUCTION FOR AN OUTRIGHT GIFT OF A PAID-UP POLICY

When donors make an outright gift of a whole-life or other cash-accumulation life insurance policy, they should name the charity as owner

EXHIBIT 14.1 GIFTS OF LIFE INSURANCE

Type	Consequences
Outright gift	Deduction equal to policy's replacement value
Partially paid-up policy	Daily current value
STEP policy	Deduction equal to premiums paid
Asset replacement trust	Replace loss due to charitable gift through life insurance
Life insurance unitrust	Fund unitrust with life insurance, pay income to survivor

and beneficiary of the life insurance policy. By doing this, donors completely give up ownership of the policy, waiving the right to assign or borrow against it, or change the beneficiary. If donors name the charity as owner and beneficiary of the policy, they obtain a charitable income tax deduction for the paid-up life insurance policy's replacement value, the cost to purchase an identical policy. If the replacement value exceeds donors' basis (cost), the deduction is limited to the basis. Donors can deduct up to 50 percent of their adjusted gross income in the year the gift is made and can carry any unused amount of charitable deduction forward for up to five additional years.

OUTRIGHT GIFT OF A PARTIALLY PAID-UP LIFE INSURANCE POLICY

Donors also can name a charity as owner and beneficiary of a life insurance policy that is only partially paid up. Donors need to decide if they intend to pay for the remaining premiums or if the charity is accepting the obligation of continuing payments.

CHARITABLE INCOME TAX DEDUCTION FOR A PARTIALLY PAID-UP POLICY

A donor's charitable income tax deduction for a partially paid-up life insurance policy is based on the value of the "interpolated terminal reserve." This is an amount that reflects the daily current value of the policy when it is donated between policy anniversary dates. The charitable income tax deduction is limited to 50 percent of the donor's adjusted gross income with the five-year carryforward.

CHARITABLE INCOME TAX DEDUCTION WHEN DONOR MAKES PREMIUM PAYMENTS

If donors make insurance premium payments in cash directly to the insurer rather than to the nonprofit, the charitable income tax deduction is limited to 30 percent of the donors' adjusted gross income. This is because the gift is considered "for the benefit of" the nonprofit rather than a gift to the nonprofit. If donors make the payments directly to the charity, the charitable income tax deduction is increased to 50 percent of donors' adjusted gross income.

SHORT-TERM ENDOWMENT POLICIES

Through a short-term endowment policy (STEP), a donor makes a series of 5 to 8 annual gifts to cover the premium on the policy. In the insurance business, these policies are called 5-pay or 8-pay policies. The charity is the owner and beneficiary of the policy. The annual premiums typically produce a death benefit of 10 to 15 times the sum of the annual premiums, depending on one's age. Be careful! STEP policies can generate more of a benefit for the agent and the life insurance company than for the charity.

Board members and trustees often are approached by insurance companies that seek to promote life insurance products to the nonprofit's constituents. These products are widely promoted, so be careful before starting such a program. Insurance companies make the numbers look very attractive; be prepared to challenge the insurance company's often-unrealistic assumptions. Insurance companies' commission fees and expenses erode the premium payments. Also make sure that investment assumptions are based on realistic returns, not on artificially high returns that are uncharacteristic of market returns over longer time frames. For example, donors sometimes have financial setbacks and are unable to continue paying the annual premiums or they cease to be associated with the charity and do not wish to complete payments. The charity must decide whether to continue to make payments or cancel the lapsed policy based on the amount of premiums contributed to date, thus reducing the death benefit and the ultimate gift to the charity.

INSURANCE USED IN ASSET REPLACEMENT ARRANGEMENTS

Donors often struggle between a desire to achieve philanthropic goals and the need to preserve assets for their families. For some donors, life insurance may solve that problem, enabling them to make a major gift while putting their estates back into the positions they were in prior to making the gift through an asset replacement trust. Donors can do this by making a major gift while simultaneously funding an asset replacement trust that is irrevocable or by giving family members sufficient cash to purchase an insurance policy on the donors' lives.

The trust arrangement can be illustrated as follows: In anticipation of receiving tax benefits and possibly a stream of income from their gift, the donors, typically a husband and wife, fund an irrevocable charitable remainder unitrust naming as current beneficiaries individuals such as their children. The beneficiaries use the cash received annually from the unitrust to purchase and maintain a "second-to-die" life insurance policy on the donors. A second-to-die policy reduces the overall cost of the life insurance since the policy accumulates retained earnings and pays a death benefit only upon the death of the surviving spouse. Second-to-die life insurance policies usually can be purchased for approximately 3 to 8 percent of the death benefit or face value of the life insurance.

The actual cost depends on the insurance carrier and the donor's age and health. The donor should price shop for a carrier that offers competitive premiums, because costs vary. Since the death benefit will not be paid for some time, the individual who purchases the policy should select a life insurance company that is financially secure. Upon the death of the survivor, the beneficiaries (typically the donors' children) receive the death benefit from the insurance policy. Because the death benefit is not part of the parents' estates, federal estate taxes on the benefit are avoided. Note that if parents transfer assets to children to enable them to purchase a life insurance policy or to an irrevocable life insurance trust that purchases a policy for the ultimate benefit of the children, the transfers will be treated as a gift for gift tax purposes. However, if structured correctly, such gifts can qualify for the $10,000 annual gift tax exclusion. Through a wealth replacement arrangement, a donor can make a major gift to a charity but still provide for family members.

FUNDING A CHARITABLE REMAINDER NET INCOME UNITRUST/FLIP WITH LIFE INSURANCE

As discussed in Chapter 10, a donor can fund an income-only charitable remainder unitrust. An income-only unitrust pays to a beneficiary, for life, the lesser of the stated percentage or net income earned. This type of unitrust can be funded with life insurance on the life of the grantor, with the trust naming the grantor's spouse as a life-income beneficiary. Such a trust, structured as a so-called flip unitrust that, upon the death of the grantor, flips to become a straight percentage unitrust, provides the spouse with an annual payment based on the fair market value of the assets. The grantor, through the unitrust, is able to make a series of payments to cover the cost of the premiums. The payments will be treated as additional contributions to the unitrust and as such will produce a charitable income tax deduction.

REPORTING REQUIREMENTS

A life insurance gift is a noncash property item and must be reported on Form 8283 if the donor claims a charitable income tax charitable deduction for $500 or more. In addition, if the value of the life insurance policy donated to a charity is $5,000 or more, the donor also is required to provide a qualified appraisal for the policy.

The next part of this chapter focuses on ways donors may make gifts of retirement plan assets.

GIFTS OF RETIREMENT PLAN ASSETS

Retirement vehicles such as employee benefit plans, individual retirement accounts (IRAs), Roth IRAs, corporate savings plans, 401(k) pension and profit-sharing plans, and tax-sheltered 403(b) annuities provide individuals with opportunities for tax-deferred investments that also may be used to help charities. Individuals who shelter income through retirement plans are not taxed on either the income earned or the capital appreciation of the assets until the funds are withdrawn. When donors participate in a 401(k) or 403(b) plan, their employers may make an additional contribution to the retirement plan, thereby increasing the retirement benefits. Moreover, the initial 403(b) and 401(k) contributions are made pretax, prior to income taxes being assessed against employees' contributions.

Federal law limits the amount an individual can contribute each year to a retirement program. For example, if donors qualify, they can contribute a maximum of $2,000 per year to a traditional IRA and meet certain income limitations. The Roth IRA also has a $2,000 ceiling, but donors can establish one even if they participate in a retirement plan if certain income limitations are met. The Economic Growth and Tax Relief and Reconciliation Act of 2001 allows for increases in contributions. The $2,000 ceiling on contributions to a traditional IRA and a Roth IRA will gradually increase each year, rising eventually to $5,000. Unlike the IRA, there is no ceiling on the amount of money that donors can contribute to a charitable gift, although donors' charitable income tax deduction may be limited by the annual percentage limitation applicable to charitable contributions.

In theory, retirement vehicles such as IRAs, tax-sheltered annuities, or qualified employee benefit plans may be used to make gifts to a charity; in practice, there are a variety of obstacles. Some plans only permit the participant to name his or her spouse or certain other individuals, such as children, as beneficiaries of the plan. When a charity can be named, federal law also requires, in most cases, that the spouse of the participant consent to the designation of a charity as beneficiary of a retirement plan at the employee's death. Because most retirement plans are funded with pretax income, the Internal Revenue Code requires that the assets of such plans be taxed at ordinary income rates upon any distribution of the asset during the donor's lifetime, even if the asset will be used to make a gift to charity. Donors obtain an offsetting charitable income tax deduction but only subject to the applicable income percentage limitations. Some attractive options do still exist if donors' retirement plans do not prohibit the transfer of plan assets to a charity or other planned gift vehicles.

Legislation has been proposed in Congress that would allow donors to make gifts of individual retirement accounts directly to a charity without first having to pay income taxes on the withdrawal and without receiving a charitable income tax deduction. If passed, this legislation will allow donors to make charitable gifts of IRA assets and, if future legislation is broad enough, perhaps other retirement plan assets, such as 401(k), 403(b), SEP, and other related employer-sponsored plan assets, without being affected by the income percentage limitations. At the time this book went to print, legislation had not been passed. Check with senators, representatives, certified public accountants, or charity's general counsel or planned giving consultants for more information on the status of this legislation. If passed, it would open desirable avenues and avoid income taxation on withdrawals transferred to charity.

TAX CONSEQUENCES OF CHARITABLE GIFTS OF RETIREMENT ACCOUNTS AT DEATH

As discussed, most withdrawals of or distributions from retirement account assets are fully taxable as ordinary income to the plan participant or to any noncharitable beneficiary. In addition, for estate tax purposes, the value of these assets is includible in the participant's estate. If the donor's spouse (a U.S. citizen) is designated as beneficiary, the estate tax is avoided because of the estate tax marital deduction; however, the assets are taxed in the estate of the donor's surviving spouse. If a nonprofit organization is designated as beneficiary, the estate tax also is avoided due to the estate tax charitable deduction. Retirement accounts are characterized as income in respect of a decedent (IRD). IRD items are taxable to the beneficiary and also are includible in the decedent's estate. The beneficiary may obtain an income tax deduction for estate taxes paid, with respect to the IRD assets. Retirement accounts transferred to a charity at death avoid income tax because of the charity's tax-exempt status. Assets transferred to a charitable remainder trust will avoid income tax upon distribution because the trust itself is tax exempt. Although ordinary income will be carved out with distributions, estate taxes also will be reduced by the charitable income tax deduction in respect of the remainder interest.

TYPES OF RETIREMENT PLANS

There are many types of retirement plans. The most common types include:

- *Traditional individual retirement accounts (IRAs).* Individuals make contributions to traditional deductible IRAs up to a maximum of $3,000 per year (gradually increasing to $5,000) subject to various limitations and tax consequences upon distribution.

- *Roth IRAs.* Roth IRA provisions enable taxpayers to transfer up to $3,000 (again increasing to $5,000) posttax to an IRA account, provided their adjusted gross income is below certain limits. Any capital appreciation or income produced by the principal may be withdrawn tax-free so long as the taxpayer is $59^{1}/_{2}$ years old or older and the principal has been in the account for five years or more. Penalties are imposed for withdrawals prior to a five-year period. The new IRA provisions apply even if the taxpayer is covered under an employer's retirement program. Both the traditional IRA and Roth IRA allow for catch-up pensions for taxpayers age 50 and above.

- *Section 401(k) plans.* Pretax voluntary contributions by an employee often are matched by the corporate employer up to a certain percentage of salary.

- *Section 403(b) plans (sometimes referred to as tax-sheltered annuities).* These are retirement plans for employees of nonprofit (501)(c)(3) organizations and public schools.

- *Qualified pension plans.* Regular contributions by an employer are used to fund retirement benefits for qualifying employees. The contributions are required annually and are based on a percentage of salary.

- *Qualified profit-sharing plans.* These are similar to pension plans, but the employer contributions are based on profits and the amount of the contribution may vary from year to year.

- *Self-employed retirement plans.* These include Keogh and SEP-IRA plans along with other self-directed retirement plans.

Many wealthy donors, especially those with fully funded retirement programs, were adversely affected by a 15 percent excise tax on excess distributions from qualified retirement plans, tax-sheltered annuities, and individual retirement accounts. The Taxpayer Relief Act of 1997 repealed this excise tax, which acted as a deterrent to donors wishing to make a gift of such assets. Donors who now make a lifetime gift of retirement plan assets will pay federal and state ordinary income taxes on the distribution (as ordinary income, not capital gain) but will receive a charitable income tax deduction that may largely offset the income tax effects of the distribution.

WAYS TO TRANSFER RETIREMENT ASSETS TO A NONPROFIT

There are several ways to make gifts of retirement accounts to a charity. These options include: outright gifts, designation of a beneficiary, bequests, and transfer to a charitable remainder trust.

Retirement Assets Transferred through Outright Charitable Gifts

Donors can make an outright gift of a retirement account to a charity during their lifetime. Unfortunately, donors must withdraw the assets, pay income taxes, and transfer the balance to the charity. These assets are fully taxable to donors as ordinary income at their marginal tax rate. Donors can obtain a charitable income tax deduction although it is limited to 50 percent of their adjusted gross income for gifts to public charities. If donors are under age $59^1/_2$, then additional penalties are imposed for early withdrawal unless they have retired and are at least 55 years old. Individuals must commence withdrawal of their retirement accounts by age $70^1/_2$; many donors choose to make the gift at that age because they want to offset the additional income. The inclusion in donors' income of distributions from the retirement account and the subsequent charitable income tax deduction for the value of the donation results in a wash, at best, and the income percentage limitations may mean that the income will not be offset fully. Since donors do not obtain favorable tax consequences, and may incur relatively unfavorable tax consequences for a gift of a retirement plan, the use of this option is limited, but it is one way to make a gift.

Designation of Beneficiary

If a donor's retirement plan is not depleted at death, she can designate a charity as a beneficiary to receive all or a stated percentage of her retirement account upon death. The donor receives an estate tax charitable tax deduction for the value of the assets distributed to a nonprofit organization. Like a bequest, a beneficiary designation provides the donor with an opportunity to make a considerable gift while avoiding income and estate tax on the assets remaining in the retirement account upon her death. The donor's estate obtains an estate tax charitable deduction for the value of the gift, and the charity is not taxed on the income arising from distribution. Unless the donor has created a separate account within the retirement plan and has designated the charity as the beneficiary of that separate account, designating both an individual and a charity as partial beneficiaries of a retirement plan will severely limit the individual beneficiary's withdrawal options and may have adverse income tax consequences.

Bequest of Retirement Account

Donors transfer retirement accounts by designating a recipient as a beneficiary at death. In the absence of a beneficiary designation, the account generally will be payable to the donor's estate, if not the donor's spouse, and the donor may then transfer the retirement account through a bequest in his will. The bequest should technically be a specific transfer. A specific transfer identifies the particular account to be distributed as compared to a gift through the donor's residuary clause. A transfer of a retirement account to charity, if properly made, avoids income taxation on the assets remaining in the retirement account at death. Because the transfer is made to a tax-exempt organization, the donor's estate also obtains an estate tax charitable deduction for the value of the account.

Transfer to a Charitable Remainder Trust

If the retirement plan permits it, a donor may transfer the retirement account to a charitable remainder trust. The plan participant will be taxed on distributions from the retirement account as they are paid during life. At death, the assets remaining in the retirement account will be transferred to a charitable remainder trust, providing income to an individual beneficiary for life, with the remainder going to a nonprofit organization at the individual beneficiary's death. Ordinary taxable income is distributed to the income beneficiary according to the terms of the trust. The retirement account also is included in the donor's estate, but the estate receives an estate tax charitable deduction for the remainder value of the unitrust. CAVEAT: The full value of the account is included in the donor's estate, and the estate tax charitable deduction for the remainder is significantly less than the value of the account. Since a qualified charitable remainder trust is exempt from income tax, the retirement account proceeds are not taxed to the trust and the corpus is preserved. In addition, although retirement accounts are IRD items, IRD items transferred to a qualified charitable remainder trust avoid taxation because of the trust's tax-exempt status. As the income distributions are made to the life income beneficiary, they are taxed as ordinary income to the beneficiary.

Charitable Remainder Unitrust for Spouse Funded with a Retirement Plan

A charitable remainder unitrust can be named as a beneficiary of a retirement plan that can provide income for life to a spouse, with the remainder going to a nonprofit. Upon the death of the first spouse, the qualified plan assets are distributed to the charitable remainder unitrust. The estate of the first spouse to die receives an estate tax charitable deduction for the remainder of the trust. However, the difference between the remainder and the initial transfer passes as a surviving spouse's income interest that qualifies for the marital deduction and therefore avoids estate taxes completely.

IN SUMMARY

The use of planned giving vehicles to assist in retirement planning is well accepted. The real challenge is finding ways to access the retirement plans to benefit nonprofits and satisfy a donor's financial and estate planning goals. Exhibit 14.2 summarizes key points about gifts of retirement assets.

CONCLUSION

In some circumstances, life insurance can be an effective tool to make a charitable gift. It works best for donors who are younger to middle age so that premiums will be relatively more affordable. From the charity's standpoint, many other options might be more attractive, such as outright gifts, life income gifts, or gifts through an estate. Life insurance can be used effectively when used as part of an asset replacement arrangement. These can help place the donor's family back in the financial position it was in prior to the charitable gift. Last, be cautious about insurance companies that offer mass-marketed life insurance programs to charities, donors, and prospects. Some of these programs could be more beneficial to the insurance company than to the charity.

EXHIBIT 14.2 GIFTS OF RETIREMENT ASSETS

- Many plans prohibit the transfer of assets to a charity whether by outright gift or beneficiary designation.
- In cases where there is no prohibition, there may be little net tax benefit because the donor must withdraw assets that will be fully taxed. The donor receives a charitable income tax deduction equal to the withdrawal, but it may not fully offset the income.
- Retirement plan assets are characterized as IRD income. They are includible in the donor's estate for federal estate tax purposes and are subject to an income tax assessed to the beneficiary recipient. The recipient does receive an income tax deduction for the estate tax paid attributable to the retirement account.
- If the plan permits, donors may transfer retirement plan assets at death by designating the charity as the beneficiary or by making a bequest of the assets to a charity or to a charitable remainder trust. This may avoid or at least defer income taxation because the charity is tax exempt and income realized by the charitable remainder trust is not taxable until distributed to the income beneficiary.
- In the case of a charitable remainder trust funded at the donor's death and paying income to a survivor beneficiary, the value of the retirement account assets are included in full in the donor's estate but the donor's estate receives a charitable estate tax deduction for the value of the charitable remainder.
- However, in the case of a charitable remainder trust that provides only for the donor's spouse for life with no other income beneficiary (either concurrent or subsequent), the spouse's interest qualifies for the estate tax marital deduction and the entire value of the plan assets thus escapes federal estate taxation.
- Watch for legislation that will allow for transfers during lifetime of retirement plan assets to charities without having to pay income taxes on the withdrawal but also without receiving a separate charitable deduction.

If their plans permit it, donors may may make distributions from retirement plan assets to a nonprofit organization. In the future, Congress may pass legislation that would allow transfer of retirement fund assets without individuals first paying taxes on the withdrawal. If so, gifts of retirement fund assets will provide valuable tools to donors who want to make charitable gifts.

PART FIVE

Working with Donors

CHAPTER 15

The Planned Giving Prospect

INTRODUCTION

Why do donors make planned gifts? To be successful at the business of planned giving, planned giving staff members need to understand why individuals make gifts and how to work with donors to increase the number of planned gifts to nonprofit organizations. This chapter examines several topics related to planned giving donors: the motivations behind donors' gifts, how to find planned giving prospects, and how to work with donors interested in making gifts.

PROFILE OF A PLANNED GIVING PROSPECT

Planned giving prospect profiles are somewhat different from other development prospects, and their demographics need to be distinguished to better identify them. In general, planned giving prospects and donors share the following characteristics.

Age

Although planned giving vehicles benefit donors of all ages, many planned giving prospects tend to be older. These prospects value the work that nonprofit organizations perform, and they have lived long enough to accumulate wealth and are comfortable with giving some of it away. Many no longer need savings for a new house or children's education.

Wealth

The majority of planned giving prospects are at least moderately wealthy, able to make a significant gift to a nonprofit organization. They make gifts from disposable income, accumulated assets such as stock or real estate, or through their estates. They often see charitable giving as a way to obtain favorable tax benefits. On the other hand, many planned giving donors supplement their retirement benefits with income streams from life income gifts.

Involvement with Charity

The typical planned giving prospect is well connected to one or more nonprofit organizations, knows their needs, and has provided supported for many years at lower levels. As prospects become more involved with charities, they seek ways to make larger and more meaningful gifts. Planned giving enables donors to increase their financial support without depleting their reserves.

Childless Couples and Single Individuals

Many planned giving prospects are childless and seek a place to leave their accumulated wealth. Many are single and do not have immediate family members whom they wish to benefit at their death.

Surviving Spouses

Once alone, many planned giving prospects develop close relationships with nonprofit organizations. Often they want to honor the wishes of their deceased spouse who was connected to a charity or to memorialize loved ones. The nonprofit organization is likely to have played a significant role in one or both of their lives.

PLANNED GIVING FROM THE DONOR'S PERSPECTIVE: DONOR MOTIVATIONS

Planned gifts are attractive to donors for many reasons. Through planned gifts, donors often can make larger gifts than they thought possible, and for some donors a planned gift is the only way to make a substantial gift to charity. When donors learn that they can make a gift that pays a stream of income for life, increases the yield they may currently receive from other investments, provides a charitable income tax deduction, and reduces or eliminates capital gains taxes or estate taxes, they feel more inclined to make the gift. Planned gifts also allow donors to be creative when making a gift. Real estate or securities can be gifted to a nonprofit organization and provide a donor with an income stream and various tax advantages. Conservative "blue-chip stocks" paying a 1 to 2 percent yield can be gifted through a life income gift and provide the donor with a substantially higher income stream, such as 6 to 9 percent. Planned giving options can encourage the charitably minded donor to move forward and make the gift. The following is an overview of common motivators for planned giving donors. Planned giving staff members reading this section should think about individuals who might fit each profile.

Philanthropic Donors

Philanthropic donors are truly the most noble and most scarce donors. They make gifts because they wish to better the world and view philanthropy as a personal duty. These donors often make their gifts anonymously and shun the spotlight. Attempts to recognize or honor these donors are politely declined. Unfortunately, there are not enough of these donors. When they are ready to act, they usually proactively seek out the nonprofit organization.

Grateful Donors

Grateful donors are those who wish to repay a debt to the nonprofit. Often grateful donors are individuals who received a service or benefit from the organization and feel indebted to it. The donors may be college graduates who feel that everything they have achieved in life is due to the education they received, patients who feel that medical care saved their lives or greatly improved their quality of life, individuals who received social services in a difficult time, or donors who wish to support the religious organization they have believed in all their lives. Like philanthropic donors, grateful donors generally seek out the nonprofit organization. They move the gift-giving process along and enjoy seeing their names included on recognition lists.

Honoring Loved Ones

Many donors make gifts to honor loved ones. Gifts can be in honor of a person who is living, but more often they are made as a memorial tribute to someone who has died. These donors usually seek out the organization and have very specific ideas about how they wish to pay tribute. Often they are motivated to create a named endowed fund that allows them to permanently honor the loved one. An entire family or several family members may be involved in supporting the fund. Planned gifts are an excellent way to build family funds because each contributor has different financial, estate planning, and tax needs that can be satisfied by various planned giving options or by using different assets. One donor may benefit most by making a gift of appreciated securities through a pooled income fund, while another family member benefits more from a charitable gift annuity or a deferred gift annuity. Donors also may make a gift through their estate to substantially augment an endowed fund. Individuals who are motivated to honor loved ones are excellent planned giving prospects.

Charity as a Family Substitute

Many donors make gifts to nonprofit organizations because they simply do not have heirs to transfer their assets to, or they do not want family members to receive all or a portion of their estates. In effect, they are looking for substitute heirs and use nonprofit organizations as replacements for a natural family. Many are older donors who are surviving spouses and do not have children. They have been treated well by the nonprofit organization and enjoy the attention and recognition that philanthropy provides. Small charities are able to develop more intimate relationships with key donors and prospects. Capitalize on this opportunity to educate these individuals fully about the charity's mission and charitable gift options. For these donors, personal visits and correspondence are extremely important.

Often these are the wealthiest donors. Following a long and successful relationship with the nonprofit organization and its staff, they make major gifts through their estates. It is especially important to show these donors that bequests can benefit the organization; they may have the capacity to make gifts of 25 to 50 percent of their estates.

Tax Benefits

One reason donors make gifts is for financial or tax incentives. However, donors first must have the philanthropic intent necessary to make a gift. As economic conditions change, tax benefits become increasingly attractive to the philanthropically minded donor. Tax benefits from charitable gifts are sometimes sufficient incentives to convert a prospect into a donor.

Financial Benefits

Sophisticated donors, such as business professionals, have increasingly turned to nonprofit organizations as a way to maximize financial returns while minimizing taxation. This relatively new breed of donors often uses assets other than cash, such as securities, closely held stock, or real estate, to fund charitable gifts. Most often they seek a stream of income greater than the yield they currently receive from low-paying investments. These donors usually are already working with financial advisors or are in the financial service business, which helps facilitate the gift-giving process. Planned giving staff members need to identify these donors through marketing and educational efforts.

Social Standing and Prestige

Some donors give to certain organizations because they wish to become its "insiders." They see their contribution as a form of membership dues. Some donors give to well-established, long-standing traditional organizations so that they can be known as a benefactor of those organizations. They perceive that their social standing will rise with each gift. Planned giving officers should pay special attention to events that allow donors at specific giving levels to socialize with each other. In addition to providing donors with a perceived gain in social status, these events foster business and professional relationships among attendees.

Insurance Policy

Some donors give to an organization because they want an "insurance policy" for the future. This is most prevalent at hospitals, but is also seen at other organizations. These donors want to make a gift so that they become known at the hospital. If anything happens to them, they feel they will be assured of getting first-class treatment (medical care) because they are a "big donor." Other donors may make the gift to influence decisions about a son or daughter being accepted into a school, college, or university. Donors may even express this when making the gift by asking, not so jokingly, "Does this mean that if something happens to me, you'll take care of me?" or "I hope the university remembers this when my son applies for admittance."

Unfortunately, donors who promise to make gifts sometimes also provide excuses to avoid making the gifts. They say that although the care they received and the physician were excellent (they do not want to jeopardize their relationship with their physician), they had to wait a long time to be admitted, the nurses were inferior, or the food was bad. Or they say that they were planning to make a gift, but their nephew's application to the college was turned down.

Help to refocus these donors on the reason that led them to want to make a gift in the first place. Remind them that the organization will benefit from their financial assistance or that a particular type of research needs to continue. Do not let donors use one negative experience to negate all of the positive things that came before that experience.

Recognition

For some donors, philanthropic intent becomes overshadowed by a desire for recognition. These donors seek the most from their gifts and tend to favor naming opportunities. They crave high-profile opportunities, such as having their names engraved on a building. Unfortunately, they also complain the loudest if their names are inadvertently omitted from the published donor list. Some of these donors want the maximum visibility for the least financial cost. They may argue about the terms or size of the gift and try to work a "deal" to give them the most recognition for the least amount of money. These donors love the chase and feeling of self-worth the planned giving staff member and nonprofit provide. Some may name-drop and mention the names of other nonprofits courting them.

To pursue these types of donors, remind them of how important they are to the organization. Remind them about the publicity, social events, and recognition they will enjoy from making a gift. It may take several years to close the gift with these types of donors, and reassurance is required that the planned giving officer will not abandon them once the gift is made. They love the attention, but do not want to risk losing it by actually making the gift.

No Donative Intent

At least once in every planned giving professional's career, repeated efforts are made to close a gift from a prospect who has no donative intent. This prospect profile often is someone who is "just looking" for planned giving information, to see if planned giving is a better (financial) option than a commercial alternative. The prospect may be someone looking for a "buyer" for an alleged "gift" of real estate or who sees a planned gift as a type of solution to a problem, such as a way to avoid paying capital gains taxes. Unfortunately, some people turn to nonprofit organizations, especially smaller ones, when they want to get rid of an asset that they cannot sell. If the prospect cannot sell the property, it is unlikely that the nonprofit organization can sell it.

Do not spend too much time on these prospects. If the donor does not have a connection to the organization or a strong desire to make a real gift, the gift will never happen, no matter how hardworking, clever, or persistent the actions of the planned giving officer. Cut losses early and move on to real prospects with donative intent.

IDENTIFYING THE PLANNED GIVING PROSPECT

Planned giving donors come from all backgrounds. Be open-minded about seeking planned giving donors and prospects, and recognize that they can be found from all socioeconomic backgrounds. Keep the following in mind to identify planned giving prospects.

Referrals from Development Staff

Educate the internal development staff about planned giving so that they feel comfortable referring prospects. Ideally other development officers will refer planned giving prospects to the planned giving office. Development colleagues must feel assured that the planned giving officer will not "steal" their prospects and become too technical or cautious, scaring donors away from making the gift. Acquiring planned giving prospects from other development officers assumes that colleagues have donors or prospects to send to the planned giving office. If this happens, be sure to share the credit for the gift.

Marketing

One important feature of a planned giving program is its ability to attract new donors to the nonprofit organization. One way to do this is through marketing. Marketing identifies new planned giving donors, and a dialogue can begin with individuals who have identified themselves as interested in learning more about planned giving. Marketing is a long-term proposition, so begin as soon as possible. See Chapter 18 for a complete discussion of marketing.

Annual Fund Upgrades

A significant number of planned giving prospects exist in the charity's annual fund base. To upgrade these prospects to a planned gift, target annual fund donors who have made gifts at a particular dollar level over a number of years. For example, identify donors who have made gifts of $500 or more for each of the last three years. If the pool is too large, reduce it by narrowing it to donors over a certain age—for example, 65—who have made a gift of $500 or more for each of the last three years. Then begin a targeted marketing and direct mail program to provide information to this population throughout the year. Information can include letters about planned giving benefits, a planned giving brochure, gift calculations, invitations to events, news articles featuring the nonprofit, and newsletters. Follow up with these prospects over time, maintaining regular contact to remind them of the benefits of planned giving.

Rehabilitate Old Cases

Review stale office files to uncover prospects who once had requested information about making a planned gift or bequest. Every development office has files containing correspondence from prospects or donors who wrote to inquire about how to set up an endowed fund or make a bequest. Send these prospects information about the planned giving program, some personal calculations, and news about the nonprofit and the need to raise funds. It is likely that after a few attempts, some viable planned giving prospects will emerge.

Events

When the nonprofit organization or development office hosts events for donors and prospects, be sure to attend. Before the event, go through a list of attendees and identify individuals who fit the planned giving profile. At the event, seek out prospects and be prepared to discuss the nonprofit organization's services. Inform prospects about charitable giving and planned giving and how planned giving benefits help donors to make gifts. If an individual is a potential prospect, follow up with a letter and include information about planned giving. Educate and cultivate these prospects. Over time new planned giving donors will emerge.

Suspects

"Suspects" are individuals who are thought to have the capacity to make a gift to the organization but may have little connection to the nonprofit. Conduct suspect meetings with individuals who may be able to screen and identify planned giving prospects, such as trustees, volunteers, and staff members. For a suspect meeting, create a list of people known to the individual attendees at the meeting. For example, when working at a hospital and meeting with a physician, have a list of the physician's patients so that the physician can help identify individuals who may have the financial capacity to, and interest in, supporting the hospital and the physician's work. It is particularly helpful if the physician or any member at a suspect meeting is willing to identify prospects and then become involved in the solicitation process. Try to conduct suspect meetings with individuals who can bring new sources of money into the organization.

Board of Trustees

Another excellent source of planned giving prospects is an organization's board of trustees. Trustees are well acquainted with the organization's constituents, and they may be willing to assist in soliciting prospects. Ask each trustee to identify potential planned giving prospects, and see if each will make an introduction for the planned giving officer. Introductions made at the trustee level often lead to successful gift solicitations because the trustee and prospect may be professional or social acquaintances, and the prospect may feel more inclined to make a gift at a higher amount.

CONCLUSION

Understanding the motivations of planned giving donors, identifying planned giving prospects, and learning to work successfully with these donors are critical to a successful planned giving program. Planned giving donors are special; they cannot be grouped together with all other individuals who make gifts to nonprofits. Understanding their unique qualities and attributes enables planned giving staff to better provide services.

CHAPTER 16

Solicitation Strategies

INTRODUCTION

Philanthropy is an investment in the present and the future. Donors, through their financial support, make investments in nonprofit organizations by providing resources for immediate and future needs. Philanthropy affords individuals the opportunity to preserve and promote ideals and concepts that they cherish and that uphold their moral and philosophical beliefs. Philanthropy gives individuals a chance to belong not only to the nonprofit, but to a larger group whose members have made financial commitments. Professionals who enter the field of planned giving and development often ask for advice on ways to solicit prospects. Their assumption is that a special script or dialogue will elicit a positive response and consequently a gift from a prospect. Of course, there is no magical array of words or one correct way to solicit a prospect for a gift. Successful solicitations are based on the donor's interest in the nonprofit, the planned giving officer's knowledge of both the nonprofit and the donor, strong planning and preparation, a positive interpersonal relationship between the officer and the prospect, and perseverance.

This chapter is divided into three parts. The first part deals with preparing for a solicitation from the perspective of a planned giving staff member; the second part discusses the solicitation process; and the third part focuses on negotiation strategies to increase success.

SOLICITATION FROM THE PERSPECTIVE OF THE PLANNED GIVING STAFF MEMBER

Think Positively

To be successful in fundraising, staff must develop a positive mind set in working with donors. The following is a comparison of successful and unsuccessful approaches:

Successful Approaches	Unsuccessful Approaches
Be positive.	Start apologizing right away.
Be confident.	Feel that you are imposing.
Practice.	Act afraid or with uncertainty.
Understand and explain the nonprofit's needs.	Make the nonprofit sound needy.

Believe in the Mission

Before commencing a solicitation, a planned giving staff member should understand and be completely conversant with the charity's mission and its charitable services. A rereading of the organization's mission or case statement reinforces the central themes and purposes of the nonprofit. Planned giving staff should meet with a variety of the charity's representatives to obtain firsthand knowledge of its services and the people who make its work essential.

Asking Is Not Taking

Individuals new to development sometimes view a solicitation as tantamount to taking the prospect's assets instead of facilitating a gift in support of a nonprofit. A gift is a free act of the donor whereby the donor parts irrevocably with an asset. A solicitation matches the financial resources and interests of the prospect with the charity's need to raise money to fulfill its mission. Planned giving staff members serve as matchmakers, bringing donors together with a charity's organizational needs while satisfying the donor's interests and goals. The process is interactive. The donor should be a full participant in the process and is the true decision maker.

Needs vs. Needy

It is important to differentiate between a charity's needs and a charity appearing needy. Nonprofits have needs, but should never appear needy. Donors want to make gifts to successful charities, knowing that their gifts have a positive impact on enhancing an already successful program. Occasionally staff members may convert needs into expressions of neediness, which evokes pity, but does not usually elicit financial support. It is more effective to show a donor blueprints and scale models of proposed new construction than to show an existing deteriorating building. Nonprofits and their staff must practice making solicitations to make certain that they demonstrate the nonprofit's organizational needs, putting the organization in the most favorable light.

The Right Time Is Now

Some professionals hesitate, waiting for the right time to solicit the prospect. There is no one right time, the right time is now. Falsely assuming that there is a correct time effectively reduces the solicitation to an act of happenstance, and procrastination should be avoided at all costs. Few solicitations are perfect; a solicitation need not be perfect to be successful. If perfection is the goal, no solicitation will ever take place. The more planned giving staff is involved in soliciting prospects, the more comfortable they will become with the process. Develop an appropriate timetable for soliciting a donor and move forward rather than wait for a more ideal time because a perfect time is unlikely.

Be Direct

The business of planned giving has changed over the years, but one thing is true: It will always remain a people business. Planned giving is also teamwork, building effective working relationships with donors, donors' advisors, and fundraising colleagues. It is a complex business that depends on skilled individuals who utilize multidisciplinary approaches to solving problems.

A successful planned giving staff cultivates solid development skills and maintains a professional image. These staff members approach the donor at arm's length, treating the interaction as the business relationship it truly is. Experienced staff members address business issues at the outset of a meeting, resolving the business matters first and leaving time for more relaxed informal conversation later. Both the planned giving staff and donors know why meetings are arranged; tend to the business portion of the meeting as early as possible. Donors make their gifts to fundraisers who are the most professional and skilled.

Know the Technical, Tax, and Legal Information

There is no substitute for knowledge when it comes to the tax consequences of charitable gifts or estate planning. Confusion can deflate the donor's interest and directs attention away from gift giving. Reread Chapters 7 through 14 to become conversant with some of the technical aspects of planned giving. Planned giving officers who do not know the answer to a donor's question should be up front and offer to research the answer. Anticipating likely technical questions is an effective form of preparation.

Know What Not to Say

Inexperienced development officers, because of nervousness or anxiety, often tend to speak too much and provide too much detail, becoming overly technical about the tax and financial aspects of a planned gift. Often, less said is more effective and creates opportunities for the donor to participate fully in the conversation. Each approach must contemplate the persona of the prospect, matching the needs of the nonprofit with the prospect's interests and matching the planned gift option with the prospect's financial needs.

Practice

As in most activities, practice makes perfect. For a solicitation, this is no different. Individuals new to planned giving should practice before a mirror or in front of family and friends who can provide direct feedback on approach, style, level of sincerity, and effectiveness. A videotape recording also provides an ideal opportunity to self evaluate a solicitation. The object of the practice session is not to memorize lines or make a speech but to anticipate the flow of conversation and prepare for prospective questions and develop appropriate responses. Role-playing also can be an effective and insightful strategy to prepare for a solicitation.

People Give to People

Philanthropy is a people business, and donors make gifts because they are asked to make a gift. Staff members or volunteers, serving as ambassadors on behalf of nonprofit organizations, communicate the organization's needs and mission to donors. These representatives establish long-term relationships with prospects and donors because major gifts secured through planned giving solicitations often take years to close. Staff must be patient and invest time in building relationships that permanently bond prospects with the charity. Staff members should possess strong interpersonal skills and should be well versed in the donor's areas of interest and in the nonprofit's services and mission. Planned giving is truly a people-to-people business.

Volunteer Involvement

At many charities, staff members work with volunteers and board members in making a solicitation. When volunteers are included, the staff member may not make the solicitation directly, but serves as an assistant to the volunteer, making introductions, facilitating conversation, and providing technical support to the volunteer who is not an expert in planned giving. Depending on the circumstances, the nature of the relationship, and the volunteer's motivation, the volunteer may play either an active or a passive role in the solicitation. Prior to the solicitation, the staff member should practice with the volunteer so that together they present a cohesive and coordinated message to the prospect. Properly trained volunteers can be exceptionally effective solicitors.

Involving New Staff Members

Soliciting a prospect with a previous giving record is a good way for new staff members to develop skills and confidence in soliciting and become comfortable interacting with donors. Donors with a gift history have already demonstrated loyalty and commitment to the nonprofit and are most likely to provide additional current and future support. Planned giving staff soliciting previous donors should begin the conversation with an expression of appreciation for the donors' past support, which may even serve as the basis of the visit. A conversation about donors' past support opens lines of communication and sets the stage for discussions about additional support.

Always Consider the Donor

Planned giving staff should view a solicitation from both the donor's and the charity's perspective to better understand the donor's frame of mind and potential reaction to the solicitation. Consider the following issues from the donor's perspective:

- Financial resources
- Family circumstances
- Relationship to the nonprofit
- Motivation for making the gift
- Available assets
- Experience with philanthropy

During conversations, be alert to the various types of assets that the donor may choose to use to fund a gift. All too often the focus is on cash when noncash assets, such as real estate or appreciated securities, should be considered.

Educating the Prospect about the Charity

Development professionals should assume that a prospect is unfamiliar with the specifics of the charity's mission. While most prospects have a general understanding of the services provided by the charity, the delivery or the nature of those services may change from time to time. Hospitals develop new centers of care or provide service to different constituents; museums may offer a new perspective or exhibit; educational institutions may introduce new programs, centers, institutes, or projects; religious organizations may offer elder care programs or children's libraries, and community playhouses may offer children's theater. Educating the prospect on innovations, changes in service, or changes in the charity's mission is an essential preliminary step in a successful solicitation.

In addition to educating prospects about the charity's mission, the planned giving staff must educate them about the available planned giving options. Carefully prepared letters and accompanying software calculations can focus prospects on one or two of the most appropriate gift options. A planned giving officer who takes the time to educate a donor will tend to produce larger gifts and more frequent gifts.

Research

Gathering basic background information is the first step in preparing for a donor meeting. Prior to a solicitation, the planned giving officer should develop a profile on the prospect that contains biographical, family, and occupational data and gift record information. More sophisticated donor profiles may contain additional data on the prospect's interests, affiliations, civic and community involvement, and relationship with the nonprofit. In addition, the profile should provide data on the prospect's giving history, including the date of the donor's last gift, largest gift, cumulative gift total, and gift designation. An excellent source of information about prospects is their paper file, which provides essential information on prospects' relationships with the nonprofit. Former or long-term staff members and volunteers of long standing also may have a mental record of key nonprofit prospects and donors.

The charity's computer system can supplement donors' paper files with information on prospects' giving history and also can record the names of nonprofit personnel with whom prospects have had contact. At many charities, computer activity codes are used to record a donor's participation in select events, programs, and activities.

Although the importance of research should never be understated, practicalities and realities may require that planned giving officers rely on listening skills and solid interpersonal skills when developing a donor profile in cases where none exists. In the absence of a profile, the first meeting with a prospect can be used primarily for orientation; second or future meetings can focus more directly on a solicitation. Planned giving officers should not be afraid to meet with a donor without having a full research profile of the donor.

SOLICITATION PROCESS

Now that the planned giving prospect and the donor's motivation for making a gift have been identified, we look at how to work with the planned giving prospect as the solicitation begins.

Long-Term Relationship

The relationship with the planned giving prospect is an ongoing one. The planned giving officer becomes well acquainted with this donor, learning intimate details of financial and personal matters. Conversations are ultimately about making a gift to the organization, but much is learned about the donor's feelings for the organization, family situation, relationships, finances, and long-term hopes and fears.

Basic Skills

If the planned giving staff member listens, the donor will tell what is needed to be known. Facilitate conversation by asking donors questions about themselves. Find topics of common interest. Let donors know that the organization cares about them. Be honest; if not, prospects will recognize insincerity quickly; trust is hard to recover once it is lost.

Donor's Background

What should the planned giving staff know about the donor when meeting with them for the first time? First, understand the donor's connection to the organization—is the donor a graduate? Grateful patient? Retired dean, physician, administrator, staff member, or friend of the organization? This should be learned at the office before meeting personally with the donor.

Then look at the donor's past giving record to the organization. How long has the donor been making gifts to the organization? At what level? Has the giving been consistent every year? If not, what interrupted the giving? Has the donor made a planned gift? If so, what type? See if there have been any dealings with the development office and if the dealings have gone smoothly. Perhaps an existing situation is causing difficulties for the donor; the staff member may be able to solve it. Files and databases tell only a portion of the story; the real story comes directly from the donor during a face-to-face meeting.

Let all donors indicate the area or program they wish to support. Do not rely solely on what a donor's file indicates as his or her area of interest. Development officers can pursue a donor's supposed area of interest, and then not understand why the prospect seems disinterested in making a gift.

Over time, relationships and feelings can change. What may have been of interest to a donor earlier may no longer be of interest today.

Learn about donors' assets and if they are trying to achieve a financial goal by making a planned gift. This information will help the development officer to discuss the best way to structure the gift appropriately. Donors may tell planned giving officers about their assets themselves, and a planned giving staff member can pick up clues when seeing a donor's home, material possessions, and accomplishments.

Seek to uncover any outstanding personal matters that may be relevant. For example, does the donor have a particular physical ailment, sick spouse, or disabled child? What personal factors may contribute to making or not making the gift? These issues can play a significant role in negotiations with a planned giving donor.

Contacting the Prospect

Solicitations may be conducted by mail, by telephone, or in person and usually involve a combination of all three. Unless the prospect contacts the nonprofit inquiring about a gift, the nonprofit must begin contact with the donor. To initiate the contact, the planned giving officer may call or send a letter to the prospect to set up an appointment to meet. Before the meeting, become familiar with the nonprofit's mission and planned giving options. Also determine how much time can be allocated toward personal visits with planned giving prospects; be realistic about the number of donors who can be seen. Determine what types of materials to take on personal visits, such as brochures, calculations, bequest language, and marketing pieces. Planned giving brochures and guides can elicit responses from donors and prospects. However, one-on-one personal contact is the key to successful planned giving solicitations.

Telephone Conversation

A telephone conversation with a prospect sensitizes the planned giving officer to a number of key factors:

- *Relationship with the nonprofit.* Speaking to a donor for the first time gives the planned giving staff member the opportunity to learn how the donor and the nonprofit are connected. At an educational institution, the staff member can learn about the donor's contacts and whether there are professional relationships still in existence with faculty. At a healthcare organization, the planned giving staff member can explore similar relationships to staff and whether the donor has attended public programs in the past.

- *Donor's motivation.*   During the conversation the planned giving officer can learn about the donor's motivation to make a gift, the seriousness of the donor's interest in pursuing the gift, and the anticipated timing of the gift.

- *Gift option.*   Staff members also may learn about the various gift options of interest to the donor, numbers of beneficiaries for a life income gift, and their ages. This valuable information enables the planned giving officer to prepare in advance planned giving calculations to be discussed during a meeting and can be sent with an accompanying letter prior to the meeting. This information can be obtained only if the conversation develops into a discussion about charitable giving.

- *Assets.*   Probe for information about the donor's assets that may be used to fund the gift. Gifts of cash pose few problems, but it is helpful to know in advance the cost basis of noncash assets such as securities and whether there is a mortgage on property likely to be used to fund a gift.

- *Designation.*   Comments from the donor regarding the anticipated designation of the gift may provide the planned giving officer with an opportunity to prepare an agreement or fund description for a named endowed fund.

Letters

A letter may be sent to a donor prior to or following the telephone call and always should be sent to follow up after a personal visit. A letter also can be used to provide information on the technical aspects of a planned gift option including calculations and tax benefits specific to the donor. Most important, letters are used to confirm the date, time, place, and next step in the process. Unlike a telephone call, a letter is one dimensional; it only carries information one way. It does, however, provide an opportunity to set the tone for or following a meeting and convey complex material.

- *Tone.* The letter sets the tone for the next stage of the solicitation and can be used effectively to show appreciation to the prospect. It also provides opportunity to reinforce the mission of the nonprofit and its charitable services.

- *Complex information.* A letter provides an opportunity to present information about planned giving options. Failing eyesight is common in later years, and large-print letters assist donors in understanding planned giving data.

- *Supporting materials.* Enclose additional materials about the nonprofit, its culture, heritage, and traditions.

The Personal Visit

A telephone call is usually the first step in setting up a donor meeting. In some cases, the staff member must speak to an intermediary (secretary or spouse) prior to speaking with the prospect. Most intermediaries are protective of the prospect and also are adept at deflecting requests. Say little to the intermediary about the nature of the telephone call.

A face-to-face personal visit is the preferred choice for a solicitation. A personal visit enables the planned giving officer to observe subtleties and nuances in the prospect's demeanor and reaction to the conversation. Prior to the personal visit, a member of the development staff should call to confirm the appointment. During the meeting, refer to materials previously sent by letter and bring an extra set in case the donor does not have the materials available.

The Role of Planned Giving Calculations in a Solicitation

In most cases, a planned giving officer should arrive at a donor meeting with material to leave with the donor at the end of the meeting. Gift calculations are ideal to leave with the donor, but a "Ways to Give" brochure or any type of news piece about the organization is also effective. The object is to keep the organization and information before the donor while emphasizing the need for funding.

Making the Ask

A planned giving solicitation is different from any other type of development solicitation. A planned gift includes calculations and tax benefits. By discussing these necessities with a donor, the ask is being made. The planned giving staff member certainly needs to discuss the organization's need for funding and the area at the organization that the donor is interested in supporting, but a planned giving solicitation often focuses on the financial benefits that the donor receives by making the gift. By illustrating these benefits, the staff member is making the solicitation. If the donor possesses donative intent, then whatever the financial obstacle is to the gift, it is likely to be overcome. A planned giving solicitation tends to focus more on how the gift will be made than on whether the gift will be made.

The solicitation of a planned giving prospect focuses on educating the donor about different types of planned gifts. Prior to meeting with a prospect, become completely familiar with each element of the gift option and anticipate questions regarding the tax consequences and financial advantages of the options. Reconfirm information about the relevant vehicles and be conversant with all data included in the planned giving calculations.

The presentation to the donor should not be overly technical or complex because too much detail can confuse a prospect, and a confused prospect is not likely to become a donor. It may be most effective to outline a general description of the mechanics of the gift and its financial benefits. Potential detriments, such as tax disadvantages, also should be explained to provide complete disclosure to the prospect. At the end, summarize the key elements of the gift options, then confirm everything in writing in a follow-up letter.

For most donors, the financial benefits are one part of the equation; the other, more important part is the satisfaction of providing financial support to a worthwhile cause. At the conclusion of the letter, reconfirm the donor's philanthropic intent.

Follow-up

One of the most important aspects of the solicitation is the need to follow up. The follow-up is more business oriented and focused on completing the gift. During the follow-up, any unresolved issues should be concluded, leaving no confusion in the prospect's mind. The follow-up may take place in the form of a letter, a telephone call, or a subsequent meeting, with or without the prospect's spouse or professional advisor.

- *Telephone call.* A follow-up by telephone is effective in resolving issues and is helpful to relationship building. The call reinforces the people-to-people aspect of the solicitation.

- *Letter.* A letter serves to reconfirm technical information and provides an additional opportunity to present supplementary material about the nonprofit and its mission. A letter also may contain specific information about one of the nonprofit's departments or programs of particular interest to the prospect.

- *Meeting.* A subsequent meeting combines the best of following up by telephone and letter. In addition, it enables the prospect's spouse or professional advisor to participate in the process and in any decision about a gift. Sometimes professional advisors can be obstacles; meeting the donor and his or her advisor to discuss issues associated with the gift can resolve confusion and dissension.

Closing the Gift

Bringing the solicitation to closure is one of the most important parts of the solicitation and one that tests a planned giving staff member's skills. At this point the solicitor's presence is important in refocusing attention on linking the prospect's financial support to achieving the nonprofit's mission through the funding of a specific objective. One's ability to organize and synthesize information in a logical and coherent message is critical. Bringing the gift to resolution is the greatest challenge of the job and is the most rewarding.

To bring a solicitation to a successful conclusion, it is helpful to use mutually agreed upon deadlines to encourage the donor to make a decision within a specified time frame. Deadlines, whether artificial or real, promote action and encourage prospects to become donors. The deadline may coincide with one or more of the following:

- Year-end closing—December 31
- Campaign stages
- Class reunions
- Homecoming
- Nonprofit's fiscal year-end

NEGOTIATIONS

In some cases, after a solicitation it is necessary to negotiate the terms, timing, or scope of the gift. The gift may be made much later or in a different tax year.

Fundamental Concepts

A solicitation is like a negotiation. Two fundamental concepts of negotiating are the recognition that all parties have a role and a stake in the process and outcome, and that areas of common ground must be established. Areas of common ground include the prospect's interest in one or more of the nonprofit's programs and the nonprofit's need to secure financial support. Negotiating with donors requires flexibility and room for maneuvering by both the donor and the charity. No donor ever likes to feel locked into a specific gift amount; the donor must be in control of the process and must determine the nature, timing, and scope of the gift.

Never Get to No

Donors need time to reach a conclusion about making a planned gift. Most initial personal visits do not result immediately in a planned gift. It is unrealistic to expect that a staff member can return to the nonprofit with a gift; if he or she does so, the gift is usually substantially smaller than it could have been. Allow adequate time for the donor to become involved in the process and comfortable with the concept of making a substantial gift. Short-circuiting the process by rushing the donor to make a gift produces small gifts.

Inexperienced staff members can phrase a solicitation in terms of a question, which results in a yes or no answer. In planned giving, the questions involved are much more complex, so the answers are unlikely to be a simple yes or no. Reinforcing of the nonprofit's mission, service, and the prospect's commitment, coupled with presenting the prospect with fundable alternatives and appropriate gift options, increases the chances for success.

Many gifts are lost because inexperienced staff members see a solicitation as an all-or-nothing proposition. A successful solicitation produces a gift that is appropriate from the donor's perspective and can benefit the nonprofit. It is important to remember that a gift at any level is always welcome and that a display of disappointment on the part of the planned giving officer is always inappropriate. The solicitor should remember that the first planned gift may be followed in later years by a larger gift. When soliciting a donor for a planned gift, a fundraiser can help the donor make a gift by spreading the gift over two to three years. Many major gifts are lost because the prospect is left with few alternatives. Be prepared to offer a variety of gift options using a variety of assets to assist a prospect in becoming a donor.

Overcoming Obstacles

Gifts can be lost because the staff member is unprepared for a donor's response. Donors, especially major donors, have more expertise at being the object of the solicitation than the planned giving officer has in making the ask. Major prospects are pursued by a variety of nonprofit organizations and are quite adept at deflecting or discouraging requests for financial support. Anticipating the prospect's deflection and being prepared to counter it is an important aspect of solicitation. Each of the following deflections can either be true or be used as an excuse to not make the gift:

• "I'd like to think about it."

   Delay.   Donors must take the time necessary to consider the appropriate response to a request that affects their financial resources. Prospects for a planned gift sometimes become overwhelmed by the complexity of the gift options. Some prospects delay in making the gift because they are more motivated to obtain favorable financial benefits and tax treatment and are less inclined to move forward due to an absence of philanthropic motivation. Uncovering the reason for the delay is likely to unlock a truthful response from the donor and shed light on the donor's motivation. Prospects who lack donative intent are unlikely to move forward in the process. Staff members must respect the wishes of the prospect but, at the same time, must seek needed funding for the nonprofit. Helping to set a reasonable and timely deadline for a decision while reinforcing the importance of the financial support can move the case forward.

- "I need to talk with my spouse."

  Spousal approval. Often a prospect pursues philanthropic interests on behalf of self and spouse. Sometimes the prospect is closer to the nonprofit and takes the lead in the couple's combined philanthropic pursuits while the other spouse remains passive. Dealing with a passive spouse who is absent from the cultivation and solicitation is a challenge. Even the most active spouse generally consults with the passive spouse, who not so surprisingly is often a key player in the decision.

  The solicitor can help the process along by making efforts to include both spouses, including addressing letters to both spouses, especially in cases where both spouses are the nonprofit's alumni, where both serve on one or more of the nonprofit's boards, or where both have personally made previous gifts. In the case of prospects who have not made previous gifts, the solicitor must determine if the issue of spousal approval is genuine or an attempt to deflect the request. This situation may be resolved by either having a meeting with both spouses to test the motivation of the active spouse or by establishing a mutually agreed upon deadline to complete the gift.

- "Not as long as he is president."

  Displaced Anger. During the cultivation process, prospects may have an opportunity to get to know the personalities and philosophies of the nonprofit's key players. Many prospects are favorably disposed to give but are put off by the actions, decisions, demeanor, personality, or philosophy of the nonprofit's president or by a policy or decision made by a board. Sometimes nonprofits are unintentionally adept at providing prospects with excuses not to give. A solicitor needs to refocus the prospect on the mission of the nonprofit and on the good work it performs on behalf of its constituents. One way to do this is by reminding the prospect that individuals, whether presidents or board members, come and go and the nonprofit has consistently provided valuable service for decades. The nonprofit outlasts any single individual, and a donor's financial support provides the nonprofit with the resources to do its work.

CONCLUSION

Soliciting donors for gifts is the most important part of a planned giving staff member's job. It is also the most fascinating, stimulating, and exciting aspect of the job. A nonprofit organization depends on the skills of its staff members, as do donors who rely on their expertise, knowledge, and interpersonal skills to make charitable giving a pleasant and rewarding experience. Anticipate potential responses by donors and be prepared to deal with obstacles. Solicitations are not all-or-nothing propositions. Negotiate to bring about a result that helps the charity and is in the donor's best interest.

CHAPTER 17

Ethics and Planned Giving

INTRODUCTION

Planned giving staff members have the opportunity to become intimately familiar with a donor's entire personal, professional, and business life. Consequently, conflicts can arise between doing what is best for the nonprofit organization and what is best for the donor. Nonprofit organizations and development offices have insatiable appetites for money, but this financial support cannot be obtained to the detriment of the donor. Due to the long and close relationship that can develop between a planned giving staff member and a donor, planned giving lends itself to more potential ethical dilemmas than other areas in the development profession. This chapter examines ethical issues that arise in planned giving, regardless of the size of the institution.

WHOM DOES THE PLANNED GIVING OFFICER REPRESENT?

While working with a prospect or donor to the organization, the planned giving staff member may find himself asking "For whom am I working? The organization that is paying me to raise money, or for the donor who is confiding in me?" It is important to remember that the planned giving staff member is hired by the organization to raise money and must keep the employer's goals in mind at all times. However, raising money cannot be done at the expense of an individual donor. Staff members bear an ethical responsibility to protect donors from giving away more money than they can afford to give. Striving to be honest, fair, and objective, the planned giving staff member can work with the donor to reach the organization's fundraising objectives while protecting the donor's interests.

HOW TO AVOID DONOR-RELATED CONFLICTS

A donor-related conflict can arise when a planned giving staff member is trying to raise money for the organization but learns something about the donor that causes him to question whether the proposed gift should be made. For example, a planned giving staff member may work with a donor who, just before (or after) making a gift, demonstrates that she does not fully understand the tax consequences or financial ramifications of the gift. When making a life income gift, the donor might ask whether she can receive the money back if she later becomes ill. Or the donor may be confused when actually writing out the check and is concerned about the amount of the tax deduction, income stream, or the size of the gift. These are warning signs that donors are not fully aware of the consequences of their actions.

A way to avoid a donor-related conflict is to suggest that the donor have a financial or legal advisor review a planned giving proposal or attend the meetings between the planned giving staff member and the donor. If possible, send a copy of all correspondence to the financial advisor. Also, when corresponding with a donor, include the statement "We advise you to consult with your attorney or financial advisor." Be sure that a donor has an appropriate amount of time to consider all of the gift options. Always try to meet personally with donors to learn more about them and determine competency. If donors do not understand the option, do not move forward.

Be certain that the prospect understands that the planned giving staff member represents the organization, not the donor. This is especially true when the planned giving staff member has an advanced degree, such as a law degree, that may encourage the donor to rely on the planned giving staff member's advice. Encourage donors who do not have their own advisor to speak with the nonprofit's attorney or outside manager, keeping in mind that these professionals are paid by the nonprofit. The goal is to promote as much input as possible for the donor. All of these things can help avoid a possible conflict of interest. In the end, the decision always belongs to the donor.

Following is a checklist for ways to help avoid potential donor conflicts:

- Have the donor consult with an outside financial advisor, lawyer, trust officer, or certified public accountant before making the gift.

- Include the outside advisor in meetings with the donor. Keep the advisor involved by sending him or her copies of correspondence. Try to speak directly with the outside advisor if possible.

- Include a statement on all correspondence that indicates that the donor should seek outside representation before making a planned gift. The statement should appear in letters to the donor and on gift calculations. The statement should not be a disclaimer; rather it should represent a genuine effort by the charity to enable the donor to confirm the appropriateness of the gift using independent advisors.

- Give the donor enough time to consider a gift proposal—two to five weeks may be appropriate.

- During conversations, the planned giving officer should remind the donor that the planned giving officer represents the nonprofit, not the donor.

- Meet personally with a donor to help judge whether the donor really understands the tax consequences of making the gift.

HOW MUCH MONEY IS TOO MUCH?

Sometimes their organization or management wants planned giving professionals to suggest a specific gift amount to a donor. Sometimes the donor will even ask, "How much should I give?" The staff member must balance the organization's need for financial support and development success with the donor's welfare. The organization would be embarrassed, perhaps humiliated, if the donor were left in an unsound financial position after making gifts to the nonprofit. For example, a donor who makes many gifts to a nonprofit could be unable to afford healthcare or be denied Medicaid coverage because of recent gifts. A nonprofit would feel uncomfortable knowing that the organization was benefiting at the expense of the donor's health or well-being. This is especially true if an individual development officer is involved, who may have known about the donor's health or financial position.

Consider accepting gifts gradually, over a period of time, if it is possible that donors may be too generous in making gifts above their means. When asked by a donor to suggest a specific gift amount, show the donor how much several gift levels "cost," such as the amount needed to endow a fund, name a patient room, or reach a particular club level. The size of the gift is up to the donor, but never accept a gift if it is possible that the donor is jeopardizing financial well-being.

HOW FRIENDLY SHOULD A PLANNED GIVING OFFICER BECOME WITH A DONOR?

Sometimes natural friendships develop between prospects and planned giving staff members. However, this really should be the exception rather than the rule. Maintain an appropriate professional distance from prospects because a close friendship can confuse the business relationship. Planned giving staff members should be aware of a potential conflict when donors invite them to off-hour social events, brings gifts, telephones a staff member at home, invites him or her to stay overnight when in the donor's town, or wants to leave the staff member something in the donor's will.

It is especially important to maintain some distance from older donors and prospects, especially those who are alone. Sometimes older donors can mistake business advances as acts of friendship and will continue meeting because it provides them with company and conversation. They may feel that making gifts to the organization assures them of continued attention.

Keep an appropriate distance by focusing conversations on business. Try to begin each meeting and telephone call by talking about the business at hand. Every meeting should relate to making gifts to the organization. For donors who seem more interested in building personal relationships than in making gifts to the nonprofit, invite other associates to participate in the meeting. If necessary, remind the donor that a staff member's role is to raise money for the nonprofit and while it is wonderful to get to know the donor, the primary reason for the relationship is to raise funds.

COMPLETE DISCLOSURE

Many times planned giving staff members become so involved with the positive aspects of the planned giving options that they forget or ignore potential negatives. Try to provide complete disclosure to donors at all times, including possible negative effects of making a gift, such as potential tax consequences and the legal fees incurred when creating such gifts as charitable remainder trusts and bequests. When working with donors who make gifts of securities, be sure to explain that the organization will sell the securities, not keep them in its portfolio.

PHILANTHROPY PROTECTION ACT OF 1995

The Philanthropy Protection Act of 1995 (PPA) requires charities to provide written disclosure to donors who retain an interest in the property if the property will be commingled with other charitable funds. The following items typically are included in PPA disclosure documents:

- Name and address of the charity
- Name and membership of the charity's governing board and committee responsible for managing the fund
- Description of the objective of the fund with an explanation about the method of distributing earnings to the fund
- Name and address of investment advisors and fund managers who invest assets on behalf of the charity
- Annual statement regarding the value of the principal in the account
- Statement describing whether the fund is a trust, corporation, or pooled fund
- Representative list of the types of securities held by the fund
- Statement that the donor's funds will be commingled with other donors' funds in a collective investment vehicle
- Statement that the fund is exempt from registration under federal securities laws
- Statement regarding the total market value of the fund
- Statement regarding restrictions or limitations for the investments of the fund
- Statement regarding the impact of risk on the market value of the investments in the pool

The act provides that employees, volunteers, officers, directors, and trustees who solicit funds on behalf of a charity are exempt from the registration requirements of federal securities laws, providing they have not received a commission or special compensation based on the number or value of donations collected for the fund. The PPA applies to charitable income funds, which include pooled income funds, collective trust funds, collective investment funds, and other funds maintained by charities exclusively for the investment and reinvestment of charitable gift annuities, charitable remainder trusts, lead trusts, or common endowment funds.

GIFT BROKERS AND FINDERS' FEES

Planned giving and development officers can find themselves in awkward situations regarding finders' fees. Over the last few years there has been an increasing amount of charitable gift brokering by agents acting or purporting to act on behalf of prospective donors. In some cases, there is no prospective donor and the agent is merely trying to obtain a consultant relationship with the nonprofit. In other cases, the agent is genuinely acting on behalf of a donor. In both cases, the agent, in exchange for a fee, is offering to deliver a donor who will make a gift to the nonprofit organization. In particular, small nonprofit organizations are targeted because of their purported inexperience in dealing with "gifts" of this type. The fee may be a lump-sum amount but it is usually a percentage of the value of the prospective gift. Because tax shelters have disappeared, planned giving options that shelter income, avoid capital gains taxes, and generate charitable income tax deductions have precipitated more aggressive gift brokering. Agents and some prospective donors shop around for the best deal that a nonprofit will offer, and life income gift discussions can center around the highest yearly rate of return the donor will receive. This new type of "philanthropist" has no donative intent and is treating the charitable gift purely as a business transaction.

Any agent who requests a fee for the service of identifying a prospective donor should be told that the organization does not wish to become involved with the transaction or know the name of the potential donor. This usually brings the conversation to an end and, at the very least, puts the agent and the donor (if there is one) on notice that this form of transaction is prohibited. Sometimes when an agent knows a fee cannot be earned, the agent will disclose the name of the prospect to the organization or may resurface several months later and offer the name of the donor free of charge in a show of good faith.

COMMISSIONED REAL ESTATE AGENTS OR BROKERS

Sometimes an agent representing a prospective donor is a commissioned agent, stockbroker, real estate broker, or chartered life underwriter acting in the normal course of business, on behalf of a client. When a piece of property is sold, the broker normally receives a commission, but gifted property produces no commission. If property has just been listed on the market and is then gifted, then the broker has rendered little or no service to the owner of the property; therefore, no fee should be paid to a broker who delivers such property to a nonprofit organization from a donor making a gift of property.

If a piece of property has been on the market for an extended period of time and the broker delivers the owner to the nonprofit to make a gift, then the broker usually will ask for a commission. A nonprofit organization should inform the broker that it is against the organization's policy to pay a commission for a gift of property. The organization should have a policy statement in place, approved by the board of trustees, to this effect. It may be appropriate to reimburse the broker for reasonable costs incurred in listing the property, such as advertising, multiple listing service fees, and other marketing costs. If the organization receives the property as a gift, it may choose to list the property with the broker, which will put the broker back in the same position prior to the donor's gift. Be certain that there is no formal documentation obligating the nonprofit to list the property with a specific broker.

COMMISSIONED STOCKBROKERS

When donors make a gift of securities from a brokerage account to a nonprofit, they often wish to generate a commission for their brokers. Some stockbrokers do not encourage clients to make gifts because it reduces the donors' portfolios and therefore the brokers' commissions. As described in Chapter 10, it takes an extra step for the donor's broker to set up an account in the nonprofit's name and then sell the securities; the broker could more efficiently transfer the securities to the nonprofit and have the nonprofit sell the securities; however, no commission would be generated for the donor's broker.

The planned giving officer needs to work with donors and let them decide how to transfer the securities. The planned giving officer should tell donors that is unnecessary and perhaps more costly for the donors' brokers to handle the transaction, but if donors are concerned with providing their brokers with a commission, the organization is happy to oblige the donors' wishes.

PAYMENT OF PROFESSIONAL ADVISORS' AND LAWYERS' FEES

Professional advisors, such as attorneys and certified public accountants, charge their clients fees in conjunction with the clients' business transactions. Donors occasionally request that the nonprofit pay for these costs when making a planned gift to the organization. This occurs most often seen when documents like wills and trusts must be drafted and donors feel that since the nonprofit is a primary or sole beneficiary, the nonprofit should absorb the cost. Prospects can become quite upset when they are asked to pay the drafting fees when making a substantial gift.

Donors have the legal obligation to pay for these services and can deduct, as miscellaneous deductions, expenses and fees paid to professional advisors for tax-related advice and services. A nonprofit that steps in to pay for these services is accepting an obligation of donors and is conferring a benefit on them. When a nonprofit confers such a benefit on donors, the payment for these services may be treated as a gain for federal income tax purposes. Advise donors that they may jeopardize their charitable income tax deduction if the nonprofit pays the fees.

Each organization must decide whether to pay for various legal expenses. Many organizations are uncomfortable with paying for the drafting of a donor's will, perhaps because a bequest to a nonprofit is revocable. Many organizations are, however, willing to pay for outside counsel to draft a donor's charitable remainder trust, especially if the charity is sole or primary beneficiary. If the nonprofit organization is willing to pay for the cost of drafting a charitable remainder trust, the planned giving officer needs to urge donors to have the trust reviewed by their own attorneys. Do not allow donors to rely solely on the nonprofit for legal advice. If for any reason donors are not satisfied with the trust arrangement, they may later blame the nonprofit organization.

PRIOR EXISTING AGREEMENTS

For a donor to claim a charitable income tax deduction for a gift of an asset to a nonprofit, the donor must make the gift free of any conditions or strings attached. Restrictions that create problems are found most often with gifts of real estate and closely held stock. These restrictions include:

- A specific timeframe for disposing of the gift
- A preexisting written agreement that binds the nonprofit to resell the gift to a specific third party
- A requirement that the donor will oversee the investment of the gift
- An agreement that binds the nonprofit to list property with a specific broker

A nonprofit should not accept a gift that restricts the right to do with the property whatever the organization, as rightful owner, could do with it. Planned giving staff members must tell donors that once a gift is made, the donor will no longer retain control over it. It is up to the organization to decide whether to sell the asset, hold onto it, or invest it. Talking openly with donors before a gift is made can reduce the likelihood that they will want to exercise subsequent control over the asset.

NONPROFIT ORGANIZATION SERVING AS TRUSTEE

An important issue for any small nonprofit organization is whether it should serve as a trustee of a charitable remainder trust that benefits the organization. There is a potential conflict of interest if the organization serves as a trustee and receives the remainder of the trust while being obligated to provide income streams to living income beneficiaries. The potential conflict occurs when the nonprofit organization, as a trustee, makes investment decisions about how the trust should be invested. Income beneficiaries of a charitable remainder trust are likely to prefer maximum current income streams, while the remainder beneficiary (nonprofit) wishes to preserve the corpus for its ultimate use. These two goals can be mutually exclusive, and it is a challenge to keep both income and remainder beneficiaries satisfied.

To avoid this conflict, a nonprofit may choose not to serve as trustee of the charitable remainder trust. If the donor insists on having the nonprofit organization serve as trustee, the nonprofit should disclose and explain the potential conflict of interest to the donor. If the organization is the only remainder beneficiary and the donor or spouse is the only income beneficiary, then it may be acceptable to serve as trustee as long as the income beneficiaries are told of the potential investment conflict. The charity also may choose to serve as co-trustee with a bank or trust company that is responsible for the investment decisions and can balance the needs of the income beneficiaries while protecting the remainder beneficiary.

NONPROFIT SERVING AS EXECUTOR OR PERSONAL REPRESENTATIVE

Sometimes nonprofit organizations are asked to serve as the executor or personal representative of an estate. The executor or personal representative is responsible upon the testator's death to gather all assets, discharge debts, and dispose of property in accordance with the donor's wishes. This time-consuming process can be fraught with problems. A nonprofit should discourage donors from naming employees as personal representative or executor of a donor's estate. The wishes of the organization as a beneficiary may compete with the wishes or rights of other individual beneficiaries. Additionally, most small nonprofits are not equipped to go through the time-consuming probate and estate settlement process.

ETHICS IN MARKETING

Charitable gift planners must be aware of potential ethical issues when marketing planned giving options. All marketing pieces, such as ads, should inform the potential donor that gifts to the nonprofit organization are irrevocable. While the focus of the ad may be on the financial benefits of making a gift, the nonprofit must not be presented as an alternative to a bank or an investment firm. The donor who makes a planned gift to a nonprofit must, above all else, have the desire to make a gift to the organization.

PLANNED GIVING STAFF MEMBER AS SALESPERSON

Planned giving staff members should not be viewed as salespeople who are selling a financial product. Staff members should present themselves as professional advisors whose expertise is in charitable gift planning. A quota-driven development program conflicts with a quality planned giving program, which requires an appropriate amount of patience and time.

ETHICAL DILEMMAS WITH OTHER DEVELOPMENT OFFICERS

In most organizations, because several members of a development staff are likely to come in contact with a specific prospect or donor, there is the possibility of a conflict among members of a development staff when the gift is made from a donor. A prospect control/prospect management system can help to avoid such conflicts, but the potential for problems still exists. As a development staff member, always consult with the central filing system in the office to check for the existence of correspondence that has been sent to a donor and obtain clearance from the director of prospect management prior to pursuing a prospect.

If the prospect is from a specific college, department, or program—for example, a graduate of the College of Business or a cardiac patient—the development officer assigned to that area should be consulted regarding all activity with that prospect. Planned giving staff members in most organizations are central office employees who work for the entire organization, and they often can find themselves at odds with other development staff. Full disclosure about activity with a prospect is the best course of action.

MODEL STANDARDS OF PRACTICE FOR THE CHARITABLE GIFT PLANNER

The Model Standards of Practice for the Charitable Gift Planner were adopted by the National Committee on Planned Giving to encourage responsible charitable gift planning by anyone involved in the charitable gift planning process. The Model Standards of Practice address some of the primary ethical concerns in planned giving and should be read by everyone in the planned giving business. Exhibit 17.1 presents the Model Standards of Practice for the Charitable Gift Planner.

DONOR'S BILL OF RIGHTS AND AFP CODE OF ETHICAL PRINCIPLES

A Donor Bill of Rights and AFP Code of Ethical Principles and Standards of Professional Practice (see Exhibits 17.2 and 17.3) is reprinted below.

EXHIBIT 17.1   MODEL STANDARDS OF PRACTICE FOR
THE CHARITABLE GIFT PLANNER

Preamble

The purpose of this statement is to encourage responsible charitable gift planning by urging the adoption of the following Standards of Practice by all who work in the charitable gift planning process, including charitable institutions and their gift planning officers, independent fund-raising consultants, attorneys, accountants, financial planners, and life insurance agents, collectively referred to hereafter as "Gift Planners."

This statement recognizes that the solicitation, planning and administration of a charitable gift is a complex process involving philanthropic, personal, financial and tax considerations, and as such often involves professionals from various disciplines whose goals should include working together to structure a gift that achieves a fair and proper balance between the interests of the donor and the purposes of the charitable institution.

I.   Primacy of Philanthropic Motivation

The principal basis for making a charitable gift should be a desire on the part of the donor to support the work of charitable institutions.

II.   Explanation of Tax Implications

Congress has provided tax incentives for charitable giving, and the emphasis in this statement on philanthropic motivation in no way minimizes the necessity and appropriateness of a full and accurate explanation by the Gift Planner of those incentives and their implications.

III.   Full Disclosure

It is essential to the gift planning process that the role and relationships of all parties involved, including how and by whom each is compensated, be fully disclosed to the donor. A Gift Planner shall not act or purport to act as a representative of any charity without the expressed knowledge and approval of the charity, and shall not, while employed by the charity, act or purport to act as a representative of the donor, without the expressed consent of both the charity and the donor.

IV.   Compensation

Compensation paid to Gift Planners shall be reasonable and proportionate to the services provided. Payments of finder's fees, commissions or other fees by a donee organization to an independent Gift Planner as a condition for the delivery of a gift are never appropriate. Such payments lead to abusive practices and may violate certain state and federal regulations. Likewise, commission-based compensation for Gift Planners who are employed by a charitable institution is never appropriate.

V.   Competence and Professionalism

The Gift Planner should strive to achieve and maintain a high degree of competence in his or her chosen area, and shall advise donors only in areas in which he or she is professionally qualified. It is a hallmark of professionalism for Gift Planners that they realize when they have reached the limits of their knowledge and expertise, and as a result, should include other professionals in the process. Such relationships should be characterized by courtesy, tact, and mutual respect.

VI. Consultation with Independent Advisers

A Gift Planner acting on behalf of a charity shall in all cases strongly encourage the donor to discuss the proposed gift with competent independent legal and tax advisers of the donor's choice.

VI. Consultation with Charities

Although Gift Planners frequently and properly counsel donors concerning specific charitable gifts without the prior knowledge or approval of the donee organization, the Gift Planner, in order to insure that the gift will accomplish the donor's objectives, should encourage the donor, early in the gift planning process, to discuss the proposed gift with the charity to whom the gift is to be made. In cases where the donor desires anonymity, the Gift Planner shall endeavor, on behalf of the undisclosed donor, to obtain the charity's input in the gift planning process.

VIII. Explanation of Gift

The Gift Planner shall make every effort, insofar as possible, to ensure that the donor receives a full and accurate explanation of all aspects of the proposed charitable gift.

IX. Full Compliance

A Gift Planner shall fully comply with and shall encourage other parties in the gift planning process to fully comply with both the letter and spirit of all applicable federal and state laws and regulations.

X. Public Trust

Gift Planners shall, in all dealings with donors, institutions, and other professionals, act with fairness, honesty, integrity, and openness. Except for compensation received for services, the terms of which have been disclosed to the donor, they shall have no vested interest that could result in personal gain.

*We thank the National Committee on Planned Giving for allowing us to reprint the Model Standards of Practice for the Charitable Gift Planner. Additional copies are available from the National Committee on Planned Giving.

EXHIBIT 17.2   A DONOR BILL OF RIGHTS

A Donor Bill of Rights

PHILANTHROPY is based on voluntary action for the common good. It is a tradition of giving and sharing that is primary to the quality of life. To assure that philanthropy merits the respect and trust of the general public, and that donors and prospective donors can have full confidence in the not-for-profit organizations and causes they are asked to support, we declare that all donors have these rights:

I.
To be informed of the organization's mission, of the way the organization intends to use donated resources, and of its capacity to use donations effectively for their intended purposes.

II.
To be informed of the identity of those serving on the organization's governing board, and to expect the board to exercise prudent judgement in its stewardship responsibilities.

III.
To have access to the organization's most recent financial statements.

IV.
To be assured their gifts will be used for the purposes for which they were given.

V.
To receive appropriate acknowledgement and recognition.

VI.
To be assured that information about their donations is handled with respect and with confidentiality to the extent provided by law.

VII.
To expect that all relationships with individuals representing organizations of interest to the donor will be professional in nature.

VIII.
To be informed whether those seeking donations are volunteers, employees of the organization or hired solicitors.

IX.
To have the opportunity for their names to be deleted from mailing lists that an organization may intend to share.

X.
To feel free to ask questions when making a donation and to receive prompt, truthful and forthright answers.

DEVELOPED BY
AMERICAN ASSOCIATION OF FUND RAISING COUNSEL (AAFRC)
ASSOCIATION FOR HEALTHCARE PHILANTHROPY (AHP)
COUNCIL FOR ADVANCEMENT AND SUPPORT OF EDUCATION (CASE)
ASSOCIATION OF FUNDRAISING PROFESSIONALS (AFP)

ENDORSED BY
(IN FORMATION)
INDEPENDENT SECTOR
NATIONAL CATHOLIC DEVELOPMENT CONFERENCE (NCDC)
NATIONAL COMMITTEE ON PLANNED GIVING (NCPG)
COUNCIL FOR RESOURCE DEVELOPMENT (CRD)
UNITED WAY OF AMERICA

Please help us distribute this widely.

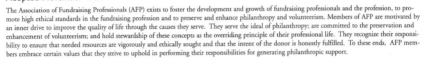

EXHIBIT 17.3 AFP CODE OF ETHICAL PRINCIPLES AND STANDARDS OF PROFESSIONAL PRACTICE

AFP Code of Ethical Principles and Standards of Professional Practice

STATEMENT OF ETHICAL PRINCIPLES
Adopted November 1991

The Association of Fundraising Professionals (AFP) exists to foster the development and growth of fundraising professionals and the profession, to promote high ethical standards in the fundraising profession and to preserve and enhance philanthropy and volunteerism. Members of AFP are motivated by an inner drive to improve the quality of life through the causes they serve. They serve the ideal of philanthropy; are committed to the preservation and enhancement of volunteerism; and hold stewardship of these concepts as the overriding principle of their professional life. They recognize their responsibility to ensure that needed resources are vigorously and ethically sought and that the intent of the donor is honestly fulfilled. To these ends, AFP members embrace certain values that they strive to uphold in performing their responsibilities for generating philanthropic support.

AFP members aspire to:
- practice their profession with integrity, honesty, truthfulness and adherence to the absolute obligation to safeguard the public trust;
- act according to the highest standards and visions of their organization, profession and conscience;
- put philanthropic mission above personal gain;
- inspire others through their own sense of dedication and high purpose;
- improve their professional knowledge and skills in order that their performance will better serve others;
- demonstrate concern for the interests and well being of individuals affected by their actions;
- value the privacy, freedom of choice and interests of all those affected by their actions;
- foster cultural diversity and pluralistic values, and treat all people with dignity and respect;
- affirm, through personal giving, a commitment to philanthropy and its role in society;
- adhere to the spirit as well as the letter of all applicable laws and regulations;
- advocate within their organizations, adherence to all applicable laws and regulations;
- avoid even the appearance of any criminal offense or professional misconduct;
- bring credit to the fundraising profession by their public demeanor;
- encourage colleagues to embrace and practice these ethical principles and standards of professional practice; and
- be aware of the codes of ethics promulgated by other professional organizations that serve philanthropy.

STANDARDS OF PROFESSIONAL PRACTICE
Adopted and incorporated into the AFP Code of Ethical Principles November 1992

Furthermore, while striving to act according to the above values, AFP members agree to abide by the AFP Standards of Professional Practice, which are adopted and incorporated into the AFP Code of Ethical Principles. Violation of the Standards may subject the member to disciplinary sanctions, including expulsion, as provided in the AFP Ethics Enforcement Procedures.

Professional Obligations

1. Members shall not engage in activities that harm the member's organization, clients, or profession.
2. Members shall not engage in activities that conflict with their fiduciary, ethical, and legal obligations to their organizations and their clients.
3. Members shall effectively disclose all potential and actual conflicts of interest; such disclosure does not preclude or imply ethical impropriety.
4. Members shall not exploit any relationship with a donor, prospect, volunteer or employee to the benefit of the member or the member's organization.

5. Members shall comply with all applicable local, state, provincial, federal, civil and criminal laws.
6. Members recognize their individual boundaries of competence and are forthcoming and truthful about their professional experience and qualifications.

Solicitation and Use of Charitable Funds

7. Members shall take care to ensure that all solicitation materials are accurate and correctly reflect the organization's mission and use of solicited funds.
8. Members shall take care to ensure that donors receive informed, accurate and ethical advice about the value and tax implications of potential gifts.
9. Members shall take care to ensure that contributions are used in accordance with donors' intentions.
10. Members shall take care to ensure proper stewardship of charitable contributions, including timely reports on the use and management of funds.
11. Members shall obtain explicit consent by the donor before altering the conditions of a gift.

Presentation of Information

12. Members shall not disclose privileged or confidential information to unauthorized parties.
13. Members shall adhere to the principle that all donor and prospect information created by, or on behalf of, an organization is the property of that organization and shall not be transferred or utilized except on behalf of that organization.
14. Members shall give donors the opportunity to have their names removed from lists that are sold to, rented to, or exchanged with other organizations.
15. Members shall, when stating fundraising results, use accurate and consistent accounting methods that conform to the appropriate guidelines adopted by the American Institute of Certified Public Accountants (AICPA)* for the type of organization involved. (*In countries outside of the United States, comparable authority should be utilized.)

Compensation

16. Members shall not accept compensation that is based on a percentage of charitable contributions; nor shall they accept finder's fees.
17. Members may accept performance-based compensation, such as bonuses, provided such bonuses are in accord with prevailing practices within the members' own organizations, and are not based on a percentage of charitable contributions.
18. Members shall not pay finder's fees, commissions or percentage compensation based on charitable contributions and shall take care to discourage their organizations from making such payments.

Amended October 1999

The Donor's Bill of Rights is endorsed by a variety of organizations including the Association of Fundraising Professionals (AFP).

CONCLUSION

Charitable gift planners have an ethical obligation to nonprofit organizations, donors, and themselves. The most ethical choices must be made when working with donors and other individuals who are involved in the gift planning process. Regularly ask if the right thing is being done and remember that no gift is ever worth receiving if it is not obtained ethically.

PART SIX

Marketing

18

Marketing Planned Giving in Small Nonprofit Organizations

INTRODUCTION

Planned giving is not just the mastery of charitable gift planning techniques, it is similar to starting a small business start-up with the planned giving staff member serving as the entrepreneur. The most successful businesses are clear about the products they offer, understand the audience they are trying to reach, and use marketing strategies to reach the targeted audience. Often marketing is the most overlooked part of a planned giving program. Marketing attracts donors and prospects to a nonprofit organization.

Marketing is a comprehensive, integrated campaign designed to educate an organization's constituents about the organization and its needs for funding. Marketing creates a heightened level of visibility and awareness and projects a positive image about the planned giving program and the nonprofit organization. Marketing is concerned not only with educating prospects about planned giving vehicles but also about articulating the needs of the organization. This chapter discusses the elements of marketing and provides an overview of the ways to market using printed materials, programs, and electronic communications to promote a planned giving program to donors and prospects at small nonprofit organizations.

THE MESSAGE, THE AUDIENCE, AND THE MEDIUM

The *message* is the most important aspect of marketing, yet it is often overlooked. For some reason the message is taken for granted, although to recipients the message is often the most important part. What is the message that needs to be conveyed? What do the recipients need to know? How will the message impact recipients? Answering these questions in advance will improve the effect of the message.

To market successfully, it is also critical to define the *audience* that is being targeted and to use the most effective marketing strategy to reach that audience. The message must be focused to reach its intended audience. Audiences can be young or old; sophisticated or unsophisticated; male or female; black, white, Hispanic, or another ethnicity; wealthy or of modest means; from rural, urban, or suburban areas; with unique interests, experiences, and education.

A small nonprofit organization can reach a wide variety of audiences. Consider the demographic profiles just discussed above when marketing to the following audiences:

- Donors
- Prospects
- Families/parents
- Senior administrators
- Faculty/staff
- Professional advisors

A small nonprofit organization's demographics influences the medium used to deliver the message. The *medium* is the method used to communicate the information to the intended audience. The medium may be specific types of printed materials, media marketing, verbal communications, or electronic communications.

MARKETING FUNDAMENTALS

Marketing fundamentals should be understood to successfully attract business to a planned giving program. To educate donors and prospects, a planned giving program needs to be marketed in a regular and systematic fashion over a long period of time. Each marketing effort—whether printed materials like a planned giving newsletter, advertisement or brochure, or electronic forms of communication such as e-mail—should be produced in a similar style. Printed ads should be placed in approximately the same location in a nonprofit's publications each time they appear. Programs for the public or for targeted audiences such as workshops, recognition events, or luncheons must occur annually to sustain the effort and maintain interest. Remember that planned gifts do not generally close right away, and it is the cumulative impact of marketing over time, along with follow-up and staff involvement, that results in a donor making a planned gift. The following four components are part of a marketing program:

1. *Continuity.* Continuity shows the recipient that each individual marketing effort is part of a whole.

2. *Consistency.* The message should be consistent visually and in terms of content.

3. *Repetition.* Once the process of marketing has begun, it must be repeated over time with each effort reinforcing and building on the previous efforts.

4. *Cumulative effect.* No single marketing effort is responsible for causing a donor to act or develop a positive impression; rather, all of the marketing efforts have a cumulative effect. This is why marketing cannot be done occasionally. Marketing must be done frequently and regularly to produce the ultimate results.

MARKETING THROUGH PRINTED MATERIALS

Marketing lets donors know that the nonprofit organization has a planned giving program, even if it is a modest program and consists only of bequests, trusts, and gifts of cash and securities. Develop marketing materials such as ads, buckslips, newsletters, and brochures to promote those options. Buckslips are about the size of a dollar bill and can be easily inserted in general mailings. Consider the following specific marketing ideas to promote a planned giving program in the first year.

Advertisements

At a small nonprofit organization, staff members should determine which gift vehicles to promote, draft advertisements for those gift vehicles, and place them in publications already produced by the organization, such as an alumni magazine, donor newsletter, or publication for subscribers or patrons. Always include a response form for donors to request additional information about leaving a gift to the organization in their will or to indicate that they have already made a bequest to the organization. Consider including a check-off box that allows donors to ask for more information about creating a charitable remainder trust to benefit the charity. Exhibit 18.1 is a response form for a life income gift.

Annual Fund Appeals

At a small charity, the delineation of duties and departments of a development office is not always clear. This can be a positive influence on developing collaborative working arrangements among staff members. Annual fund staff and planned giving staff can collaborate on many projects. As part

---

EXHIBIT 18.1 FORM: RESPONSE MECHANISM—LIFE INCOME GIFT

<ORGANIZATION>
OFFICE OF DEVELOPMENT

Please send me more information about:

Receiving income from my gift
____ Your age
____ Spouse's age (if applicable)
____ My gift will be funded with cash.
____ My gift will be funded with stock.
____ My stock is valued at $ _____.
____ My stock was purchased for $ _____.

Name: _____
Address:
City: _____ State: _____ Zip: _____
Telephone:
_____

Send to:
<ORGANIZATION>, <NAME>, <TITLE>, <ADDRESS>, <CITY, STATE ZIP>, <TELEPHONE>.

of a planned giving effort, include a check-off box on the annual fund appeal that urges donors to request information about making a planned gift. The response letter to the donor should discuss the benefits of planned giving, including a life income stream, a charitable tax deduction, and possible avoidance or reduction of capital gains taxes. This collaborative approach among development office staff members increases the chances of success.

Annual giving and planned giving also can team up to market gifts of securities. Many donors make gifts of securities of their own volition. Actively promoting gifts of securities during annual giving appeals increases the chances that additional donors will make these gifts. Describe the ways securities are transferred and the benefits of these gifts (charitable income tax deductions and avoidance of capital gains tax on gift of securities held long-term), and donors will ask for information. Exhibit 18.2 is an example of an advertisement marketing gifts of securities.

Targeted Mailings

A major part of a planned giving program is identifying, cultivating, and soliciting planned giving prospects. Begin the process by sorting through files to rejuvenate relationships with any prospects who have requested planned giving information in the past.

EXHIBIT 18.2 AD: GIFT OF APPRECIATED SECURITIES

Do you own low-yielding or appreciated securities?

The ‹ORGANIZATION› Pooled Income Fund can help you while you help ‹ORGANIZATION›. For a minimum gift of $5,000 you can:

- Increase your yield substantially (current rate is ‹ % ›)
- Avoid capital gains tax on gifts of appreciated securities
- Receive an income for life
- Receive an immediate charitable income tax deduction
- Become a member of a ‹ORGANIZATION› leadership club

The Office of Development will send you a personalized financial analysis that shows you how a contribution to the Pooled Income Fund can benefit both you and ‹ORGANIZATION›. Please contact ‹NAME›, ‹TITLE›, ‹ORGANIZATION›, ‹ADDRESS›, ‹CITY, STATE ZIP›; ‹TELEPHONE›.

Use targeted mailings to identify prospects rather than for soliciting them. Consider targeting all donors to the annual fund who have made gifts for 2 to 3 years and are over a certain age, such as 65. Send a personal letter describing what the organization offers in planned giving and include a way for them to request more information. A trustee, the president, or a volunteer who has made a planned gift can sign the letter, or the development director can. The letter may target donors who have recently made stock gifts to the annual fund, or, depending on the size of the development program, it can be mailed to all donors. Be sure to distribute the letters in a way that allows the office to respond adequately to inquiries. Rather than being inundated with inquiries, send letters over time, so that follow-up can be done in a timely manner.

A special letter also can be mailed to trustees. The aim of this letter is twofold; it shows the trustees that a planned giving program is being launched, and it enables a trustee to jump-start a planned giving program with a planned gift. A lead planned gift from a trustee can be used to encourage other trustees to give, and the trustee can be profiled in an upcoming newsletter.

Brochures

A third part of the marketing effort should be brochures. Depending on which gift option is offered, a new brochure may be needed that is different from the one the office currently uses. Prepare one that describes the history and philosophy of the organization and includes information on ways to make a cash gift, a gift of securities, a gift through a bequest, and a trust. Small nonprofit organizations can offer charitable gift annuities and pooled income funds. Outline the benefits to the donor of making each kind of gift, including areas and programs that need private support.

A brochure does not need to be expensive or complicated. To keep expenses down, try to produce it in the office. Fancy brochures do not necessarily produce greater responses. Instead, get results with "homegrown" marketing materials produced in-house that deliver real messages about the services offered to those who need to know. Ask a planned giving colleague to review the brochure and suggest appropriate changes. Exhibit 18.3 is an example of a short guide to planned giving.

EXHIBIT 18.3 BROCHURE: PLANNING GIVING MINI-GUIDE

TAX PLANNING AND CHARITABLE GIVING AT ‹ORGANIZATION›

The Office of Development presents donors with financial options that benefit both the donors and ‹ORGANIZATION›. Most of our financial vehicles, such as gift annuities, deferred gift annuities, the pooled income fund, and trusts, provide the donor with income for life. These vehicles pay a rate of return that often exceeds money market and CD rates. In addition, some of these vehicles avoid capital gains taxes and reduce estate taxes. We also work with donors who make gifts through their estates while preserving assets for their current needs. Let us help you while you help ‹ORGANIZATION› by making a gift to ‹ORGANIZATION›.

Gift by Check

A gift by check may be made outright or pledged over a period of up to five years. If you itemize your tax deductions your gift is fully deductible up to 50% of your adjusted gross income. Any excess can be carried forward for up to five additional years.

Appreciated Securities

Your outright gift of long-term, appreciated securities (stocks, mutual funds, and bonds) is exempt from capital gains taxes and, in most cases, enables you to obtain a charitable income tax deduction equal to the market value of the securities at the time of transfer for up to 30% of your adjusted gross income. Any excess can be carried over for up to five additional years.

Life Income Gifts

A donor can make a gift to ‹ORGANIZATION› and receive direct financial benefits. The benefits include an income for life for the donor and/or the donor's spouse and a charitable income tax deduction. The following three options—the charitable gift annuity, the pooled income fund, and the deferred gift annuity—require a minimum gift of ‹ $ ›, which may be designated to benefit any department or program at ‹ORGANIZATION›.

Charitable Gift Annuity

A gift annuity is a contract between the donor and ‹ORGANIZATION› that provides advantages to both. The donor makes a gift and receives a guaranteed payment for life and a charitable income tax deduction. The payout rate on a gift annuity is based on the age of the donor at the time the gift is made. Charitable gift annuities may be funded with cash, securities, or property. Payouts may be made annually, semiannually, quarterly, or monthly.

Benefits from a $5,000 Charitable Gift Annuity*

Age	Payout Rate	Annual Income	Tax Deduction
65	‹ % ›	‹ $ ›	‹ $ ›
70	‹ % ›	‹ $ ›	‹ $ ›
75	‹ % ›	‹ $ ›	‹ $ ›
80	‹ % ›	‹ $ ›	‹ $ ›

*Figures based on current discount rate of ‹ % ›.

EXHIBIT 18.3 BROCHURE: PLANNING GIVING MINI-GUIDE
(CONTINUED)

The Pooled Income Fund

The pooled income fund is similar to a mutual fund. Your gift is pooled with other donors' gifts and assigned a proportionate interest in the fund. The rate is variable and currently pays ‹ % › to each participant. You may name a second beneficiary to receive a life income from your gift after your death. Ultimately, the gift will pass to ‹ORGANIZATION› to be used in accordance with your wishes.

Benefits from a $5,000 Gift to the Pooled Income Fund*

Age	Payout Rate	Annual Income	Tax Deduction
50	‹ % ›	‹ $ ›	‹ $ ›
55	‹ % ›	‹ $ ›	‹ $ ›
60	‹ % ›	‹ $ ›	‹ $ ›
65	‹ % ›	‹ $ ›	‹ $ ›
70	‹ % ›	‹ $ ›	‹ $ ›

*Figures based on current discount rate of ‹ % ›.

Deferred Gift Annuity

A deferred gift annuity is similar to a charitable gift annuity, except that the payments are deferred to a future date. In addition, the donor obtains a substantial charitable income tax deduction in the year the gift is made. A deferred gift annuity is an excellent way for younger donors to make a gift and receive a charitable income tax deduction while providing income for the future.

Benefits from a $5,000 Deferred Gift Annuity deferred to age 65*

Age	Payout Rate	Annual Income	Tax Deduction
30	‹ % ›	‹ $ ›	‹ $ ›
35	‹ % ›	‹ $ ›	‹ $ ›
40	‹ % ›	‹ $ ›	‹ $ ›
45	‹ % ›	‹ $ ›	‹ $ ›
50	‹ % ›	‹ $ ›	‹ $ ›

*Figures based on current discount rate of ‹ % ›.

Charitable Remainder Trust

A charitable remainder trust provides a lifetime income and a charitable income tax deduction. The donor selects the payout rate, usually between 5 and 7 percent. The higher the payout rate, the lower the charitable income tax deduction. This gives the donor, and perhaps the donor's spouse, an income every year for life.

Annuity Trust and Unitrust

An annuity trust pays a fixed, guaranteed dollar amount regardless of the trust's investment performance.

A unitrust pays the donor a predetermined percentage of the fair market value of the trust's assets as revalued annually.

EXHIBIT 18.3 BROCHURE: PLANNING GIVING MINI-GUIDE
(CONTINUED)

Capital gains taxes are avoided on transfers of appreciated assets.

Estate taxes may be avoided or diminished.

Benefits from a $100,000 Charitable Remainder Trust for a Donor Age 70*

Payout Rate	Annual Income	Charitable Income Tax Annuity Trust	Unitrust
5%	‹ $ ›	‹ $ ›	‹ % ›
6%	‹ $ ›	‹ $ ›	‹ % ›
7%	‹ $ ›	‹ $ ›	‹ % ›
8%	‹ $ ›	‹ $ ›	‹ % ›

*Figures based on current discount rate of ‹ % ›.

Gifts of Real Estate

You can make a gift of commercial or residential real estate to ‹ORGANIZATION› and receive substantial financial benefits. If you wish to give the property outright, you qualify for a charitable income tax deduction based on the appraised value of the property. If you are contemplating leaving your home to ‹ORGANIZATION› through your will, you may want to consider giving it now but retaining the right to live in it for your lifetime. You will continue to pay taxes, insurance, and maintenance costs. However, by giving now, you receive a substantial charitable income tax deduction in the year the gift is made.

Gifts Through Your Estate

For many donors, making a gift through your estate is the most realistic way to provide a substantial contribution to ‹ORGANIZATION›.

Summary of Benefits:

A gift through your estate reduces or may eliminate federal estate taxes.

Most states provide estate or inheritance tax benefits for gifts through an estate to nonprofit organizations.

Specific Bequest

‹ORGANIZATION› receives a specific dollar amount, a specific piece of property, or a stated percentage of the estate. This is one of the most popular forms of bequests.

Residuary Bequest

‹ORGANIZATION› receives all or a stated percentage of an estate after distribution of specific bequests and payment of debts, taxes, and expenses.

Contingent Bequest

‹ORGANIZATION› receives part or all of the estate under certain specified circumstances.

Trust Established Under a Will

A trust may be established that provides for both ‹ORGANIZATION› and other beneficiaries.

EXHIBIT 18.3 BROCHURE: PLANNING GIVING MINI-GUIDE
(CONTINUED)

Scholarship Funds

Endowed scholarship funds provide financial assistance to worthy and needy students at ‹ORGANIZATION›. Scholarship funds can be tailored to meet your specific goals.

Endowed Scholarships

The minimum level at ‹ORGANIZATION› is ‹ $ › to establish a named endowed scholarship fund. You may fund it now with cash or fund it partially or completely through a planned gift and/or through a bequest from your estate.

Current Use Scholarships

Current use scholarship funds are awarded the year the gift is made. These funds do not grow but provide immediate financial assistance to ‹ORGANIZATION› students. You can create a named current use scholarship for as little as ‹ $ ›.

Your Own Endowment Fund

Creating an endowed fund provides permanent support to ‹ORGANIZATION› for teaching, learning, and research each year in perpetuity. The endowed funds of many friends of ‹ORGANIZATION› have helped fund projects, scholarships, professorships, lecture series, athletic programs, operation of facilities, and much more.

There may be no finer way to honor the memory of a loved one than to establish a scholarship or an endowed professorship in his or her name. A named endowed fund becomes a lasting symbol of the bond between ‹ORGANIZATION› and those who are permanently honored.

Endowed Naming Opportunities

Distinguished ‹ORGANIZATION› Chair	‹ $ ›
‹ORGANIZATION› Chair	‹ $ ›
Professorship	‹ $ ›
Lectureship	‹ $ ›
Scholar-in-Residence	‹ $ ›
Full Tuition Scholarship	
Room and Board	‹ $ ›
Fellowship	‹ $ ›
Full Tuition Scholarship	‹ $ ›
Endowed Fund	‹ $ ›

Policies vary on guidelines for naming opportunities, some of which require approval.

Office of Development

Our staff is available to assist you in achieving your tax, estate planning and charitable giving objectives. We are pleased to provide personal financial projections to you and your financial advisors. For further information, please complete and return the response form below or call ‹TELEPHONE›.

EXHIBIT 18.3 BROCHURE: PLANNING GIVING MINI-GUIDE
(CONTINUED)

‹ORGANIZATION›
Office of Development

Please send me more information about:

☐ Establishing a named fund
☐ Making a gift of appreciated securities
☐ Receiving income from my gift
☐ Making gifts of real estate
☐ Making a gift through life insurance
☐ Providing for ‹ORGANIZATION› in my will

Name: _____

Address: _____

City: _____

State: _____Zip: _____

Phone: _____

Send to:

    ‹NAME›, ‹TITLE›
    ‹ADDRESS›
    ‹CITY, STATE, ZIP›
    ‹TELEPHONE›

Bequest Language

Standard bequest language should be available to donors who request information about making a gift through their estate. Donors usually want to learn how the gift is made and obtain bequest language for their attorney. The attorney usually wants the legal name of the nonprofit, proof that the organization is a nonprofit organization, and the name of the program or department the donor wishes to support (see Exhibit 18.4). See Chapter 7 for more information on bequests and sample bequest language that may be distributed to donors and/or professional advisors.

Create a standard letter to send donors who request information that details the financial benefits donors receive from creating a trust or bequest and the areas or programs that they can support when making a gift. Even if the organization does not yet have planned giving software, educate prospects about the basic tax and financial benefits of charitable remainder trusts without discussing specific numbers. If a prospect materializes, ask a

EXHIBIT 18.4 EXHIBIT BEQUEST NEWSLETTER

YOUR BEQUEST

Bequests have always played an important role in supporting ‹ORGANIZATION›. For many donors, a gift made through a will is the most realistic way to provide a substantial contribution to ‹ORGANIZATION›. Property, including cash, securities, jewelry, works of art, and real estate, may be given through your will. A will is a legal document that allows you to decide to whom your assets are to be distributed and in what amounts or proportions.

TYPES OF BEQUESTS

Specific Bequest
‹ORGANIZATION› receives a specific dollar amount, a specific piece of property, or a stated percentage of the estate. This is one of the most popular forms of bequests.

Residuary Bequest
‹ORGANIZATION› will receive all or a stated percentage of an estate after distribution of specific bequests and payment of debts, taxes, and expenses.

Contingent Bequest
‹ORGANIZATION› will receive part or all of the estate under certain specified circumstances.

Trust Established Under a Will
A trust may be established that provides for both ‹ORGANIZATION› and other beneficiaries.

BEQUESTS TO ‹ORGANIZATION›

A bequest to ‹ORGANIZATION› is a way of perpetuating a donor's support for the role ‹ORGANIZATION› plays in the lives of others. It also enables a donor to make a major gift that might not otherwise be possible.

Through a bequest a donor may leave to ‹ORGANIZATION› a specific dollar amount, for example, ($10,000) or may reserve for ‹ORGANIZATION› all or a certain percentage of the estate after provisions for family members and other beneficiaries have been made. The donor may stipulate whether the bequest is for the general support of the ‹ORGANIZATION› or for a specific purpose. A bequest may also be made in honor or memory of another individual.

In addition to cash and securities, bequests to ‹ORGANIZATION› may include real estate, works of art, or patent rights. All outright bequests to ‹ORGANIZATION› are exempt from federal estate taxes, and there is no limitation on the size of the gift.

colleague or an attorney who specializes in charitable gift planning to produce the financial calculations. See Chapter 7 for more information about bequests.

PROGRAMS

A variety of programs can serve to expand the marketing efforts of the nonprofit organization. Discussing the planned giving program at functions and meetings also will help to attract new planned giving prospects. Consider the following programs to promote planned giving.

Planned Giving Committee

One effective way to promote planned giving is through a planned giving committee. Its purpose is to promote awareness of planned giving as a way to make charitable gifts. The committee is composed of donors, professional advisors, friends, and community representatives. Planned giving staff or consultants may present planned giving training programs to the committee. Invite staff members, such as the nonprofit organization's general counsel, treasurer, and vice president of development, to serve as ad hoc committee members. The committee is encouraged to identify the names of prospects and assist in the cultivation and solicitation of prospects.

Bequest/Planned Giving Societies

Bequest societies that recognize donors who have made gifts through a bequest (or planned giving societies that recognize donors who have made planned gifts through bequests, life income gifts, assets other than cash, or an endowed fund) are excellent ways to acknowledge donors for their support. Societies help to make donors feel a part of the nonprofit organization and are great ways for staff members to get to know the donors better. Exhibit 18.5 is a sample membership application.

Seminars/Workshops

Planned giving seminars and workshops can be offered to donors, prospects, the community at large, staff, or professional advisors. These events are "risk-free" to attendees. They can learn about planned giving without feeling that they are obligated to make a gift.

EXHIBIT 18.5 FORM: GIVING SOCIETY MEMBERSHIP APPLICATION

‹PLANNED GIVING SOCIETY› MEMBERSHIP APPLICATION

Name _____

Mailing Address _____

‹COLLEGE/IF ALUMNUS OR ALUMNA› _____

Relationship to the ‹ORGANIZATION› (if non-alumnus or alumna) _____

_____

Type of Provision

I have made a provision for ‹ORGANIZATION› in my estate plan as follows:

Estimated Amount

1. Outright bequest in will:
    (a) Specific dollar amount $_____
    (b) Specific property (please describe) _____ $_____

    _____
    (c) Share of entire residue of estate (____%) _____ $_____

    _____
2. Conditional bequest or will (please describe conditions) $_____

    _____

    _____
3. Trust under will or to be funded by will (please describe)
    (a) Charitable Remainder Trust _____ $_____

    _____
    (b) Charitable Lead Trust _____ $_____

    _____
    (c) Other _____ $_____

    _____
4. As beneficiary of a life insurance policy _____ $_____

    _____
5. Other (please describe) _____ $_____

    _____

If your gift to ‹ORGANIZATION› is for other than ‹ORGANIZATION›'s general purposes, please describe any restrictions on the back of this form. Attachments or letters that further describe the above provision(s) are encouraged. In particular, a copy of the section of your will, trust agreement, or other document containing the provision(s) will be appreciated. In the event of unforeseen circumstances that require any further change in the above estate planning provision(s), I agree to notify ‹ORGANIZATION› of such change.

_____   _____
       Date   Signature

Please return this form to: ‹NAME›, ‹TITLE›, ‹ADDRESS, CITY, STATE ZIP›; ‹TELEPHONE›.

Professional Advisory Committee

This committee, discussed in detail in the next chapter, includes attorneys, certified public accountants, financial planners, trust officers, and other types of investment advisors. These individuals have clients who need information about charitable gift planning.

ELECTRONIC COMMUNICATIONS

For some audiences, the most effective way to market is through electronic communications. Electronic communications include e-mail and the Internet. The following sections discuss the use of electronic communication as a way to reach and engage planned giving audiences.

E-mail

E-mail can be used passively to respond to donors who write asking for information about planned giving options. In addition, e-mail can be used actively as a way to disseminate information to targeted audiences, such as e-mailing a message to a select group, based on, for example, demographics or geography. At year-end, from October to December, planned giving staff members can send charts showing rates of income and tax deductions for deferred gift annuities for donors between the ages of 25 and 50. With the chart include the benefits of deferred gift annuities.

Maintaining and updating e-mail addresses is important and time consuming. However, e-mail is an efficient and cost-effective way to deliver the message to select audiences.

Internet

The Internet (World Wide Web) has expanded opportunities to communicate with a wide variety of audiences. The nonprofit organization's home page should include information about the charity along with information about charitable gift planning and the planned giving vehicles. Ideally the webpage has an easy-to-use e-mail connection to allow prospective donors and prospects to communicate with the planned giving office staff.

CONCLUSION

At a small nonprofit organization, marketing is an important part of the planned giving staff member's job. No one else within the development office is as likely to engage in marketing as the person charged with building a planned giving program. Marketing raises the level of awareness about the nonprofit organization and the planned giving options. Each marketing effort should build on the previous efforts. Carefully defining the audience, the message, and the medium increases success. Marketing includes a variety of mediums, including printed documents, programs, and electronic communications. Use each of these to reach the nonprofit organization's many audiences.

CHAPTER 19

Marketing to Professional Advisors

INTRODUCTION

Marketing planned giving to professional advisors is a significant part of an overall marketing strategy, especially at smaller nonprofit organizations. Professional advisors include attorneys, trust officers, financial advisors, certified public accountants, stockbrokers, and insurance agents. These advisors represent donors, prospects, faculty, staff, volunteers, and virtually all of a nonprofit organization's key constituents. Professional advisors often have extensive client bases and are very familiar with their clients' net worth, tax situations, and investment holdings. Advisors who work with these individuals are in a unique position to suggest the need for making charitable gifts and can recommend appropriate nonprofit organizations to make gifts. For most large planned gifts, donors seek the advice of a professional advisor. Planned giving staff members at all charities, whether large or small, should reach out to professional advisors. Small nonprofit organizations should develop a core list of professional advisors who work in the region in which the charity is located. These advisors need to be educated about the charity's mission, services, and charitable gift planning options offered to its constituents.

WAYS TO BEGIN

Settlement of Estates

During the settlement of estates for which the organization is a beneficiary, the charity's planned giving officer and the donor's attorney should develop a solid business relationship. Good relationships ensure that the estate settlement process will move along properly and quickly, and that the organization will obtain its maximum estate distributions or personal distributions as early as possible. This relationship enables the planned giving staff member to check on the status of the case and inquire about the anticipated timing for the distribution of assets. The planned giving officer also may be needed to provide information about the charity or draft endowed fund descriptions if the bequest is used to establish an endowed fund. Planned giving staff members are ambassadors of their organizations. They have opportunities to educate professional advisors about the services the charity performs and the administration of donors' funds.

Outreach Mailing List

A planned giving officer who is starting a new planned giving program or expanding an existing one should compile a list of professional advisors who have large estate, tax, or financial planning practices. Ask board members, trustees, and professional advisors for the names of advisors who have extensive practices. To educate these advisors about the organization and its planned giving program, place their names on a mailing list to receive select publications about the organization. Send publications that carry planned giving advertisements and promotional material to educate them about planned giving and how the planned giving office can act as a resource for them. If advisors feel comfortable with planned giving concepts, they may discuss the benefits of making planned gifts to the organization with appropriate clients or perhaps even consider making a personal gift.

Personal Visits to Advisors

Next, select advisors to meet with personally to explain the concept of life income vehicles such as charitable gift annuities, gifts to a pooled income fund, and charitable remainder trusts. Do not be surprised if some of these professional advisors are not familiar with the intricacies of planned gifts. Although they have specialized knowledge in their fields, planned giving is not something usually covered in law, accounting, or financial planning courses.

Offer to run calculations for these advisors. It is likely that the nonprofit has planned giving software that outside advisors do not have. Some professional advisors, especially those in the business of investment management, may seem to resent or be disinterested in the program. These advisors may mistakenly believe that the nonprofit organization is competing with them for business. For example, stockbrokers paid on a commission basis receive their compensation based on the pool of assets they manage or based on the trades they make on behalf of their clients. Any transfer of stock to a nonprofit organization removes assets from their management, thereby reducing their opportunity for compensation or commissions. A gift of stock is neither a buy nor a sell; therefore, no commission is produced. One way to work with a broker is to have the donor transfer the stock to an account the broker creates in the name of the nonprofit. Once the stock has been transferred to the nonprofit's account, the nonprofit orders a sale, and the broker receives a commission. Some trust officers also see nonprofits as competition because the nonprofit may serve as a trustee for a trust or a donor may have a pooled income fund located at a different trust company or bank.

Through a personal visit, a planned giving staff member has an opportunity to build a relationship with advisors, perhaps utilizing advisors' skills to benefit the nonprofit or inviting them to serve as volunteers. Professional advisors can create gift opportunities that otherwise would not happen by considering the positive benefits that philanthropy offers to donors with no previous connection to the organization. In some cases, professional advisors may help to introduce clients to a charity.

PROFESSIONAL ADVISORY COMMITTEE

Another way to market a planned giving program to outside professionals is by establishing a professional advisory committee. Invite board of trustee members, donors who are professional advisors, and other outside professional advisors in the region to attend a meeting of professional advisors.

Schedule a lunch or breakfast meeting, draft an agenda, select a chairperson for the group, and ask him or her to invite additional members to attend. At the meeting, offer an overview of the planned giving vehicles and cover some estate planning concepts. Explain to participants how charitable gift planning can help their clients. If the planned giving staff member is uncomfortable making a presentation, hire a planned giving consultant to do so.

Exhibit 19.1 is a letter that may be sent to professional advisors inviting them to serve as members of a professional advisory committee.

EXHIBIT 19.1   LETTER: OUTREACH TO ADVISORS VERSION 1

‹DATE›

‹NAME›
‹ADDRESS›
‹CITY, STATE ZIP›

Dear ‹NAME›:

In an effort to increase our outreach to professionals in the legal and financial service areas, we have included your name on our mailing list to receive selected publications of ‹ORGANIZATION›. Enclosed is our latest copy of ‹PUBLICATION›. We are also considering hosting a luncheon at ‹ORGANIZATION› where you can hear from some of the ‹ORGANIZATION›'s specialists about recent discoveries and changes in healthcare. In the event that ‹ORGANIZATION› can help you, I hope that you will telephone me at ‹TELEPHONE› for a gift calculation or with questions you may have about charitable donations.

‹ORGANIZATION› has been serving the local, national, and international communities since its founding in ‹YEAR›. ‹ORGANIZATION› strives to provide the very best in every aspect of planned giving.

If you have a client who is considering making a charitable gift, I hope that you will remember ‹ORGANIZATION›. We offer donors the opportunity to receive an income from their gifts, a charitable income tax deduction, a higher yield than they may currently receive from other investments, avoidance of capital gains taxes, and most importantly a chance to support a remarkable institution. Best wishes.

Sincerely,

Next form a subcommittee of the professional advisory committee to present a financial planning workshop. Invite the organization's constituency and staff members to attend. Prepare a one-page brochure, advertise the workshop, and send it to the development staff, donors, prospects, and advisory members. If possible, include it as an advertisement in a local newspaper. The workshop accomplishes two purposes: It educates prospects and donors about planned giving, and it showcases the professional advisory committee at an organizational gathering that indirectly may promote business for the advisors. Invite members of the committee to plan next year's workshop. Offer additional regional workshops involving local professional advisors who are professional advisory committee members.

Calculations and Handouts

The *Planned Giving Workbook,* by Ronald R. Jordan and Katelyn L. Quynn, contains a master set of overheads that can be used to illustrate various planned giving options at workshops for professional advisors. Before the workshop, call two or three attendees to obtain their ages and run personalized calculations. Using the names and ages of real people helps to educate prospects and advisors, and conceptualize planned giving points. Provide hard copies of these calculations as handouts for attendees to take with them when they leave.

Maintenance and Use

Professional advisory committees are generally easy to maintain and require limited attention between meetings. Committee members have their own professional commitments, and their time is limited and valuable. However, members usually are pleased to provide advice on technical aspects of their particular profession, often at no cost. By sharing the workload among committee members, planned giving staff members are able to obtain answers to questions while building solid professional working relationships with well-connected players in the community. Consider the merits of establishing a regional panel or a professional advisory committee to serve as a referral service to answer donors' questions about charitable gift planning.

Communications: A Newsletter

One way to stay in touch with advisory committee members is through a newsletter. By utilizing a desktop publishing package, communicate new information to members about tax and estate planning, and include information on particular gift options or gifts using types of assets such as real estate or closely held stock. The newsletter may be photocopied and circulated throughout the professional advisor's office and distributed to clients.

PLANNED GIVING PRESENTATIONS FOR OUTSIDE AUDIENCES

Another way to market to outside professionals is to take the organization's message outside of the organization. Either the planned giving staff member or the nonprofit organization's consultant can make a presentation to a variety of audiences. This can be accomplished by speaking regularly to outside groups about the planned giving program, the services offered, and the gift options available. The following are possible speaking opportunities: civic clubs including Lions and Rotary clubs; certified public accountant associations; estate planning councils; bankers' associations; cultural groups, such as theater, museum, and library associations; and athletic booster clubs. Take a laptop to planned giving workshops to show advisors or prospects personalized calculations on the spot.

MAILINGS TO PROFESSIONAL ADVISORS

When the development office produces new brochures, publications, or newsletters, send copies to as many professional advisors as possible. By sending them the latest newsletters and planned giving information, they become educated about planned giving options and the needs of the organization are reinforced. Exhibit 19.2 is an excerpt from the *Professional Advisors Committee Resource Manual* including the opening page and table of contents. This document is provided in full in the *Planned Giving Workbook*.

Take an altruistic approach to the outreach program; sometimes working with a professional advisor on a particular situation will benefit another nonprofit. Do not despair; next time the gift may benefit the

EXHIBIT 19.2 BROCHURE: PROFESSIONAL ADVISORS COMMITTEE RESOURCE MANUAL

Planned Giving: Management Marketing and Law
by Ronald R. Jordan and Katelyn L. Quynn
© 2002, John Wiley & Sons, Inc., New York, NY

PREFACE

‹ORGANIZATION›
Professional Advisors Committee Resource Manual

The Office of Development at ‹ORGANIZATION› assists donors in achieving their tax, estate planning and philanthropic goals by offering charitable gift options that can benefit both the donors and ‹ORGANIZATION›.

Increasingly, professional advisors including attorneys, certified public accountants, investment advisors and bank trust officers are consulted by donors regarding charitable giving. We are pleased to enclose a copy of ‹ORGANIZATION›'s Professional Advisors Committee Resource Manual. This manual focuses on the following:

1. Tax consequences of charitable giving, including the charitable income tax deduction and the estate and gift tax deduction.
2. Utilizing a donor's assets, including gifts of cash as well as appreciated securities, mutual funds, closely held stock, real estate, tangible personal property, and life insurance.
3. Life income gifts, including charitable gift annuities, deferred gift annuities, pooled income funds, and charitable remainder trusts.
4. Estate planning, including bequests.

We hope that this guide serves as a valuable resource and planning tool for you and your clients. Our staff is ready to assist you and your clients by preparing personal charitable gift planning projections illustrating the benefits of the most appropriate gift options. For more information, please call or write us or complete the attached client questionnaire.

TABLE OF CONTENTS

organization and the professional advisor may be the key player in making that happen.

PUBLICATION IN TRADE PAPERS

Write a planned giving article for a local trade magazine. Publications that cater to lawyers, certified public accountants, trust officers, and bankers are often looking for new topics that will benefit their readership. Write a piece that focuses on the benefits of charitable gift planning. It is likely that new inquiries will be made from it and new connections formed. This promotes both the planned giving professional and the charitable organization. Exhibit 19.3 proposes a series of resolutions for the new tax year.

EXHIBIT 19.3 COLUMN: TAX RESOLUTIONS

RESOLUTIONS FOR THE ‹YEAR› TAX YEAR

Now that your ‹YEAR› tax returns are filed, it is time to make your resolutions for the new tax year.

Resolve to review your existing estate plan.

If you have not reviewed your estate plan (will, trust, durable power of attorney, living will), you may need an update. Changes in state or federal tax laws may have turned your plans into something that you did not intend. In addition, you should update your will if you have married, separated, or divorced, had a child, inherited money, or moved out of state.

If you are interested in contributing to specific charities, such as ‹ORGANIZATION›, you should review your will to make provisions for charitable giving. This is an excellent way to reduce your taxable estate. Federal estate tax rates are assessed from 37% to 50% and the rate declines in future years. The unified credit increases until 2009. If you have not yet drafted a will or if your will is stale, have a new one drafted today.

Estate and Gift Tax Rates and Credit Exemption Amount

Calendar Year	Estate and GST Tax Death Transfer Exemption	Gift Tax Credit Exemption	Highest Estate and Gift Tax Rates
2002	$1 million	$1 million	50%
2003	$1 million	$1 million	49%
2004	$1.5 million	$1 million	48%
2005	$1.5 million	$1 million	47%
2006	$2 million	$1 million	46%
2007	$2 million	$1 million	45%
2008	$2 million	$1 million	45%
2009	$3.5 million	$1 million	45%
2010	N/A (taxes repealed)	$1 million	Maximum gift tax rate equal to maximum income tax rate (35%)

EXHIBIT 19.3   COLUMN: TAX RESOLUTIONS (CONTINUED)

Resolve to reduce your taxes.

Understand the tax rates. Depending on your taxable income, tax rates are as follows:

Timetable for Marginal Income Tax Rate Reductions

2000	2001*	2002–03	2004–05	2006–10
15%	10%**	10%	10%	10%
	15%	15%	15%	15%
28%	27.5%	27%	26%	25%
31%	30.5%	30%	29%	28%
36%	35.5%	35%	34%	33%
39.6%	39.1%	38.6%	37.6%	35%

*Blended rates for the year that reflect 1% reduction effective July 1, 2001.
**On the first $6,000 of earnings for single filers, $10,000 for heads of households, and $12,000 for married couples, filing jointly.

If you itemize your deductions, you can reduce your taxes through charitable gifts. Charitable gifts reduce your taxable income, which may also reduce your tax rate.

Resolve to examine your investment strategies.

You may be holding stocks, bonds, or mutual funds that are no longer producing sufficient dividends or interest. Perhaps your needs have changed; you may have previously invested for growth, but now need income. You may be holding securities that have greatly appreciated in value and have incurred significant capital gains taxes. If this is the case, you may wish to consider making a gift of appreciated securities to a pooled income fund or to a charitable remainder trust, which offer you the following advantages:

1. You receive a charitable income tax deduction.
2. You avoid capital gains taxes.
3. You receive full fair market value credit for your gift.
4. An income stream based on the fair market value of your gift.

Resolve to examine your financial plans for retirement.

If you are contributing to a company pension plan, see whether you are investing the maximum, especially if the company is matching your contribution. You will also need to reexamine your IRA investments. In addition, you may wish to consider establishing a charitable deferred gift annuity, which will provide an immediate charitable income tax deduction and an income when you are in a lower tax bracket, perhaps at age 65. This is a new and exciting way to make a gift and plan for retirement.

Resolve to review your insurance needs.

Find out whether you need additional insurance. Be sure to reexamine your needs if you have recently had a child, bought a home, or acquired valuable property.

EXHIBIT 19.3 COLUMN: TAX RESOLUTIONS (CONTINUED)

Resolve to learn more about investments.

It is smart to know all you can about your investments, because your finances are your future. The more you learn, the easier and more interesting it becomes.

‹ORGANIZATION› can help you keep your tax resolutions. If you are interested in making a bequest, contributing to a pooled income fund or a charitable remainder trust, or establishing a charitable gift annuity, please call ‹NAME›, ‹TITLE›, at ‹TELEPHONE› or write ‹ORGANIZATION›, ‹ADDRESS›, ‹CITY, STATE ZIP›.

NONTECHNICAL OUTREACH PROGRAM

Another way to bring outside advisors closer to the organization is to host an outreach program consisting of a breakfast or lunch followed by a program on any topic. For example, at an educational organization, consider having guest faculty members speak about their area of academic expertise or have someone from the administration speak about trends in education or policies of academic institutions. At a hospital, have a physician talk about new medical discoveries, research, or treatments; or have an administrator talk about healthcare reform. Arts organizations have opportunities that other nonprofits do not have; show attendees a new exhibit or performance at the organization.

Whatever topic, speaker, or program chosen, make it something that professional advisors will want to attend. The purpose is to promote the organization and inform attendees that the nonprofit is seeking funds and is interested in identifying prospects who can be potential donors to the organization. Include on the guest list professional advisors worked with in the past, such as lawyers who have settled estates of which the organization was a beneficiary and trust officers who have made charitable trust distributions to the organization. Invite the outside planned giving manager and stockbrokers who process gifts of securities to the organization. Strive to make the outreach program a positive, memorable event that professional advisors will want to attend each year. Careful cultivation of professional advisors will result in some unexpected valuable gifts.

CONCLUSION

Marketing a planned giving program to outside professional advisors is a way to educate professionals who may be in a position to bring gifts, through their clients, to the organization. Tell these professionals that the organization needs financial support, and show them how their clients can be helped by making planned gifts. When trying to reach outside professionals:

- Create a mailing list to keep professional advisors regularly informed about the organization and the planned giving services offered.

- Try to meet personally with outside professionals to talk about planned giving vehicles and help them to become comfortable with the concepts. Alleviate their suspicions that the organization is competing with them for business.

- Form relationships with attorneys who are settling estates of donors to the organization. Doing so helps to build a planned giving network as well as monitor the estate settlement process.

- Consider forming a professional advisory committee to bring these individuals closer to the organization. Host a financial planning workshop for donors. Use personalized calculations as examples.

- Try to speak regularly to outside organizations about planned giving to further expand an outside network and educate others about the benefits of planned giving.

- Showcase the organization to outside professionals by offering a program conducted by someone from the nonprofit who will speak on a topic related to the organization rather than a planned giving related topic.

- Over time new gifts will come into the organization based on continued outreach efforts. Stay with it!

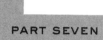

PART SEVEN

Planned Giving and Taxes

CHAPTER 20

Tax Consequences of Charitable Gifts

INTRODUCTION

Charitable giving has become big business in the United States with gifts from individuals accounting for most of the philanthropic contributions. In 2001, approximately $200 billion in current gifts and bequests were made to nonprofit organizations. To encourage continued private funding of charitable organizations, Congress has provided tax incentives for philanthropic individuals. A donor's charitable intent must be the motivating factor behind making a gift. No amount of tax benefits will cause an individual who does not have donative intent to make a charitable gift. Planned gifts provide a way for philanthropic donors to make gifts to nonprofit organizations and simultaneously enjoy financial and favorable tax consequences.

Currently, much of this country's wealth is held by older Americans, those age 60 and above. As the population rapidly ages, baby boomers become middle age, older Americans live longer, and concerns over healthcare and Medicaid increase. The years ahead will see the largest intergenerational transfer of wealth in U.S. history, as approximately $7 trillion is expected to be transferred from parents to their baby-boomer children. This transfer of assets creates the need for close examination of tax issues, beyond the traditional benefits of income tax savings. Passing wealth on to family members through planned giving options offers an attractive way to provide secure current income while receiving tax advantages and providing for charity. Charities need to emphasize planned giving techniques that provide needed benefits to donors while building for the charity's future.

As discussed, donors make gifts not because of tax considerations but because of philanthropic motivations that match their interests. However, almost all donors are still motivated to make their gift "taxwise" seeking income, capital gains, estate, and gift tax relief through charitable giving. Planned giving staff members, donors, and their professional advisors must have a comprehensive understanding of the tax consequences of charitable contributions and the underlying tax considerations that can impact charitable giving.

Potentially, four different types of taxes may be involved when a donor makes a single charitable gift: (1) income, (2) capital gains, (3) estate, and (4) gift taxes. In addition to federal taxes imposed by the Internal Revenue Code and assessed by the Internal Revenue Service, related taxes may sometimes be assessed by a state or local government. The following is an overview of the tax consequences of charitable giving.

FEDERAL AND STATE INCOME TAXES

A donor is taxed on income earned as well as investment income produced by the donor's assets. The marginal federal income tax rates under the Economic Growth and Tax Relief Reconciliation Act of 2001 (EGTR-RA) are listed in Exhibit 20.1.

EXHIBIT 20.1 TIMETABLE FOR MARGINAL INCOME TAX RATE REDUCTIONS

2000	2001*	2002–03	2004–05	2006–10
15%	10%**	10%	10%	10%
	15%	15%	15%	15%
28%	27.5%	27%	26%	25%
31%	30.5%	30%	29%	28%
36%	35.5%	35%	34%	33%
39.6%	39.1%	38.6%	37.6%	35%

*Blended rates for the year that reflect 1% reduction effective July 1, 2001.
**On the first $6,000 of earnings for single filers, $10,000 for heads of households, and $12,000 for married couples, filing jointly.

Most taxpayers who have the capacity to make major charitable gifts are in the upper tax brackets. In addition to federal income taxes, in most cases state income taxes are assessed on a similar basis, although at lower rates. Donors who are citizens and residents of foreign countries and who have no U.S. income are not subjected to federal income taxation nor do they obtain the tax benefits of charitable giving. Canadian citizens who give to certain U.S. colleges and universities, designated by Revenue Canada because they accept Canadian citizens as students, are permitted to deduct their gifts for Canadian income tax purposes.

Adjusted Gross Income

A donor's adjusted gross income (AGI; contribution base) is an important benchmark in calculating his or her allowable deductions. The adjusted gross income is the donor's total income derived from all sources, minus deductions for alimony, IRA contributions, and other specific expenses and items. The AGI is the starting point for computing the charitable income tax deduction, medical deductions, casualty losses, and miscellaneous deductions. Some deductions may be available only subject to certain limits; for example, only medical expenses (for the donor, spouse, or a dependent) in excess of 7.5 percent of one's adjusted gross income are deductible.

Taxable Income

Personal exemptions and itemized deductions are subtracted from the adjusted gross income, resulting in taxable income. One of the most advantageous deductions to income is the charitable income tax deduction. There are two types of taxpayers for federal income purposes: nonitemizers and itemizers. Charitable contributions benefit only those taxpayers who itemize their deductions.

Nonitemizers Nonitemizers most likely rent or own a personal residence without a mortgage. Home ownership provides important tax deductions for mortgage interest, real estate taxes, and home equity loan interest. Under current law, taxpayers may not deduct their charitable contributions unless charitable contributions, along with all other permitted deductions such as mortgage interest, real estate taxes, and state income taxes, exceed the estimated standard deduction levels of $7,600 in 2001 for married individuals filing jointly or $4,550 for taxpayers filing singly. Once these levels are reached, these taxpayers can become itemizers. The standard deduction levels are adjusted annually and are indexed to inflation. A donor may choose to accumulate contributions that otherwise would have been made over several years and make them all in a single year instead. By "bunching" ordinary deductions and charitable contributions, a donor may exceed the standard deduction thresholds and qualify as an itemizer. At the time this book went to press, several legislative proposals were being considered that would allow nonitemizers to obtain charitable income tax deductions for charitable gifts.

Itemizers   For gifts of cash, itemizers may deduct the value of their contributions to public charities up to 50 percent of their contribution based on their adjusted gross income. If the entire deduction cannot be used in the first year, it may be carried over for five additional years. If it is carried over, donors are required to use as much of the charitable income tax deduction as possible each year up to 50 percent of their contribution base. In other words, donors may not voluntarily apportion the contribution over several years.

For certain gifts of investment property, such as real estate or securities, if the property has been held for at least one year and a day and would produce long-term capital gain on sale (a long-term capital asset), donors may deduct the fair market value of the property, up to 30 percent of their contribution base.

FAIR MARKET VALUE

Fair market value is the price at which property would change hands between a willing buyer and a willing seller, with neither one being under an obligation to act and both having reasonable knowledge of the relevant facts. If the property is held for a year or less (a short-term capital asset), then only the cost basis of the property can be deducted, which is an amount that equals the purchase price of the property.

COST BASIS

The cost basis and the fair market value for cash are the same amount. For gifts of securities, such as stocks or bonds, the cost basis is the purchase price of the securities in addition to any costs associated with the purchase, such as commissions and transfer fees. For real property, the cost basis is the purchase price plus legal fees, recording costs, and settlement or closing costs, plus the cost of improvements less other adjustments. For lifetime transfers (property that is transferred by gift), the cost basis to the donees (or recipients of the gift) is the donor's cost basis plus the value of any gift tax paid by the donor.

For property transferred to a donee through one's estate until 2010, the basis is stepped up to the fair market value of the asset at the donor's date of death. For example, if a donor inherited property from her father, her basis is the fair market value of the property as of the date of her father's death. If a donor continues to hold the property and the property appreciates and is later sold, then a capital gains tax is due upon the sale of the asset on the difference between the value of the property at her father's death and the value of the property upon sale. Under the Economic Growth and Tax Relief Reconciliation Act of 2001, beginning in 2010, neither heirs nor beneficiaries will receive a stepped-up basis on inherited property in excess of certain amounts. Recipients will acquire the lesser of the fair market value or the decedent's basis plus up to $1.3 million for assets transferred to other beneficiaries and $3 million for certain assets transferred to a surviving spouse.

DEDUCTIBILITY OF GIFTS OF TANGIBLE PERSONAL PROPERTY

As discussed in Chapter 13, for a donor to obtain a charitable income tax deduction for the full fair market value of gifts of tangible personal property such as artwork, antiques, stamps, and coin collections, there is an additional requirement that it is reasonable to anticipate that the donated tangible personal property will be used in a way that is related to "the business of the charity." The "related use" rule is met if a donor makes a gift of a painting to a museum or a book to a library. This rule applies only to the charitable income tax deduction, not to the estate or gift tax charitable deduction. The purpose of the related use rule is to diminish the charitable income tax deduction for gifts of tangible personal property where there is no related use to the charitable organization's exempt purpose or where the property, even though related, will be sold by the charity immediately at an auction or other event. For most large charities, especially universities, arguably almost any gift of property, such as artwork, can satisfy the related use test since it could be used by at least one of the many departments or for display. However, if the donor knows that the charity intends to sell the property, the gift will fail the related use test. If the property is a gift of long-term appreciated tangible personal property and the charity uses it in a related use, a donor can deduct the fair market value of the property up to 30 percent of the donor's contribution base. If the gift of tangible personal property is unrelated, then the donor's deduction is limited to the donor's cost basis up to 50 percent of the contribution base.

If the donated property is not related to the business of the charitable organization, a donor may prefer to sell the asset and give the proceeds to the charity. In this case, a donor obtains a charitable income tax deduction equal to the proceeds less any capital gains taxes. If donors make a gift of "ordinary income property" (property used in their trade), then they may deduct the cost basis of the property, up to 50 percent of their contribution base, assuming they have not already deducted the cost as a business expense, in which case no deduction is allowed. Donors do not receive a charitable income tax deduction for the value of the use of their property, such as a ski condominium or vacation property, contributed for a weekend to a charity or that is auctioned at a charity auction. Only the donor's out-of-pocket expenses, such as cleaning or heating costs, associated with such use may be deducted as a gift.

Volunteers do not receive a charitable income tax deduction for a gift of services such as time volunteering at the charity. However, volunteers may receive a charitable income tax deduction for unreimbursed out-of-pocket expenses incurred while working on behalf of the organization, including transportation expenses.

ACCELERATION OF DEDUCTION

Taxpayers may utilize an alternative to permit an increase in the percentage of income that may be offset by the charitable income tax deduction. Donors may increase the limitation from 30 percent to 50 percent of their contribution base for gifts of property if they elect to deduct the cost basis rather than the fair market value. If the asset has not appreciated significantly, they may accelerate the deduction by choosing to deduct the cost basis rather than the fair market value limited to 50 percent of their contribution base. Example: If a donor bought real estate for $100,000 and the property has a current value of $105,000, he may choose to deduct the cost basis of $100,000 up to 50 percent of his contribution base rather than the fair market value of $105,000 limited to 30 percent of his contribution base income.

DEDUCTION REDUCTION PROVISION

The 1993 Omnibus Reconciliation Act (OBRA) reduced the value of deductions for upper-income taxpayers. Now the EGTRRA will further modify this provision. Beginning in 2006, the phase-out provisions for deductions will be reduced gradually, and by 2010 they will be repealed. Until that time, taxpayers will have the total value of their itemized income tax deductions reduced by the lesser of 3 percent of that portion of the AGI that exceeds a base level or 80 percent of their itemized deduction otherwise allowable for the taxable year. The threshold amounts are indexed and change annually.

Itemized deductions include home mortgage interest, real estate taxes, state taxes, medical expenses, excise taxes, and charitable and other miscellaneous deductions. The deduction reduction formula reduces the value of these types of deductions for certain taxpayers. This provision has a negative impact on the value of all deductions (except for medical, investment interest, or casualty and theft losses) including the charitable income tax deduction. However, most wealthy donors have involuntary types of deductions, such as state income taxes and real estate taxes in amounts that exceed the 3 percent threshold; therefore, charitable contributions, which are voluntary, may be considered on top of the 3 percent limit.

Additional Provisions of the EGTRRA of 2001

EGTRRA made a number of other changes that will impact taxpayers in the years to come. The following summarizes those changes.

- *Marriage Penalty Relief.* Beginning in 2005 and phasing in over a four-year period, the standard deduction is increased so that a married couple filing jointly eventually receives a standard deduction equal to an amount twice that of singles.

- *Itemized Deductions and Exemptions.* Beginning in 2006 and by 2010 taxpayers will receive full benefit for all income tax deductions and exemptions.

- *Limitations on Retirement Plan Contributions.* The limits on contributions to IRA and ROTH IRAs will gradually increase: $3,000 in 2002–4, $4,000 in 2005–7, and to $5,000 in 2008–10. From 2009 and forward the amount will be adjusted to inflation. Individuals 50 years or older may use catch-up provisions. The act also increases amounts that can be contributed to 401(k) and 403(b) plans ($10,500 in 2001, $11,000 in 2002, $12,000 in 2003, $13,000 in 2004, $14,000 in 2005, and $15,000 in 2006 and beyond), subject to a number of restrictions. From 2007 the limit is indexed for inflation.

- *Coverdell IRAs.* Increases the limit on contributions from $500 to $2,000 subject to income limitations and phase-out ranges. The act allows tax-deferred growth and tax-free distributions to pay for qualified expenses.

- *Qualified Tuition Programs (529 Plans).*

The withdrawal of investment gains are now tax-free, and these plans will be made available to private schools; however, withdrawals cannot be made until 2004. Taxpayers can contribute to both 529 plans and Education IRAs.

PLEDGE AND PROMISSORY NOTE

A pledge generates a charitable income tax deduction only in the year the pledge actually is paid. Likewise, a promissory note from a donor to a charity does not generate a charitable income tax deduction until the note is paid in full.

BENEFITS TO DONORS

Donors can jeopardize their charitable income tax deductions and charities can jeopardize their nonprofit status by improperly crediting the value of a charitable gift. If a donor makes a contribution and receives a benefit such as a product or service, the value of the benefit must be deducted from the contribution to determine the actual charitable income tax deduction. For example, if a donor makes a gift of $100 to a charity to attend a fundraiser, the fair market value of the meal, entertainment, and other benefits enjoyed must be deducted from the gift of $100 to determine the real value of the gift. The IRS requires charities that receive a gift of $75 and above for which a donor obtains a benefit to disclose the following two items:

1. The amount of the contribution deductible for federal income tax purposes, which is limited to the excess of the money or the value of any property other than money contributed by the donor over the value of the goods and services provided by the organization.

2. A good faith estimate of the value of such goods and services.

In addition, in order for a donor to deduct a contribution of $250 or more, the charity must issue a receipt for the gift and must state whether (and give an estimated value if) any portion of the gift was made in exchange for a benefit.

Gifts by a donor who receives goods or services from the charity are called quid pro quo contributions. Under the quid pro quo rules, goods or services having an insubstantial value may be disregarded when calculating the charitable income tax deduction. It is also possible to disregard goods or services having minimal value of the lesser of $75 in 2002 (and indexed for inflation) or 2 percent of the donor's gift, so that donors who make a gift of $1,000 and are invited to a reception where they receive food having a value of $20 may be treated as if the full gift is deductible. Volunteers may deduct out-of-pocket expenses incurred in the course of traveling or otherwise contributing their services to the charity as long as they receive an acknowledgment recognizing the date of the volunteered service and a statement that the service was a benefit to the charity.

ORDINARY INCOME REDUCTION RULE

The ordinary income reduction rule reduces the value of the charitable income tax deduction for contributions by donors of assets that are characterized as ordinary income property. The rule applies only to the charitable income tax deduction, not to the estate tax deduction. Ordinary income property is property that would result in ordinary income or a short-term capital gain if the property was sold on the date contributed. Ordinary income properties are assets that a taxpayer sells or uses to produce ordinary income, such as a retailer who sells inventory to customers or an artist who sells items that she produced or created. Property is characterized as ordinary income property based on the nature of the property in the hands of the donor.

For example, sales of the following property would produce ordinary income:

- Short-term capital assets
- Inventory in the hands of a retailer, dealer, or merchant
- Artwork in the hands of the artist; a manuscript in the hands of the author
- Section 306 stock of which any dividend produced would be treated as ordinary income
- Certain property that has been subject to depreciation recapture
- Annuity or life insurance contract

For gifts of ordinary income property, a donor is entitled to claim a charitable income tax deduction equal to the cost basis of the asset. The rule limits the value of contributions of ordinary income property by donors to charities because the value of the charitable income tax deduction is reduced.

Artists, authors, and playwrights who donate their own works of art or manuscripts are limited to a charitable income tax deduction equal to the cost basis, which for an artist usually amounts to the cost of materials used to make the artwork (such as paint, brushes, and canvas for a painting), assuming that the cost has not already been deducted as a business expense, in which case no deduction is available. However, inventors who make gifts of their own patents are entitled to a charitable income tax deduction equal to the fair market value of the patent since patents are characterized as capital gains property rather than ordinary income property.

INCOME IN RESPECT OF A DECEDENT

As discussed earlier, most assets transferred at death receive a stepped-up basis, which means that the donee obtains a new basis in transferred property equal to the fair market value of the property at the date of the donor's death. However, items that are classified as income in respect of a decedent

(IRD) do not receive a stepped-up basis. Income in respect of a decedent is taxable income that the decedent was entitled to at death but which was not included in any previous income tax return. The term "income" in respect of a decedent includes the following categories of income:

- Wages
- Accounts receivable (for a cash-basis taxpayer)
- Untaxed interest income on savings or treasury bonds
- Deferred compensation such as individual retirement accounts and qualified plans
- Series EE bond interest
- Installment contracts

These types of income are subject to an income tax and also are includible in the decedent's estate. Beneficiaries receiving IRD items pay an income tax and receive an income tax deduction for the estate tax that was assessed against the estate for the IRD items. This partial double taxation of IRD items can be avoided if these items are gifted to charities, which do not pay income taxes. Unlike the charitable income tax deduction, which is limited by a percentage of the taxpayer's contribution base, there is no limit on the amount that an individual may contribute to charities for purposes of the estate tax charitable deduction.

Items classified as income in respect of a decedent may be transferred in one of two ways, either outright or to a charitable remainder trust.

Outright Transfers

IRD items may be transferred by will to a charity. IRD items should be transferred as a specific legacy to a charity or may be transferred through the residuary clause in a will if the charity is the recipient of the residue. Series EE bonds, for example, could be transferred to a charity through a specific legacy by will, or retirement plans could name the charity directly as the beneficiary.

Charitable Remainder Trust

IRD items also may be transferred to a charitable remainder trust. A charitable remainder trust is exempt from income taxation, and IRD items transferred to it avoid income taxation until the trust makes a distribution to the beneficiaries. See Chapter 10 for more on IRD transfers to a charitable remainder trust.

DEDUCTIBILITY OF CHARITABLE CONTRIBUTIONS FOR BUSINESS ORGANIZATIONS

Business organizations, like individuals, can make tax-deductible contributions to a charity. There are several types of business organizations including regular business corporations known as C corporations, S corporations and partnerships. Each receives a different tax treatment for gifts of charitable contributions made by the business organization.

C Corporations

C corporations may deduct charitable gifts of cash or property and obtain a charitable income tax deduction limited to 10 percent of the corporation's taxable income (with certain adjustments) for the year in which the deduction is made. Like individuals, the corporation is permitted to carry over any excess for up to five additional tax years.

S Corporations

An S corporation is a special type of corporation. An S corporation is limited to no more than 75 shareholders (with certain limitations on who those shareholders can be) who, along with the corporate entity, elect to be treated as an S corporation. An S corporation does not pay income taxes but instead passes through to its shareholders income, expenses, and profit or loss, all of which are included in the shareholders' individual tax returns. An S corporation can make charitable gifts; unlike a C corporation, the gifts are not limited to a ceiling of 10 percent of taxable income. Instead, the value of any charitable gifts is passed through to the shareholders. The charitable income tax deduction available to shareholders is limited to the extent of a shareholder's basis in the stock. The deduction is still limited to the taxpayer's (shareholder's) contribution base levels of 30 percent for gifts of property or 50 percent for gifts of cash. Under previous tax law, a nonprofit organization could not own shares or an ownership interest in an S corporation; otherwise the S corporation status was lost. Now charities (but not charitable remainder trusts) may own S corporation stocks, although the value of the stock to the charity is greatly diminished. All income or loss flows through to the charity as unrelated business taxable income or loss. In addition, any capital gain on the sale of S corporation stock is taxed as unrelated business taxable income. See Chapter 12 for more information on making gifts of S corporation stock.

Partnerships

Under current tax law, a partnership is not entitled to deduct charitable contributions directly. The partnership itself files a tax return but does not pay tax because gains and losses from the partnership are passed through to the partners. A partnership's charitable contributions are passed on to the partners.

DEPRECIATION

Depreciation is a tax concept that enables a taxpayer "a reasonable allowance for the exhaustion, wear and tear of property used in a trade or business, or of property held for the production of income." The depreciation deduction is applied against ordinary income earned by the taxpayer and effectively reduces the taxpayer's income tax liability. To be depreciable, an asset must have a useful life of more than one year. Items that have a useful life of less than a year are expensed, and the cost is recovered as a deduction against revenue in the year the item is acquired. The cost of repairs is expensed unless the repairs amount to capital improvements, in which case they are depreciated. There are several ways to claim depreciation. For example, in straight-line depreciation, the asset is deducted on a prorated basis over the useful life of the capital asset. The IRS has established asset depreciation tables for tax purposes to measure the useful life of any asset.

The impact of depreciation on an asset that is gifted depends on whether the asset is considered ordinary income property or capital gains property. The difference as to whether an asset is ordinary income property rather than capital gains property is based on the nature and use of the asset in the hands of the donor. Ordinary income property is property that, if sold, would produce ordinary income, such as art in the hands of an artist or property that, if sold, would produce a short-term gain. Capital gains property is property held for investment; some property used in a trade or business is treated as capital gains property. The donor may obtain a charitable income tax deduction for the full fair market value of the asset as long as the asset was held at least a year and a day and qualifies as a long-term capital asset. Certain depreciation of assets must be recaptured or taxed on the sale of the property. Under the ordinary income reduction rule, the donor of ordinary income property must reduce the full market value of that property by the amount of depreciation that would have been recaptured had the property been sold. The basis of an asset is important for gifts made to fund a charitable gift annuity; the difference between the fair market value and the cost basis is capital gain and is taxed accordingly, although such tax, in most cases, may be deferred at the time of the annuity payout. Long-term capital gains are not taxed when capital gains property is transferred outright to a charity or to a charitable remainder trust or a pooled income fund.

CAPITAL GAINS TAXES

Long-term capital gains taxes are assessed on the sale of an appreciated capital asset that has been held by the taxpayer for more than a year. The appreciation is measured by the difference between the fair market value of the asset and the original price, or cost basis less depreciation of the asset. Currently, capital gains are taxed at a maximum rate of 20 percent for most investment assets. Donors who acquired investment assets after December 31, 2000 and hold the assets for a minimum of five years pay a capital gains tax rate of 18 percent. Donors may gift long-term appreciated assets to a charitable organization and avoid capital gains taxes while obtaining a charitable income tax deduction equal to the fair market value of the asset.

FEDERAL ESTATE AND GIFT TAXES

Federal estate and gift taxes are sometimes referred to as wealth transfer taxes. Donors can make a transfer of property during their lifetime and be subject to a gift tax or can make a transfer of property at death and be subject to an estate tax. Under previous law, the estate and gift tax rate was "uniform," meaning that the same rate of tax was assessed regardless of whether the asset was transferred during life or at death. The estate tax is assessed on the value of the asset transferred and the amount needed to pay the estate tax whereas the gift tax is assessed only on the amount transferred. Every taxpayer is entitled to an exemption, which permits a donor to transfer $1,000,000 (in 2002) of assets during their lifetimes or at death, without incurring any federal or estate taxes. Now, under EGTRRA, the estate and gift taxes are treated separately. For gift tax purposes, the new act caps the lifetime exemption equivalent at $1,000,000 and for the estate tax and generation-skipping tax, the exemption equivalent is $1,000,000 in 2002 and increases to $3,500,000 in 2009. The same tax rate is assessed on estate and gift transfer until 2009. In 2010 the estate tax is scheduled to be repealed and the gift tax will be assessed on transfers in excess of $1,000,000 at a rate equal to the taxpayer's income tax rate. Exhibit 20.2 illustrates the applicable tax rates and exemptions.

Wealthy taxpayers with significant assets may wish to make charitable gifts rather than pay hefty estate and gift taxes. Many donors are motivated to reduce their estate taxes through lifetime charitable gifts supplemented by additional gifts to reduce their estate. Charitable gifts made during one's lifetime are deductible for gift tax purposes. To be deductible for gift tax purposes, the contribution also must be deductible for income tax purposes.

EXHIBIT 20.2 ESTATE AND GIFT TAX RATES AND UNIFIED CREDIT EXEMPTION AMOUNT

	Estate and Gift Tax Rates and Unified Credit Exemption Amounts		
Calendar Year	Estate and GST Tax Credit Exemption	Gift Transfer Exemption Tax	Highest Estate and Gift Tax Rates
2002	$1 million	$1 million	50%
2003	$1 million	$1 million	49%
2004	$1.5 million	$1 million	48%
2005	$1.5 million	$1 million	47%
2006	$2 million	$1 million	46%
2007	$2 million	$1 million	45%
2008	$2 million	$1 million	45%
2009	$3.5 million	$1 million	45%
2010	N/A (taxes repealed)	$1 million	Maximum gift tax rate equal to maximum income tax rate (35%)

When making a taxable gift of assets that are likely to appreciate in value, it is more advantageous to make a lifetime gift of the assets prior to the anticipated appreciation, thereby avoiding higher taxes later. This option is better than transferring the assets at death and paying the higher estate taxes on the asset plus its appreciated value. Charitable gifts made through a decedent's estate are deducted from the decedent's gross estate, which lessens the estate tax burden. To take advantage of such a deduction, the gift must be irrevocable. It may be made through a will, an irrevocable charitable remainder trust, or a revocable trust that becomes irrevocable at the donor's death.

Philanthropically motivated donors will always make gifts through their estates, even if there is no longer an estate tax charitable deduction. For example, because donors do not exactly know how much of their estate they will need for their use during their lifetimes, many prefer to make the largest of their charitable gifts through their estates. For other donors, this legislation will be a disincentive to make charitable gifts. Check with the charity's general counsel for more information about legislative changes that may affect the estate and gift tax.

GIFT TAX ANNUAL EXCLUSION

Donors are entitled to an annual exclusion that permits them to make a present gift of up to $10,000 each year to any number of donees without gift tax consequences and without using up any of the $1,000,000 lifetime exemption equivalent. Spouses can pool annual exclusions, enabling a couple to give up to $20,000 each year to any number of donees. The annual exclusion is adjusted and will increase gradually over time. Parents and grandparents who wish to take advantage of the annual exclusion can make gifts to their children and grandchildren while substantially reducing their estate tax liability. The annual exclusion applies only to gifts of a present interest, and not a future interest such as a deferred gift annuity. Charitable gifts are unaffected by the $10,000 annual exclusion limit that exists for gifts to individuals. In addition, gifts to charity do not diminish an individual's lifetime exemption; regardless of amount, gifts to charities will not incur any gift tax.

PAYMENTS FOR TUITION AND MEDICAL BILLS

A donor also may give any amount, including an amount over $10,000, without gift tax consequences if the gift takes the form of a direct payment of tuition or medical expenses. The payment must be made by the taxpayer directly to the provider (university, hospital, etc.) rather than to an individual. For example, an individual can pay tuition to a university on behalf of another individual without being subject to a gift tax.

GIFTS BY HUSBAND AND WIFE/UNLIMITED MARITAL DEDUCTION

When spouses contemplate making gifts, they should consider whether the gift should be made by an individual or as a couple. For federal gift and estate tax purposes, each spouse is considered to have contributed one half of the purchase price of an asset if the property is held jointly. By transferring assets jointly instead of from a single spouse, they can elect to split gifts of property. In this manner, each spouse obtains one half of the charitable income tax deduction. Current federal tax law provides spouses who are U.S. citizens with an unlimited marital deduction, allowing one spouse to make an outright gift to the other of an unlimited amount of marital property without incurring any federal estate or gift tax and without using any of their lifetime gift or estate tax exemption. The transfer may be made either as a lifetime transfer (inter vivos) or a transfer at death (testamentary). There is both an estate tax marital deduction and a gift tax marital deduction. To qualify as a transfer under the gift tax marital deduction, the spouses must be married and the transfers must take place during the marriage. If a surviving spouse disclaims a property interest, then the marital deduction will not be allowed for that property. Any property interest subject to a mortgage that passes to a surviving spouse will be reduced by the amount of that mortgage. If one spouse is infirm, that spouse may wish to take advantage of the marital deduction by gifting his or her interest in the property to the other spouse and having the healthy spouse donate the property to charity. This technique allows the healthy spouse to receive the full charitable income tax deduction for the donation including any contribution carryover that would otherwise expire at the first spouse's death.

STREAMS OF INCOME AND GIFT TAX CONSEQUENCES

A future interest is created when a gift is made of an interest that begins at a point in the future, such as a charitable remainder trust that provides income to a second beneficiary upon the death of the first. A gift of a future interest to an individual does not qualify for the annual gift tax exclusion of $10,000. A gift of a future interest to a spouse (other than through a charitable remainder trust) also does not qualify for the marital deduction. In both cases, there is no present interest created. A donor can avoid creating a future interest, and making a taxable gift, by reserving the right to revoke the future interest. The reservation of the right to revoke is generally exercisable by will and must be included in appropriate language in the legal document. In the case of a charitable gift annuity with an income stream paid to someone other than the donor or the donor's spouse, the charitable gift annuity agreement should include the following language:

> The donor may, by the donor's will, revoke the annuity to be paid to Mr. Donee X.

Taxation of a Stream of Income from a Life Income Gift

Depending on the life income gift option selected (charitable gift annuity, deferred gift annuity, pooled income fund, etc.) and the beneficiary (donor, spouse, relative, etc.), there are different tax consequences associated with the gift of a stream of income. Generally, the gift of a present stream of income qualifies for the annual exclusion, but any gift of a future stream of income to another person raises gift tax considerations.

Taxation of a Present Interest

For life income gifts such as charitable remainder trusts, charitable gift annuities, and pooled income funds, all of which may create a present stream of income for the benefit of another, the stream of income is an interest that is eligible for the annual exclusion of $10,000. If the stream of income is payable to a spouse, then the stream is also eligible for the marital deduction.

Taxation of a Future Interest

If the stream is not a present interest but a future interest payable upon a contingency such as the death of a first beneficiary, the annual exclusion does not apply nor, in the case of a spouse, does the marital deduction. In this case a donor may reserve the right to revoke the income stream, exercisable by will or during lifetime although a lifetime right to revoke may disqualify a charitable remainder trust. This reservation has the effect of suspending the stream of income and making the gift incomplete. If the right to revoke is not exercised, then the present value of the gift to a non-spouse will become part of the donor's taxable estate.

In the case of a deferred gift annuity, an income stream is created to be paid beginning at a point in the future. When the annuity is payable to a beneficiary other than the donor, it is unclear under current tax law if the present value of the beneficiary's intent would qualify for the gift tax annual exclusion. If the present value of an income stream exceeds the annual exclusion or if the donor creates a future interest but fails to retain the right to revoke, there is a gift tax. Donors who create streams that exceed the annual exclusion subject to a gift tax can use the lifetime gift/estate tax exemption.

SALE OF A PERSONAL RESIDENCE

Under prior law, taxpayers were subject to a capital gains tax on any gain realized from the sale of a principal residence unless they purchased a replacement principal residence of equal or greater value within a specified period of time. Under that law, if the taxpayer was 55 years of age or older and did not replace the residence, the gain on the sale of the principal residence could have been offset by the one-time, lifetime exclusion that permitted a taxpayer to sell a principal residence and exclude up to $125,000 of the gain. New tax law permits a taxpayer of any age to exclude up to $500,000, if married filing jointly, of capital gain ($250,000 if single) upon the sale of a personal residence if the taxpayer lived in the residence for at least two of the last five years. The exclusion can be taken more than once.

GIFTS OF REAL ESTATE SUBJECT TO A MORTGAGE

Donors who make a gift of mortgaged real estate obtain a charitable income tax deduction equal to the fair market value of the property minus the value of the mortgage. See Chapter 12 for an in-depth look at gifts of real estate.

TAX IMPLICATIONS OF A BARGAIN SALE

If a donor makes a partial gift, partial sale, or transfers real estate worth, for example, $100,000 to a charity in exchange for a payment of, for example, $50,000, the donor is making a bargain sale and is taxed on the gain. Assuming the property is capital gains property, the gain is treated as a capital gain. The same is true in a charitable gift annuity situation. When donors transfer capital gains property in exchange for a gift annuity, they will receive part ordinary income and part capital gain.

A bargain sale is treated for tax purposes as two transactions: one part sale and one part gift. The basis of the property has to be allocated between the sale portion and the gift portion to determine gain. To calculate the gain, divide the sale price by the fair market value of the property. This will produce a ratio expressed as a percentage. To determine the cost basis to be allocated to the sale portion, multiply the percentage (which is a ratio of the sales price to market value) times the cost basis of the property. Last, from the sale price subtract the cost basis allocated to the sale to arrive at the reportable gain.

SUBSTANTIATION REQUIREMENTS

A taxpayer who makes a gift of $250 or more must obtain a receipt from the charity to claim a charitable income tax deduction. The receipt or acknowledgment must state the amount of cash or the nature of the property received and must state whether the donor received any goods or services in exchange for the gift. If any were so received, the value of the goods and services must be stated. If donors make a gift of property other than cash and marketable securities, they need to prove that the gift was made and also need to substantiate value. The IRS has specific requirements for the substantiation of noncash gifts, including forms and appraisals.

Form 8283

The Internal Revenue Service requires that donors who make gifts of a value of $5,000 or more of any property, other than cash or marketable securities to charitable organizations, have a formal appraisal and report these gifts on Form 8283. (Gifts of closely held stock, with a value of $10,000 or more require an appraisal.) Noncash contributions include gifts-in-kind such as artwork, musical instruments, real estate, antiques, jewelry, computer hardware and software, and securities. In each of these cases the determination of the value of the contribution is complex. The purpose of the appraisal and Form 8283 is to require taxpayers who make noncash gifts to be honest and accurate in substantiating the value of those assets for charitable income tax deduction purposes.

APPRAISALS

For situations in which an appraisal is necessary, the appraisal must be conducted by an independent qualified appraiser. Form 8283 is a summary of the gift appraisal and must be attached to the donor's federal income tax return. (A partially completed Form 8283 is also required for some gifts in which a donor requires an appraisal.) The cost of the appraisal is borne by the donor and is treated as a miscellaneous deduction subject to the 2 percent limit. The charitable organization recipient is not required to attest to the value of the property but is required to acknowledge receipt of the gift on Form 8283. The appraisal must be conducted no more than 60 days prior to the transfer of the property and no later than the date the federal income tax return is filed for the year of the donation. Failure to obtain an appraisal and to file Form 8283 will result in a disallowance of the charitable income tax deduction. A "good faith" failure to obtain an appraisal is not a defense to the disallowance of the deduction. The appraiser's signature is required.

Form 8282

In the event that the charitable organization sells the contributed assets reported on Form 8283 within two years from the date of the gift, the organization must file Form 8282 with the Internal Revenue Service. If the charity sells the asset for an amount that does not closely approximate the appraised value, the donor's charitable income tax deduction may be challenged.

PARTIAL INTERESTS

A charitable income tax deduction is not allowed for charitable gifts whether made outright or in trust that represent less than the donor's entire interest in the gift. The loss of the deduction applies to the charitable income tax deduction, the charitable gift tax deduction, and the charitable estate tax deduction. Partial interests are created when a donor retains a right or ownership interest in property transferred to a charity.

A number of important exceptions to this rule enable a donor to obtain a charitable income tax deduction:

- *Gift of the donor's entire interest where the interest is less than full property rights.* The donor may obtain a charitable income tax deduction for a gift of a partial property interest as long as that interest represents the donor's entire interest in the property and the partial interest was not created for purposes of the gift.

- *Gifts in trust.* As discussed, the donor is entitled to a charitable income tax deduction for a gift of a remainder interest in trust as long as the trust is a qualified charitable remainder unitrust, charitable remainder annuity trust, or a qualified pooled income fund. In addition, the donor may obtain a charitable income tax deduction for the gift of a lead interest (income interest) in a grantor charitable lead trust as long as the donor is taxed on the income of the trust.

- *Gifts of a remainder interest in a personal residence or farm.* This exception permits the donor to obtain a charitable income tax deduction less depreciation for a gift of a remainder interest in a personal residence or farm. For example, in a retained life estate, the donor retains a life estate or the right to occupy the property for life, with the remainder to a nonprofit organization. The donor receives a current charitable income tax deduction for the present value of the gift of the remainder. A personal residence is defined as any residence used by the taxpayer as a personal residence, although it does not need to be the donor's primary residence. A farm is defined as any land used by the taxpayer in the production of crops, fruits, agricultural products, or livestock.

- *Gifts of an undivided interest in a donor's entire interest.*   An undivided fractional interest of a donor's entire interest is often expressed as a percentage or a fraction. If the donor transfers 25 percent or a one-quarter interest in property, she is conveying a portion of her interest. It is undivided in that the nonprofit's interest does not represent a certain right to a specific area or acreage, but rather has use of the entire property for a certain fraction of the year.

- *Gift of a partial interest in real property for conservation purposes.*   A donor can obtain a charitable income tax deduction for a gift of less than the donor's entire interest if the interest is an easement or conservation restriction imposed for conservation purposes. Conservation purposes include the preservation, protection, or creation of open space, natural habitat, recreation, or historic preservation if the use is for public purposes or education. See Chapter 12 for more information on the use of conservation easements.

CONCLUSION

Nonprofit staff members and planned giving staff members must understand the tax consequences of a donor's charitable gifts. Four types of tax savings may be available:

1. Charitable income tax deduction
2. Capital gains tax avoidance
3. Gift tax
4. Estate tax deductions

In addition, taxes assessed by a state also may be avoided or reduced.

To engage fully in philanthropy, donors must first want to make a gift to help support the charity's mission. The tax benefits are provided to donors who wish to make a gift to benefit a charity. Few donors make gifts for tax purposes. The planned giving officer can help donors see the benefits of philanthropy, then show them ways to maximize the tax benefits of their gifts.

Index